DUMP ROMNEY

Why Tampa's Republican Delegates must
Dump Romney to Defeat Obama

~

A MANIFESTO

Sara and David Bethel, editors

Developed by
Jews and Christians Together
www.JewsandChristiansTogether.com

ISBN: 978-0-9858723-6-6

DUMP ROMNEY

Why Tampa's Republican Delegates must Dump Romney to Defeat Obama

~

A MANIFESTO

The Overview 3 >

The Backup 9 >

How does it play in the Swing States? 15>

Abandoning Monotheism 19>

Mormon Racism and the Hispanic Vote 22>

The Sci-Fi President 26>

Horny Prophets 28>

The Martyred Molester 31>

Mormons, Multiversers and Bill Maher 34>

Romney Spawned Gay Wedlock 47>

Prophet, Priest, King... and President 48>

Mitt's Sexual Confusions 53>

Naked Temple Rituals 57>

Same Sex as Sandusky 63>

Human Rights and Homosexuality 64>

The Founders' View 67>

L'chaim, Barney Frank! 68>

Anderson Cooper was Born Gay? 70>

Our Manhattan Project 72>

Can we really Dump Romney? 75 >

American Monotheism, Monogamy and Survival 80>

The Appendix

DUMP ROMNEY

Why Tampa's Republican Delegates must Dump Romney to Defeat Obama

~

A MANIFESTO

TO: Our fellow Tampa-bound delegates and friends; fellow conservatives, libertarians, neo-cons, soldiers, vets and Tea Partiers; and to all of our fellow *Manhattan Declaration* signatories/affirmers.

FR: Jews & Christians Together - Contact: Sara or David (davidbethel70ce@yahoo.com), Drafting Committee eds

The Overview

What if Mitt Romney is *not inevitable* at Tampa? What if his nomination makes four more years for President Obama *all but inevitable?* What if it's true that, despite Obama's governing ineptitude, the Republican frontrunner is *already* losing the Electoral College in a rout which threatens GOP Senate prospects in the overlapping swing states?[1] And, what if that's *before* all the ugly stuff really hits the fan?

Few Tampa delegates have had any disclosure on the racially-toxic texts to which Willard M. Romney is tied – and which he has yet to repudiate; same with the anti-Semitic writings.[2] No disclosure, either, on Romney's role as America's Founding Father of Gay Marriage,[3] the reason Obama could safely come out. Without a Tampa game-changer, we'll soon see how it all ties in to Romney's Big Problem, the core reason he can't carry the toss-ups.

"Purple State" voters already get it that ObamaCare is simply coercive RomneyCare writ large – each a punitive tax program for nonetheless bankrupting new entitlements,[4] each illustrating why *neither* author should be President. This fall, however, left-allied media will also be spinning our "No Apologies" social engineer, quite plausibly, as a liar and loony: For a catalog of troubling character issues, click The Romney Files or this Romney robo-audio[5]; they're examples of what millions of voters have *already* been receiving in battleground states like MI, WI, PA and OH – and partly why, despite a weak economy and incumbent, Romney's already losing the Electoral College so badly.

So, let's now face it squarely, the Big Problem: Can there be any real doubt that the fascinating metaphysics of Mitt's Mormonism – which belligerently declares all other faiths to be "ABOMINATIONS"[6] – will soon find wide distribution in Bible Belt areas of FL, VA, IA and MO? Can any of us (including our own LDS loved ones and friends) watch this animated yet accurate summary of Romney's sci-fi polytheism[7] without cringing? No mere adherent, Romney presided as the LDS equivalent of Boston's Cardinal Law. In 2008, Obama had his Jeremiah Wright problem; in 2012, Mormon Bishop Romney *is* Jeremiah Wright.[8]

Yet, *what if there's a way out?*

---

[1] Seehttp://www.realclearpolitics.com/epolls/2012/president/2012_elections_electoral_college_map_no_toss_ups.html; http://www.realclearpolitics.com/epolls/2012/president/2012_elections_electoral_college_map.html; http://www.realclearpolitics.com/epolls/2012/senate/2012_elections_senate_map.html. Also, see our list of overlapping POTUS/Senate Swing States on page 69.

[2] See pages 23-25.

[3] See, page 47 and forward, and e.g., http://massresistance.org/romney/#SSM

[4] See, e.g., "Romney's Tax Confusion," *The Wall Street Journal,* July 5, 2012 (http://online.wsj.com/article/SB10001424052702304141204577506652734793044.html?mod=googlenews_wsj)

[5] Located here http://www.massresistance.org/romney/email_030212.html and here http://www.massresistance.org/romney/jct_robo_call_NC.html,respectively.

[6] Joseph Smith, the founder of Romney's Mormonism, aka, The Church of Jesus Christ of Latter-day Saints, claims that God commanded him: "...I must join none of them [other denominations], for they were all wrong...that all their creeds were an abomination in His sight" (Joseph Smith History 1:19); "The Roman Catholic, Greek, and Protestant church, is the great corrupt, ecclesiastical power, represented by great Babylon...." (Orson Pratt, *Writings of an Apostle,* "Divine Authenticity," no.6, p.84); "There is no salvation outside The Church of Jesus Christ of Latter-day Saints..." (Bruce McConkie, *Mormon Doctrine,* p. 670); "The Christian world, so called, are heathens as to their knowledge of the salvation of God." (Brigham Young, *Journal of Discourses* 8:171); all as quoted in McCann, "How Does the Mormon Church Really View other Churches?" (http://www.spotlightministries.org.uk/morm&churches.htm). Also: "Does Mormonism Attack Other Religions?" (http://carm.org/does-mormonism-attack-other-religions).

[7] "What Mormons Really Believe" (http://www.youtube.com/watch?v=3HSlbuli7HM)

[8] http://www.youtube.com/watch?v=fGAhiVutAx4&ytsession=Al8C1pf7s66iYxcy64fiCNCW9syd3_-WMdri6g3WJQ4w81-GFeMFkmGSZnilNM3Z4Wn-FqhY14O9GFUOUhKbN5wV-xjetoZlp2_3GMLSlko3x8AKoC0bnRh4o2mDar0n1H2KFLu_ZPkTFN9Ti-meDDhqYuzEh2VXtJHU-aT4se7S2pkcv7RPTIU-tJnSK00m8MerVQNatwg

What if it's true that Romney does not and can *never* own a "bound" majority of 1,144 "Harem Delegates" – like slaves, concubines or plural wives – for a first-ballot win?[9]

- What if 100% of Tampa's GOP delegates – as a function of longstanding Republican Party Rules – are in fact **FREE TO CONSCIENTIOUSLY ABSTAIN ON THE CRUCIAL FIRST BALLOT?** [10] (For details, jump to page 75).

- What if enough of us were to realize just in time and in accord with RNC Rules – which necessarily empower "small-r" *republican* delegates to derail a doomed train – that one of the GOP primary survivors or **AN ENTIRELY NEW NAME** *can and must* be drafted as the 2012 Republican nominee?

- What if Santorum, Gingrich, Ron Paul or other liberty lovers were suddenly to recognize, as a function of the disturbing facts cited herein, what a deep betrayal, what profound negligence it would be to endorse Romney on stage in Tampa?

Who seriously doubts that Romney's exotic beliefs – e.g., that the Garden of Eden was in Missouri,[11] that Jesus is Satan's brother,[12] that G_d the Father physically and sexually penetrated the Virgin Mary, [13] that each of us can become gods[14] – will get spun this fall as those of a religious whack-o?

To grasp how the internet teems with information on Romney's Big Problem – and with eventual media and voter education from left, right and center – simply click here,[15] here,[16] here,[17] here,[18] here,[19] here,[20] here,[21] here,[22] here,[23] here,[24] here,[25] here,[26] or here.[27]

Or, visit any of *hundreds* of other websites on the Church of Jesus Christ of Latter-day Saints, the mainstream of Mitt Romney's Mormon sect, the faith of his fathers. On June 21, Gallup reported:

> **Eighteen percent of Americans say they would not vote for a well-qualified presidential candidate who happens to be a Mormon, virtually the same as the 17% who held this attitude in 1967.... Negativity toward a Mormon candidate increases from 10% among Republicans to 18% among independents to 24% among Democrats. There is virtually no difference in resistance to a Mormon presidential candidate among Protestants [18%], Catholics [17%], and those with no religious identity [20%].... as Romney's faith becomes better known this summer and fall, it could become more of a negative factor – given that those who resist the idea of a Mormon president will in theory become more likely to realize that Romney is a Mormon as the campaign unfolds.**[28]

---

9 See, e.g., "Response to "A Rogue Convention?" (http://www.fairvote.org/response-to-a-rogue-convention-how-gop-party-rules-may-surprise-in-201)

10 For the very real potential event that Presidential primaries may yield a presumptive nominee discovered to have a fatal political problem – e.g., a history of mental illness, suicide attempts, pedophilia, incest, spousal abuse, bisexuality, Satanism, embezzlement, emailing lewd photographs of himself, involvement in a kooky cult, etc.. – RNC Rules ultimately empower delegates to CONSCIENTIOUSLY ABSTAIN or vote their consciences, in entirely unbound fashion, on every ballot – *including, necessarily,* the crucial First Ballot (after which no one contends any delegate is bound). In this manner, the Republican Party sensibly protects both the nation and its brand by upholding "small-r" republicanism; by empowering elected delegates to dutifully exercise their good judgment and wisdom, rather than binding them to "small d" democratic or "mobocratic" election results which can be unduly influenced by money, mass hysteria, misleading advertising, bad journalism, foreign interests, extortion, etc. See www.thereal2012delegatecount.com; "Response to "A Rogue Convention?" (http://www.fairvote.org/response-to-a-rogue-convention-how-gop-party-rules-may-surprise-in-201); "A Rogue Convention? How GOP party rules may surprise in 2012"(http://www.politico.com/news/stories/1111/69048_Page2.html); the journalism of Ben Swann, e.g., Reality Check: Republican Delegates "Unbound"? (http://www.youtube.com/watch?v=anWsU93fFsk&feature=relmfu); and http://www.examiner.com/article/rnc-delegates-not-bound-to-any-candidate-on-first-ballot. Entirely apart from existing RNC Rules which uphold the right of all Tampa delegates to abstain -- and apart from the fact that any adverse RNC rule can be set aside or revised by the convention itself! -- Federal law also seems to protect the voting rights of Tampa delegates to abstain on the First Ballot: "Federal Law: All Delegates are Unbound" (http://www.examiner.com/article/federal-law-all-delegates-are-unbound); "Federal law proves that all delegates are unbound: All delegates must see this" (http://www.dailypaul.com/237770/federal-law-proves-all-delegates-are-unbound-all-delegates-must-see-this). In any case, it is indisputable that the Republican National Convention has the legal authority to dump Romney at Tampa and choose a more viable nominee. See page 75 and forward.

11 See, e.g., Sandra Tanner, "Was the Garden of Eden in Missouri?" (http://www.utlm.org/onlineresources/gardenofeden.htm)

12 See, e.g., Hank Hanegraaff, "Is Jesus Christ the Spirit Brother of Satan?" (http://www.equip.org/articles/is-jesus-christ-the-spirit-brother-of-satan/)

13 See, e.g., "Was the LDS Jesus born of the Virgin Mary?" (http://carm.org/was-lds-jesus-born-of-virgin-mary).

14 See, e.g., http://www.youtube.com/watch?v=3HSIbuli7HM

15 "What Mormons Really Believe" (http://www.youtube.com/watch?v=3HSIbuli7HM)

16 http://www.exmormon.org/

17 See "Mitt Romney, Mormonism and the Christian Vote: A Biblical Call to Christian Ministers and Leaders," (http://forthesakeofthegospel.com/document/)

18 http://carm.org/mormonism

19 "Top 10 Mormon Problems Explained"(http://www.youtube.com/watch?v=4ac_fLUHiBw&feature=youtu.be).

20 http://crcmin.org/What_Mormons_Dont_Tell.html

21 "The Collapse of Mormonism: Why Millions are no longer Mormons" (http://www.youtube.com/watch?v=rn1iGvXU0dI&feature=related)

22 http://www.iamanexmormon.com/

23 http://www.ldsvideo.org

24 http://www.i4m.com/think/history/mormon_christians.htm

25 http://mormoncurtain.com/

26 http://www.mormonthink.com/lying.htm

27 http://www.equip.org/articles/are-mormons-and-muslims-apples-and-oranges/

28 http://www.gallup.com/poll/155273/bias-against-mormon-presidential-candidate-1967.aspx

Weirded-out by Romney's beliefs just as swing-state voters will be, some GOP delegates and other "national leaders" take strange, cold comfort in the fact that Mitt governed Massachusetts as an amoral social engineer on abortion, homo/bisexuality, RomneyCare, climate regulation, taxation, religious liberty, etc. The pretzel logic goes:

> **Although he's a RINO[29] and I'm not, although he embraces strange Mormon doctrines I don't, and although I'd NEVER consider putting a Scientologist, Salafist or Jonestown dupe into the White House... I'm for Romney.**
>
> **Why? Well, I have Mormon friends and I like Mormons. They're a good and decent folk – despite a Tabernacle Choir's worth of wild, wing-nut beliefs which tax all credulity.**
>
> **BUT, I'm OK with Mitt – in the Oval Office, carrying the nuclear football, waging war, appointing judges, forging social policy, defending Israel, governing from the left just as we'd expect from Mr. RomneyCare, and representing the American Nation – because his appalingly liberal record proves he just *can't* be a TBM ("True Believing Mormon").**

That, however, is the cold comfort of losers, of those who already know somewhere deep down inside that Romney's nomination means Obama's reelection.

In the pages ahead, we'll be contending that Mormons are indeed a good and decent people – as are most gays, lesbians, Scientologists, Muslims, Methodists, Baptists, Jews, Catholics, libertarians, media elites, neo-cons, paleo-cons and GOP delegates.

To be sure, we're all deeply erring souls, all pretty messed-up and Prozac-prone, all more or less equally equidistant from heavenly perfection. And yet, not all *belief systems* are equal: While most Germans are good, Nazism was evil. While most Muslims are good, Sharia Islam is evil. While most of Jonestown's victims were good, the People's Church was evil. So, what about Mitt's Mormonism?

Well, for one thing, when contrasted to the USA's core premise that all human beings are "created equal" and "endowed by their Creator with certain unalienable Rights," we're convinced Romney's unrepudiated racist dogmas[30] will seem so hateful ... that we'll all look like fools if we make him our 2012 nominee.

How about his ethics? To many, Romney presents a handsome, clean-scrubbed, All-American face. How could *he* be a fibber, a charlatan, a con-man? How could *he* dissemble so robotically, so constantly? The answers seem to be buried somewhere deep within the irrationalist DNA, polytheistic tenets and lie-filled history of the mind-controlling enterprise into which the GOP frontrunner and his forebears were born – and perhaps also in the manipulative, exemplary sex predators whom Romney and all good Mormons must regard as holy prophets.

How about his governance? As we'll see herein, Romney's lawless authoritarianism is in fact *deeply consistent* with the faith of his fathers, with the relativistic core of his Mormonism. One native Mormon says "LDS culture — along with the institutional LDS church — is the most authoritarian, controlling culture on the face of the earth."[31]

One of the few constants of Romney's flip-flopping career has been his fidelity to a statist and intolerant GLBT (Gay, Lesbian, Bisexual and Transgender) Agenda. In fact, Romney simply willed same-sex marriage onto American shores as a legal precursor to the reinstatement of polygamy.[32]

Unless willfully blind, any Tampa delegate with eyes will quickly be able to see that Romney was weaned on ideas utterly alien to most of the USA, especially to swing-state voters who will determine the next President. We'll discover how Romney can be so "religious" and yet, even to this day, so very RINO. We'll grasp how and perhaps *why* Romney's statism so closely mirrors Obama's.[33]

We'll see that the USA is indeed a "Chik-fil-a Nation" – a country committed to traditional marriage and sexuality – partly because we're loaded with "Chik-fil-a Swing States."[34] And yet, Romney's been unable to find a good word to say for the pro-marriage, pro-family Judeo-Christians behind that company. [35] It figures.

---

[29] "RINO" stands for "Republican In Name Only" or "Republican in Obama-mode."
[30] See pages 23-25.
[31] "Understanding Mitt's Mormon Culture" (http://www.renewamerica.com/romney_mormon.htm)
[32] See, page 47 and forward, and e.g., http://massresistance.org/romney/#SSM
[33] See, e.g., this offering from Ron Paul's camp: http://www.youtube.com/watch?v=IWDJEc92d38
[34] See table, page 74.
35 "At a press conference in Las Vegas, Romney wouldn't weigh in on either the fight over comments by the president of the fast food restaurant Chick-Fil-A over gay marriage or an effort spearheaded by Michele Bachmann calling for an investigation into ... alleged Muslim Brotherhood infiltration of the federal government. 'Those are not things that are part of my campaign,' Romney said." (http://www.politico.com/blogs/burns-haberman/2012/08/romney-chickfila-huma-abedin-not-part-of-my-campaign-131040.html).

We'll look at how the coital libertinism of a 19th Century sect (and historic sex cult) could enable Romney to rationalize a career's worth of cover for our ugly national habits of child sacrifice: abortion and pedophilia.[36] And, we'll hear how Mitt's marriage doubletalk echoes, so eerily, lies told two centuries ago by his Holy Prophet Joseph Smith, the frisky, philandering founder of his faith. Brainwashing may be too strong a word,[37] and yet:

> **Hostile to hetero-monogamy, it's as if Mitt's the Manchurian Candidate from GOProud, the Log Cabiner from some rustic den of sodomy in the Utah backwoods: Romney has been grinding hard to deliver on state-sanctioned SSM/SSS (Same-Sex Marriage/Same-Sex-as-Sandusky[38]) in domestic, military or foreign policy from way back when Obama was all talk.**
>
> **Who seriously imagines that Romney's creeper roots – naked temple rites[39] and all – won't soon be subject to blistering media heat? In his embrace of an enduring Mormon subculture of pedophilia, polyamory and homoeroticism – plus childlike faith in the left's demonstrably anti-scientific premise that some people are born gay[40] (like being born black-skinned, blue-eyed or female) – Romney has even undercut the Boy Scouts for their prudent good sense on homo/bisex Scoutmasters.[41]**
>
> **It's a clueless (or clever?) position which Romney still embraces as of August 2012, post-Sandusky.[42] On his way to making himself America's Founding Father of Gay Marriage,[43] Romney was signing Gay Youth Pride Proclamations[44] and promising to exceed Teddy Kennedy's extremes[45] on GLBT-pedophile issues, years before Obama came out and Fox News went all wobbly. If the GLBT movement ever carves its own Mount Rushmore, Romney will be rock-hard and right up there with Obama, smiling over the nation they conquered.**

As we'll see, the GOP's presumptive nominee has been waging steady war against American monotheism and hetero-monogamy. Mitt's man-dates on the GLBT front correlate with myriad others – for example, on RomneyCare and CO2 regulation – each one, in its own special authoritarian way, raping liberty. To bury this lead, to blind ourselves to the Elephant in the Temple, to pretend that this would-be emperor is actually clothed – or rather, *unclothed* by mystical Mormon undergarments – is a Republican death wish: Watch this.[46]

But, what if there's really a way out?

What if faithful Jews, Christians and totally-unbound GOP delegates were to grasp, before it's too late, that we have the right (and no other responsible choice but) to dump Romney in Tampa?

If you're a thoughtful, responsible and open-minded Tampa delegate; if you're a dutiful "small-r" republican whose time is tight – yet your mind's still your own – here's the good news: You've *already* read everything you really need to know! (Especially if you just click some of the links so far). Everything else – every shocking fact which follows in the Backup Content – simply expands on what we've just said; you can read the steamy stuff at the beach or on your flight to Tampa. You can skim the rest, or skip it all.

---

[36] On July 17, the Boy Scouts of America once again rejected Romneyesque relativism on homo/bisexuality and the attendant pederast risks, a courageous stand which many of us believe, based on years of evidence, would be unlikely to endure a Romney Presidency. See, e.g., "Romney on Boy Scouts" (http://www.youtube.com/watch?v=uEOJNw4lmlI); "Romney's Gay Youth Pride Proclamation" (http://www.massresistance.org/docs/marriage/romney/GayYouthProclamation.pdf); "Romney's Abortion Record: Spin vs. Truth" (http://www.slatev.com/video/romneys-abortion-record-spin-vs-truth/) and "The Conversion" (http://www.slate.com/articles/news_and_politics/the_conversion/2012/02/mitt_romney_s_abortion_record_flip_flop_or_conversion_.html)

[37] We say this because, although Mitt Romney has been drip-fed Mormon dogma from his birth, he may by now be wise to the manipulative falsehoods, false prophets and cruel deceptions upon which, as we will see, Joseph Smith's house of cards has been built. The survival of Mormonism to date is no argument for its veracity; Muhammad's 7th Century amendments to the Bible, and his prescriptions for the ill treatment of women, Jews, Christians and black-skinned people, live on as well.

[38] Anal intercourse which, coerced or uncoerced, is toxic to human health – a practice for which human beings are not designed – yet central to the broad GLBT/pedophila-pederast movement (see page 56 forward). In this appalling sense, it is the Republican frontrunner who has led from behind: Whether adult-youth, youth-youth, or adult -adult interaction, Romney has been joined to them at the figurative hips for years: Romney's chiding of the Boy Scouts (http://massresistance.org/romney/videos/index.html), for example, could have been scripted by NAMBLA (the North American Man-Boy Love Association), despite well-known cases of LDS pedophiles within the Boy Scouts. Likewise with Romney's infamously obsequious, brown-nosing letter to the Log Cabin Republicans. (http://www.boston.com/news/daily/11/romneyletterbaywindows.pdf).

[39] See page 57.

[40] See page 70 and forward.

[41] "Boy Scouts reaffirm ban on gays" (http://www.foxnews.com/us/2012/07/17/apnewsbreak-boy-scouts-reaffirm-ban-on-gays/). The pederast outrages of Jerry Sandusky and so many others; the willful blindness of Penn State, public K-12 school officials, religious institutions and liberal officials like Romney; all of these illustrate how ludicrous it is to contend – as do the Left and the GOP's Romney-Mehlman-Grenell-GOProud-Log Cabin wing – that there's no swollen connectivity between gay/bisex pedophilia and the "GLBT community," ie, Gay, Lesbian, Bisexual or "Transgender" practitioners who've spurned faithful hetero-monogamy. For the empirical science, see page 38 and forward.

[42] "Mitt Romney Disagrees With Boy Scouts Gay Ban" http://www.ontopmag.com/article.aspx?id=12596&MediaType=1&Category=26

[43] See, page 47 and forward, and e.g., http://massresistance.org/romney/#SSM

[44] "Romney's Gay Youth Pride Proclamation" (http://www.massresistance.org/docs/marriage/romney/GayYouthProclamation.pdf)

[45] See, e.g., http://www.massresistance.org/romney/email_030212.html.

[46] For an animated yet essentially accurate summary of LDS Mormom polytheism -- which even the children and grandchildren of 2012 RNC delegates can easily understand when they eventually ask what their elders did to avert 2012 disaster -- go to http://www.youtube.com/watch?v=3HSlbuli7HM. See also http://carm.org/mormonism.

We all know this much: Four more years of President Obama will devastate the United States of America. The Republican Party needs to do everything within its power to prevent his reelection. And, it's within the power of Tampa's delegates to dump Romney. (See page 75).

He can't win. Or more precisely, after months of campaigning, at a time when the U.S. economy is at its lowest point in decades, and against one of the most inept Presidents in U.S. history, if Romney's trailing as badly as he is now… the odds are very long he can close this fall. Yet the odds for Romney's outlook, for his odd, bizarre beliefs, are very different: They're likely to bite the GOP hard.

SEXUAL PIONEERING: Left: "Brigham Morris Young (son of Brigham Young) in drag as Italian opera diva 'Madam Pattirini' (circa 1901 photographic placard advertising 'her' appearance in the Sugar House Ward, Salt Lake City, Utah; photo by C. R. Savage)"[47] Right: America's Founding Father of Gay Marriage.[48] Why did Romney bring solemnized sodomy to the USA via Massachusetts? [49] Why does Romney, with Obama, wish to transgenderize and "homogenize" the US military and US work places? Maybe this: From the start, Mormonism has been hostile to American monotheism and hetero-monogamy: Systemic adultery, "spiritual wifery," polygamy, polyandry, "buggery" (homosexuality), celestial sex and terrestrial confusion. Romney has a gold-plated Mormon pedigree going back to Nauvoo, Illinois, where Mormonism's founding holy prophet Joseph Smith was "martyred" after molesting his foster daughters. Smith's second in command, whom Smith appointed as mayor of Nauvoo, was the notorious "buggerer" (homosexual) and abortionist, John C. Bennett. Romney's great-great grandfather, Parley Pratt, was one of Smith's original "Twelve Apostles" – and got killed by the estranged husband of his twelfth "spiritual wife". Romney's great grandfather, Miles Park Romney had five wives and fled to a polygamy colony in Mexico, from whence Romney's father George would eventually return to the USA to make his fortune — and set up son Mitt to fulfill Smith's White Horse Prophecy.[50]

Take a Rorschach test, but instead of an ink-blot, look at this famous 2012 online photo[51]: It shows a US Marines sergeant wrapped around his male partner, living out a policy Mitt Romney was pushing long before Obama

---

[47] Connell O'Donovan, *"The Abominable and Detestable Crime Against Nature": A Revised History of Homosexuality & Mormonism, 1840-1980*; 1994, 2004 (http://www.connellodonovan.com/abom.html); http://en.wikipedia.org/wiki/B._Morris_Young

[48] See, page 47 and forward, and e.g., http://massresistance.org/romney/#SSM

[49] See, page 47 and forward, and e.g., http://massresistance.org/romney/#SSM

[50] See page 21.

[51] http://gothamist.com/attachments/nyc_arts_john/022712pride.jpg

became President. If you see something good (or irrelevant, or inconsequential, because it's "not about the economy")… then you and your progeny win either way, with Obama or Romney, when it comes to our sinking culture.

If you are a "Rombot" or "Harem Delegate" or an "LDS-GOP Stepford Wife," please read no further; your mind (such as it is) is already made up! On the other hand – even if you're part of the Utah or Massachusetts delegations to the Republican National Convention – perhaps you too feel something's just not right about that picture, about the amoral direction in which both Obama *and* Romney wish to take our nation? Maybe you recognize that they're *both* AWOL on issues of limited government and sexual sanity? If you see something troubling, if you see something that's just not right, then you may wish to read on, because Tampa's delegates can still save the day.

Perhaps you're so fear-filled about the White House "devil you know" that you're willing to jump into bed with the "devil you don't"? Well, if you really want to settle, like some naive child bride or hopeless Salt Lake spinster, for the embrace of a "lesser evil" sure-loser, then we'd suggest you skip everything that follows. And, if you're a conservative defeatist, cowed Christian, self-loathing Jew, religious syncretist, Country Club multiculturalist or access-hungry accomodationist who's short on vision and attention span… you might as well just quit this now. Go to Orlando, go entertain yourself, go do something else… *because this text is for others.*

Summary

However, if you're a thought leader or thoughtful Tampa delegate, you already know that the original purpose of major party conventions was to nominate *the best possible candidate,* even if he or she requires drafting. Were frontrunners simply *entitled* to the nomination, a convention wouldn't be necessary; some RNC bureaucrat would just tally up all the votes from the 50 states. So in sum, here are the essentials:

- **ROMNEY IS ALREADY LOSING THE ELECTORAL COLLEGE BADLY.** [52]
- **WHEN THE MEDIA EXPLAINS ROMNEY'S WEIRD POLYTHEISTIC BELIEFS (AND CORRESPONDING PUBLIC RECORD) TO THE SWING STATES, IT'S LIKELY TO SEAL THE GOP'S DEFEAT.**[53]
- **NO TAMPA DELEGATE IS "BOUND" TO ROMNEY; EVERY DELEGATE HAS THE RIGHT TO CONSCIENTIOUSLY ABSTAIN FROM HIM ON THE CRUCIAL FIRST BALLOT.**[54]
- **WHILE MOST RIVALS DEMURRED FROM FACING THE FRONTRUNNER'S MILLIONS IN THE GRUELING PRIMARIES, THERE'S NO SHORTAGE OF CONSERVATIVE LEADERS WHO, IF NOMINATED AT TAMPA, WOULD COURAGEOUSLY RISE TO THE CALL TO LEAD THE GOP TICKET INTO NOVEMBER.**[55]
- **AFTER ENOUGH DELEGATES CONSCIENTIOUSLY ABSTAIN FROM ROMNEY ON THE FIRST BALLOT – FOR SAKE OF THEIR CHILDREN AND GRANDCHILDREN, THEIR NATION, THEIR PARTY, AND THE MONOTHEISTIC FAITH OF THEIR FATHERS – NO ONE EVEN DEBATES THAT ALL DELEGATES ARE "UNBOUND" AND FREE TO CHOOSE A DIFFERENT NOMINEE IN A SUBSEQUENT VOTE. ROMNEY HAS NO ENTITLEMENT TO THE 2012 REPUBLICAN NOMINATION.**[56]

Why should faithful American Jews, Christians and Tampa's totally-unbound GOP delegates DUMP ROMNEY?

Because even if we could win, we'd all be acquiescing in polytheism at the very pinnacle of our leadership – and steering the USA away from the monotheistic Faith of our Fathers, the American Founders.

Because we *won't* carry the swing states by nominating the Bishop of a kooky sex cult.

Because we need someone better, or we'll lose. *Because we need a game-changer.*

What follows are merely the details.

---

[52] Seehttp://www.realclearpolitics.com/epolls/2012/president/2012_elections_electoral_college_map_no_toss_ups.html; http://www.realclearpolitics.com/epolls/2012/president/2012_elections_electoral_college_map.html; http://www.realclearpolitics.com/epolls/2012/senate/2012_elections_senate_map.html; Nate Silver's forecast/now-cast at http://fivethirtyeight.blogs.nytimes.com/.

[53] See, e.g., "What Mormons Really Believe" (http://www.youtube.com/watch?v=3HSlbuli7HM)

[54] See page 75 and forward.

[55] For possible examples, see page 75.

[56] See page 75 and forward.

DUMP ROMNEY

Why Tampa's Republican Delegates must Dump Romney to Defeat Obama

NOTE: If you've skipped the preceding Overview, skip this Backup section instead. The Overview – especially if you click the links – is all you really need to need to know. What follows, including the Appendix, are the drill-down details.

What's inside Mitt Romney's head?

There are plenty of official and unofficial bios on Mitt Romney; look elsewhere for them.[57] Here, however, is what they all tend to overlook, or at least downplay: Romney has a gold-plated Mormon family pedigree going back to Nauvoo,[58] home to his revered and sexually-pioneering Holy Prophet (and 1844 U.S. Presidential candidate) Joseph Smith. [59] Romney's great grandfather, Miles Park Romney had five "plural wives."[60] Two of Romney's great-great grandfathers had about a dozen wives apiece.

Yet, it's not all ancient history. Consistent with his sect's proudly-defiant heritage of authoritarian rule and psycho-sexual relativism, it was indeed Mormon Bishop-turned-Gov. Romney who spawned gay wedlock in the USA[61] – historic payback, perhaps, for the emancipation of child brides from Mormon pedophiles by abolitionist Republicans who rightly saw institutionalized polygamy and slavery in the same light.

After all, it was Abraham Lincoln, the first Republican President, who signed a law banning polygamy in 1862. In public policy, Lincoln resisted the harem lifestyles of Smith and Brigham Young, just as Lincoln's better-known deeds undercut the racist outlook of the man for whom Romney's alma mater is named.

> **Brigham Young is generally credited with having been responsible for revoking the priesthood and temple blessings from black members of the LDS Church.... In 1863, Young reported that he said, "Shall I tell you the law of God in regard to the African race? If the white man who belongs to the chosen seed mixes his blood with the seed of Cain, the penalty, under the law of God, is death on the spot. This will always be so." (Journal of Discourses, vol. 10, p. 110) After settling in Utah in 1848, Brigham Young announced a priesthood ban which prohibited all men of black African descent from holding the priesthood. In connection, Mormons of African descent could not participate in Mormon temple rites such as the Endowment or sealing.[62]**

These racial rules remained until 1978, when another LDS "living prophet" undid the ban. That Romney was over 30 at the time and had dutifully accepted it until then says much about the man.

Still, one's heritage is a weighty thing. As Romney seeks the GOP nomination and Presidency now at age 65, a giant question remains: Is he finally ready to repudiate *the doctrinal basis* for the ban on black priests, is he finally ready to condemn the racism inherent in his own holy Mormon scriptures? As we'll see, that inherent racism is ugly, and it is politically toxic. The media hasn't "discovered" by now because, no doubt, it's all being saved for October.

---

[57] See, e.g., http://www.mittromney.com/learn/mitt
[58] http://en.wikipedia.org/wiki/Romney_family
[59] http://en.wikipedia.org/wiki/Joseph_Smith_Jr.
[60] http://en.wikipedia.org/wiki/Miles_Park_Romney
[61] See page 47 and forward.
[62] http://en.wikipedia.org/wiki/Brigham_young

No doubt about this, either:

> **On explosive matters of race, sex and the very nature of *reality itself,* Romney represents a formal and momentous potential sea change for GOP and US leadership, from the monotheism of Jewish-Christian Natural Law embraced by America's liberty-loving Founders ... into an authoritarian brand of latter-day polytheism.**

JoePa Smith

To make some sense of Romney's revered prophet Joseph Smith, Jr., picture Penn State's chief pedophile – rather than a hapless Jerry Sandusky – as a charismatic and eloquent version of a young, unsullied Joe Paterno, preaching strange new offenses to football-fervent masses from a magic, allegedly heaven-sent playbook.

Then, imagine that JoePa's adoring boosters anoint him "Prophet, Priest, King and President Pro-Tem of the World."[63] Next, imagine that it's all occurring as Paterno – before his martyrdom for child molestation – solemnly and privately empowers his coaching staff and trustees to engage with trusting fans in almost every conceivable variation of adultery, pedophilia, pederasty, homoeroticism and group sex.

Finally, let's imagine that nearly two centuries later, Paterno's pervy institution has somehow survived, after cloaking its history in conservative conventionality. Picture millions of good, decent and mind-controlled fans who keep swapping their credulity (and 10 percent of their incomes) for access to Happy Valley plus promised stardom in the afterlife – for BMOC godhood and all the curvy cheerleaders one can handle on one's own special campus in the sky.

That, in a nutshell, is a fair analogy to what gets taught as sacred doctrine at Brigham Young University – where Romney's got his undergraduate degree – and what wing-nut LDS prophets have taught him and his forebears from the very start. The rest is history. Associated Press reports:

> [T]he Republican presidential candidate's great-grandfather had five wives and at least one of his great-great grandfathers had 12.Polygamy was not just a historical footnote, but a prominent element in the family tree of the former Massachusetts governor now seeking to become the first Mormon president. Romney's great-grandfather, Miles Park Romney, married his fifth wife in 1897. That was more than six years after Mormon leaders banned polygamy and more than three decades after a federal law barred the practice.
>
> Romney's great-grandmother, Hannah Hood Hill, was the daughter of polygamists. She wrote vividly in her autobiography about how she "used to walk the floor and shed tears of sorrow" over her own husband's multiple marriages. Romney's great-great grandfather, Parley Pratt, an apostle in the church, had 12 wives. In an 1852 sermon, Parley Pratt's brother and fellow apostle, Orson Pratt, became the first church official to publicly proclaim and defend polygamy as a direct revelation from God.
>
> Romney's father, former Michigan Gov. George Romney, was born in Chihuahua, Mexico, where Mormons fled in the 1800s to escape religious persecution and U.S. laws forbidding polygamy. He and his family did not return to the United States until 1912, more than two decades after the church issued "The Manifesto" banning polygamy....
>
> Joseph Smith, who founded the Mormon church in 1830... is believed to have had 33 wives. Brigham Young expanded the practice after the church's migration from the Midwest to Utah, which began in 1846. He is said to have had 55 wives. Historical texts show Young also asked Orson Pratt to publicly proclaim the church's belief in polygamy in 1852.
>
> In 1862, while Utah was a territory, President Abraham Lincoln signed the Morrill Anti-Bigamy Act, banning plural marriage. In 1882, Congress also passed the Edmunds Act, an anti-polygamy law. That was followed in 1887 by the Edmunds-Tucker Act, which disincorporated the church and threatened to seize its nonreligious real estate as part of the crackdown on polygamy. In 1890, Mormon President Wilford Woodruff issued "The Manifesto," in which he declared the church no longer taught or permitted plural marriages.
>
> Nonetheless, the law of polygamy — Smith's revelation that God authorized polygamy — remains in Article 132 of the church's Doctrine and Covenants. In addition, Mormon widowers who remarry today believe they will live in eternity with their multiple wives. Mormon genealogical records, among the most detailed and complete of any religion, show that two of Mitt Romney's great-great grandfathers, Miles Romney and Parley Pratt, had 12 wives each.... Gaskell Romney, Mitt Romney's grandfather, was not a polygamist. He married Anna Amelia Pratt, the daughter of polygamists and the granddaughter of Parley Pratt, the apostle with 12 wives....Gaskell Romney and Anna Pratt had seven

---

[63] See page 49.

> children, including George Wilcken Romney, the former Michigan governor [and Mitt Romney's father]. He lived with his parents in Mexico until 1912, when the family returned to the United States.[64]

No one would ever fault Mitt Romney for his heritage; like Brigham Morris Young, the son of Brigham Young, Romney had no more control over of the family into which he was born than do any of us. And yet, each of us must decide whether to embrace and build upon what our forebears have handed down. Per the photo in the Overview above, it seems that Brigham Morris Young went on to do some pioneering in transgenderism, bisexuality or both.

Similarly, as a grown adult and LDS official, Romney has passively accepted Mormon racism while engendering a hostility to normal marriage to rival that of Joseph Smith, the Youngs and the Pratt brothers, his ancestors: When Romney pioneered gay marriage in Massachusetts, he was being consistent with relativistic core of the historic sex cult into which he was born.

> **Memo to our fellow leaders and Tampa delegates: *It just won't play in the sensible swing states.***

Let's not Fool Ourselves

If Romney becomes Tampa's "ROMinee," his personal beliefs will, *and indeed should,* face the same high scrutiny as those of any ticket leader who embraces Scientology, Islam, Wicca or some other unfamiliar belief system alien to America's Jewish-Christian foundation and Founders.

Simply labeling something a "religion" does not exempt it from objective standards of evaluation – logical, empirical, historical and moral – by sane and rational GOP delegates, by the media or by swing-state voters. This text, therefore, does *not* represent "blind bigotry" or "prejudice"; the facts on Romney's record and belief system are readily available to every Tampa delegate, and we have "pre-judged" nothing.

> **Rather, we have carefully examined the facts, done our due diligence and are convinced – if Tampa's totally-unbound delegates shirk their clear duty –that swing-state voters will find Willard Mitt Romney mentally unfit for our nation's highest office.**

Or at the very least, *politically unfit,* to the same devastating effect: Another term for President Obama. Therefore, RNC delegates would be acting responsibly and prudently to assign their kamikaze nominee to some other cockpit.

> **Think about it: What, exactly, is to prevent swing-state voters from warming to October media and blogosphere spin that the favorite son of a weird, authoritarian sex cult[65] is on the brink of becoming *Commander-in-Chief of the U.S. military and head of the CIA, FBI, Justice Department, Homeland Security and ATF?***

If that's no worry to blithe GOP suits, perhaps they *all* Tampa conventioneers who aim to rescue their troubled nation via the Party of Lincoln can at least see this much:

> **We will not and should not displace Obama's statism with Romney's. We cannot win by debasing our own currency; by wrecking our own brand; by going just about as gay, goofy and Big-Gov as the Left; by embracing an AP- manufactured illusion that a coreless, cult-ish, consultant-driven financier has somehow purchased, state-by-state, "bound" Republican delegates like corporate takeover targets or slaves.**

Or, like submissive plural wives in a Big Love harem.

In fact, no plurality of Tampa delegates is wed to Mitt Romney, no delegates are his "spiritual wives" or child brides, and none are "sealed to him for eternity." Even on first ballot, no GOP delegate is "bound" to Romney; this not only *is* the longstanding actuality with RNC Rules, it is *necessarily* so for any truly "republican" party.[66]

---

[64] "Polygamy Prominent in GOP Presidential Hopeful Mitt Romney's Family Tree," Associated Press, February 24, 2007, at http://www.foxnews.com/story/0,2933,254362,00.html

[65] The web and blogosphere are rife with plausible charges that everything known as Mormonism – including "mainstream LDS," Fundamentalist Latter-Day Saints (FLDS), "splinter groups," etc. – collectively derives from the predatorial, sex-obsessed teachings of Joseph Smith, Jr., Brigham Young and their successors. Examples: "Understanding Mormononism: The Sex Cult" (http://remnantradio.org/Mirror/www.jesus-is-savior.com/False%20Religions/Mormons/sex_cult.htm); "Mormon Sex Slave Tells of Horrific Abuse by Church Leaders" (http://www.moneyteachers.org/Mormon+Sex+Slave.htm); "Mormon Trolls Attempting To Censure Mormon Sex Scandals," (http://nomormoninwhitehouse.blogspot.com/2012/06/mormon-trolls-attempting-to-censure.html). Certain accounts of eccentric Mormon behavior, of course, may be apocryphal, but it would be a colossal *non-sequitur* to thereby discount all of the "colorful" history pertaining to the origin, development and even recent leadership of Romney's LDS sect.

[66] For the very real potential event that Presidential primaries may yield a presumptive nominee discovered to have a fatal political problem – e.g., a history of mental illness, suicide attempts, pedophilia, incest, spousal abuse, bisexuality, Satanism, embezzlement, emailing lewd photographs of himself, involvement in a kooky cult, etc.. – RNC Rules

Judge Not

RINO relativists may wish to judge any sound-minded Tampa delegate who recoils from Romney's statist history; from his LDS polytheism and authoritarianism; and from his creepy public policy of abortion, sodomy, lesbianism and GLBT recruitment.[67]

Such judges might even be inclined to cast stones at us for showing inadequate enthusiasm over the recently-solemnized same-sex unions of Mary Cheney and Barney Frank. The brow-beatings often begin, with no sense of irony, at the words of Jesus in Matthew 7 ("Judge not lest ye be judged"), while somehow ignoring his admonition of John 7 ("Judge not according to appearance, but judge righteous judgment").[68]

Stipulated: As deeply sinful human beings ourselves, none of us wish to cast eternal stones – nor fiery brimstone – in divine condemnation of Romney (e.g., for his "Gay Youth Pride Proclamations" and gay marriage inauguration); of Ms. Cheney and Rep. Frank (for availing themselves, and their deeply wounded self-images, of that unwisdom which Romney spawned); of Sandusky (for imagining he had cover for his gay/bisex outrages from institutions and politicians cowed by the GLBT Left); of John Edwards, JFK, LBJ, RFK, RFK Jr., Bush 41, Clinton, Gingrich, Dole, Sanford, Jesse Jackson, Jesse Jr., Giuliani, etc. (for treating their wives and marital vows with contempt).

Nor would we wish to damn: Anderson Cooper, Ellen DeGeneres or Vicki Gene Robinson (nice people who have dedicated their careers, in part, to putting a sunny face on the profound sadness of homosexual choices);[69] nor

---

ultimately empower delegates to CONSCIENTIOUSLY ABSTAIN or vote their consciences, in entirely unbound fashion, on every ballot – *including, necessarily,* the First Ballot (after which no one contends any delegate is bound). In this manner, the Republican Party sensibly protects both the nation and its brand by upholding "small-r" republicanism; by empowering elected delegates to dutifully exercise their good judgment and wisdom, rather than binding them to "small d" democratic or "mobocratic" election results which can be unduly influenced by money, mass hysteria, misleading advertising, bad journalism, foreign interests, extortion, etc. See www.thereal2012delegatecount.com; "Response to "A Rogue Convention?" (http://www.fairvote.org/response-to-a-rogue-convention-how-gop-party-rules-may-surprise-in-201); "A Rogue Convention? How GOP party rules may surprise in 2012"(http://www.politico.com/news/stories/1111/69048_Page2.html); Reality Check: Republican Delegates "Unbound"? (http://www.youtube.com/watch?v=anWsU93fFsk&feature=relmfu); http://www.examiner.com/article/rnc-delegates-not-bound-to-any-candidate-on-first-ballot. Entirely apart from existing RNC Rules which uphold the right of all Tampa delegates to abstain -- and apart from the fact that any adverse RNC rule can be set aside or revised by the convention itself! -- Federal law also seems to protect the voting rights of Tampa delegates to abstain on the crucial First Ballot: "Federal Law: All Delegates are Unbound" (http://www.examiner.com/article/federal-law-all-delegates-are-unbound); "Federal law proves that all delegates are unbound: All delegates must see this" (http://www.dailypaul.com/237770/federal-law-proves-all-delegates-are-unbound-all-delegates-must-see-this). See page 75 and forward. In any case, it is indisputable that the Republican National Convention has the legal authority to dump Romney at Tampa and choose a more viable nominee.

[67] See, e.g., http://www.amycontrada.com/;"The Romney Files" (http://www.massresistance.org/romney/email_030212.html)"Romney on Boy Scouts" (http://www.youtube.com/watch?v=uEOJNw4lmlI); "Romney's Gay Youth Pride Proclamation" (http://www.massresistance.org/docs/marriage/romney/GayYouthProclamation.pdf); "Romney's Abortion Record: Spin vs. Truth" (http://www.slatev.com/video/romneys-abortion-record-spin-vs-truth/) and "The Conversion" (http://www.slate.com/articles/news_and_politics/the_conversion/2012/02/mitt_romney_s_abortion_record_flip_flop_or_conversion_.html)

[68] Most commentators recognize Jesus to be using two senses of the term, the first being "condemnation" with regard to a person's soul or worth, the second pertaining to moral discernment. The former is not widely regarded to be the role of ordinary mortals and the latter, of course, is unavoidable by ordinary mortals in daily life: To recognize marital infidelity as wrong, for example, requires making a judgment.

[69] Endowed by their Creator with unalienable rights to hetero-monogamous marriage; to the ecstasies of heterosexual intimacy and procreation; and to the deep, abiding joys of natural motherhood, fatherhood, and grandparenthood; these and other gay media celebrities spin their eschewal of those natural rights and joys as normative to a watching nation and world of young people searching out their own identities And yet, while gay TV icons may find compensatory comforts in fame and high salaries, their social emulators may not be quite so smiling: Scientific studies cited in Peter Sprigg's *The Top 10 Myths about Homosexuality* (Family Research Council, http://downloads.frc.org/EF/EF10F01.pdf) undercut "Myth No. 5: Homosexuals do not experience a higher level of psychological disorders than heterosexuals." Sprigg writes:

> Fact: Homosexuals experience considerably higher levels of mental illness and substance abuse than heterosexuals. A detailed review of the research has shown that "no other group of comparable size in society experiences such intense and widespread pathology."(36) One of the first triumphs of the modern homosexual movement was the removal of homosexuality from the American Psychiatric Association's official list of mental disorders in 1973. That decision was far more political than scientific in nature, (37) and an actual survey of psychiatrists several years later showed that a large majority still believed homosexuality to be pathological.(38)
>
> Nevertheless, regardless of whether one considers homosexuality itself to be a mental disorder, there can be no question that it is associated with higher levels of a whole range of mental disorders. Ron Stall, one of the nation's leading AIDS researchers, has been warning for years "that additive psychosocial health problems—otherwise known collectively as a 'syndemic'—exist among urban MSM" (39) [men who have sex with men]. For example, in 2003, his research team reported in the American Journal of Public Health that homosexual conduct in this population is associated with higher rates of multiple drug use, depression, domestic violence and a history of having been sexually abused as a child.(40) Findings released in 2005 from an on-going, population-based study of young people in New Zealand showed that homosexuality is ". . . associated with increasing rates of depression, anxiety, illicit drug dependence, suicidal thoughts and attempts. Gay males, the study shows, have mental health problems five times higher than young heterosexual males. Lesbians have mental health problems nearly twice those of exclusively heterosexual females."(41)
>
> A 2008 "meta-analysis" reviewed over 13,000 papers on this subject and compiled the data from the 28 most rigorous studies. Their conclusion was: "LGB [lesbian, gay, bisexual] people are at higher risk of mental disorder, suicidal ideation, substance misuse and deliberate self harm than heterosexual people."(42) Even the pro-homosexual Gay & Lesbian Medical Association (GLMA) acknowledges:
>
> - "Gay men use substances at a higher rate than the general population . . ."
> - "Depression and anxiety appear to affect gay men at a higher rate . . . ."
> - ". . . [G]ay men have higher rates of alcohol dependence and abuse . . . ."
> - ". . . [G]ay men use tobacco at much higher rates than straight men . . . ."
> - "Problems with body image are more common among gay men . . . and gay men are much more likely to experience an eating disorder . . . ."(43)
>
> The GLMA also confirms that:
>
> - ". . . [L]esbians may use tobacco and smoking products more often than heterosexual women use them."
> - "Alcohol use and abuse may be higher among lesbians."
> - ". . . [L]esbians may use illicit drugs more often than heterosexual women."(44)

Joseph Smith and Brigham Young (for giving cover to adultery, incest, pedophilia, pederasty, homoeroticism,[70] polytheism and polyamory under the rubrics of religion, plural marriage, and Temple Endowment rituals, etc.); nor would we damn the woman who was reportedly rescued, by a Jewish rabbi from an adulterer's grim fate, in John 8.

In that rescue, however, Jesus advised that she, "Go, and sin no more" – and so far as the record indicates, he refrained from announcing that marital infidelity had suddenly become OK. The core purpose of the Torah law to which Jesus assented – and to which millions of American Jews and Christians still assent to this day – is not to condemn, but rather to point humanity, and *especially our young,* toward upright, healthful and good ways of living. All law should do so.

From the earliest moments of our nation's history to the watershed moment we're approaching now, American citizens, U.S. society and republican delegates (to party conventions and to Congress) have always had to strive for sound judgments. We cannot avoid making moral, legal and scientific/health calls about such matters as sexuality (e.g., incest, stalking, voyeurism, public nudity, pedophilia, child brides, polygamy, clitorectomy, statutory rape, honor killings, burqas, anal intercourse, *e coli,* HIV, Hepatitis B, coprophilia, fisting, prostitution, cannibalism, necrophilia, bestiality, public health, the risk of STD pandemics, etc.).

Nor can we or should we strive for amorality, strive to *avoid* good discernment, with regard to economic and political systems (e.g., treating Communism, Fascism, Nazism, Sharia Islam or Corporatist Crony Capitalism as morally equivalent to truly tolerant and capitalistic free societies). Nor can we accept an amoral "moral equivalence" approach to matters of race, ethnicity and gender (e.g., slavery, voting rights, Jim Crow, anti-Semitism, property rights, transgender toilets, sexual harassment, our daughters in front-line combat, divorce, fathers' rights, etc.).

Nor, of course, can we ever rightly shrug-off the best interests of American children (e.g., to be protected from physical abuse, from deadbeat dads, from human trafficking, from the abortionist's knife, from embryonic experiments, from child porn, from K-12 public school pedophiles,[71] K-12 gay/bisex curricula and "transgender counseling," and from a crushing $120 trillion load of national debt unfunded liabilities[72]).

And so, neither is this a "hate" document; we and swing-state voters *simply see reality very differently* from the GOP frontrunner and the racist, sci-fi cult he has led. Sure, that's a harsh way to say it, but as we'll see, it's scary-accurate – and remember, the proposition before us is the Presidency of the United States.

> Homosexual activists generally attempt to explain these problems as results of "homophobic discrimination." However, there is a serious problem with that theory—there is no empirical evidence that such psychological problems are greater in areas where disapproval of homosexuality is more intense. On the contrary, even a study in the Netherlands—perhaps the most "gay-friendly" country in the world—showed "a higher prevalence of substance use disorders in homosexual women and a higher prevalence of mood and anxiety disorders in homosexual men."

Sprigg's footnoted "Myth 5" citations are as follows:

36 James E. Phelan, Neil Whitehead, Philip M. Sutton, "What Research Shows: NARTH's Response to the APA Claims on Homosexuality," Journal of Human Sexuality Vol. 1, p. 93 (National Association for Research and Therapy of Homosexuality, 2009).
37 See the very balanced account offered in Ronald Bayer, Homosexuality and American Psychiatry: The Politics of Diagnosis (Princeton, N.J.: Princeton University Press, 1981).
38 Ibid., p. 167, citing "Sexual Survey #4: Current Thinking on Homosexuality," Medical Aspects of Human Sexuality 11 (November 1977), pp. 110-11.
39 Ron Stall, Thomas C. Mills, John Williamson, Trevor Hart, Greg Greenwood, Jay Paul, Lance Pollack, Diane Binson, Dennis Osmond, Joseph A. Catania, "Association of Co-Occurring Psychosocial Health Problems and Increased Vulnerability to HIV/AIDS Among Urban Men Who Have Sex With Men," American Journal of Public Health, Vol. 93, No. 6 (June 2003), p. 941.
40 Ibid., 940-42.
41 "Study: Young Gay Men At Higher Risk Of Suicide," 365Gay.com, August 2, 2005; online at: http://www.365gay.com/newscon05/08/080205suicide.htm (page not available February 13, 2010; on file with author).
42 Michael King, Joanna Semlyen, Sharon See Tai, Helen Killaspy, David Osborn, Dmitri Popelyuk and Irwin Nazareth, "A systematic review of mental disorder, suicide, and deliberate self harm in lesbian, gay and bisexual people," BMC Psychiatry 2008, 8:70 (August 18, 2008); online at: http://www.biomedcentral.com/content/pdf/1471-244X-8-70.pdf
43 Victor M. B. Silenzio, "Top 10 Things Gay Men Should Discuss with their Healthcare Provider" (San Francisco: Gay & Lesbian Medical Association); accessed April 1, 2010; online at: http://www.glma.org/_data/n_0001/resources/live/Top%20Ten%20Gay%20Men.pdf
44 Katherine A. O'Hanlan, "Top 10 Things Lesbians Should Discuss with their Healthcare Provider" (San Francisco: Gay & Lesbian Medical Association); accessed April 1, 2010; online at: http://www.glma.org/_data/n_0001/resources/live/Top%20Ten%20Lesbians.pdf
45 Theo G. M. Sandfort, Ron de Graaf, Rob V. Bijl, Paul Schnabel, "Same-Sex Sexual Behavior and Psychiatric Disorders: Findings From the Netherlands Mental Health Survey and Incidence Study (NEMESIS)," Archives of General Psychiatry 58 (January 2001), pp. 88-89.

[70] See, e.g., Connell O'Donovan, *"The Abominable and Detestable Crime Against Nature": A Revised History of Homosexuality & Mormonism, 1840-1980*; 1994, 2004 (http://www.connellodonovan.com/abom.html); http://en.wikipedia.org/wiki/B._Morris_Young.

[71] See, e.g., Campbell Brown, "Teachers Unions Go to Bat for Sexual Predators," The Wall Street Journal, July 30, 2012 (http://online.wsj.com/article/SB10000872396390443437504577547313612049308.html?mod=googlenews_wsj).

[72] http://www.usdebtclock.org/

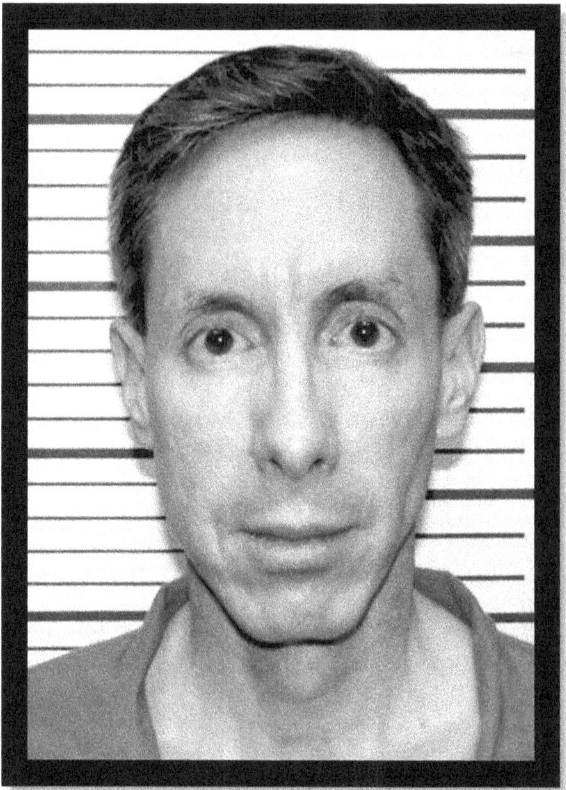

UTAH SEX OFFENDERS: Brigham Young (Left) was successor to founding Prophet Joseph Smith as head of the LDS Mormons, between them bedding over 80 known "spiritual wives" or child brides, some as young as 14. Mitt Romney's alma mater, Brigham Young University, is named for the original Utah governor – whom Romney as an LDS missionary, stake president, and Bishop is required to regard a divine prophet. Right: Warren Jeffs, a disciple and emulator of Mormonism's first two heads is leader of the Fundamentalist Church of Jesus Christ of Latter-Day Saints (FLDS Church) and was convicted of two felony counts of child sexual assault in 2011.

Wikipedia reports, "Jeffs gained international notoriety in May 2006 when he was placed on the FBI's Ten Most Wanted List [in connection with] illegal marriages between his adult male followers and underage girls.... Arizona charged him with eight additional counts, including sexual conduct with minors and incest [a practice approved of by Brigham Young] in two separate cases." Found guilty of rape in his Utah trial, Jeffs' conviction was, interestingly, reversed by Utah's Supreme Court, but he was found guilty in 2008 of child sexual assault (12 and 15-year-old girls) in a Texas polygamy commune reminiscent of the one in Mexico to which Romney's great grandfather Miles Park Romney fled with his plural wives in Mexico, where Romney's father George was born. "Jeffs' nephew, Brent Jeffs, filed a lawsuit against him alleging that ... his uncle sodomized him in the Salt Lake Valley compound then owned by the FLDS Church. Brent Jeffs said he was five or six years old at the time, and that Warren Jeffs' brothers, also named in the lawsuit, watched and participated in the abuse. Two of Warren Jeffs' other nephews also made similar abuse claims against him. One of the alleged victims, Clayne Jeffs, committed suicide with a firearm after accusing Warren Jeffs of sexually assaulting him as a child."[73] As we'll see, Jeffs wasn't misbehaving by certain historic Mormon standards; pedophilia, pederasty and homoeroticism have dogged Joseph Smith's cult from the very start.

Most of us, however, would very gladly break bread with the Romney family – or for that matter, *any* peaceful Mormon, Muslim, Scientologist, Wiccan, GLBT practitioner, etc. For one thing, such hospitality could be the only way souls genuinely troubled by heritage (or lifestyle choices) may find peace.

A welcoming Jewish or Christian dinner table, confident in the loving G_d of Abraham, Isaac and Jacob, could be a friendly bridge to appropriate therapies, counseling, books, ministries, deprogramming or support groups.[74] There's no need for traditionalists of goodwill to endorse or be neutral toward any given alien belief system or behavior in order to show basic human decency, tolerance, love and compassion to adherents, say, by warmly inviting them

---

[73] http://en.wikipedia.org/wiki/Warren_jeffs

[74] Examples: For friends fleeing homosexuality, Exodus International (http://exodusinternational.org/); for those fleeing Mormonism, Life After Ministries: Leading Mormons to the Real Jesus (http://www.lifeafter.org/); Recovery from Mormonism (http://exmormon.org/) and Christian Apologetics & Research Ministry (http://carm.org/mormonism); for those fleeing Scientology and other cults, Probe Ministries (http://www.probe.org/site/c.fdKEIMNsEoG/b.4217675/k.5019/Scientology_Religion_of_the_Stars.htm).

into our homes. Inviting Mormonism's latest White Horse to make *the White House* his home, however, is something quite different.

How does it play in the Swing States?

And yet, unless responsible Tampa delegates boldly exercise *their right and duty* to abstain on the First Ballot[75] to deny Romney the victory he demands – unless we derail his Tampa train and the fratricidal likelihood it will take its engineers and the entire GOP over a cliff – swing-state voters will, this fall, be evaluating hard, stubborn *facts* like these:

- The Church of Jesus Christ and the Latter-Day Saints (LDS), the dominant Mormon "mainstream" sect which Romney himself has helped lead, unambiguously holds as a matter of sacred doctrine that African-Americans are accursed with dark skin. Is there any doubt that this will receive intense media and voter attention?[76]

- Romney's Mormonism aggressively belittles[77] the very foundations of Judaism, Catholicism, Protestantism and Evangelicalism across the board; do GOP bosses really think pastors and worshipers – the kinds who have courageously attached their names to *The Manhattan Declaration* – are so feckless, so anemic and so moribund, that it just won't matter? Consider these utterances by Romney's fellow LDS leaders:

> **Both Catholics and Protestants are nothing less than the 'whore of Babylon'.... Any person who shall be so corrupt as to receive a holy ordinance of the Gospel from the ministers of any of these apostate churches will be sent down to hell with them, unless they repent.**
>
> - Apostle Orson Pratt, **Mitt Romney's great-great uncle**, *The Seer,* p. 255
>
> **...all the priests who adhere to the sectarian religions of the day with all their followers, without one exception, receive their portion with the devil and his angels.**
>
> - Prophet Joseph Smith , *The Elders Journal,* Joseph Smith Jr., vol.1, no.4, p.60
>
> **The Christian world, so-called, are heathens as to the knowledge of the salvation of God.**
>
> - Prophet Brigham Young, Journal of Discourses 8:171
>
> **Brother Taylor has just said that the religions of the day were hatched in hell. The eggs were laid in hell, hatched on its borders, and then kicked on to the earth.**
>
> - Prophet Brigham Young, *Journal of Discourses* 6:176
>
> **...the Book of Mormon remains secure, unchanged and unchangeable, ...But with the Bible it was not and is not so....it was once in the sole and exclusive care and custody of an abominable organization (Christianity), founded by the devil himself, likened prophetically unto a great whore, whose great aim and purpose was to destroy the souls of men in the name of religion. In these hands it ceased to be the book it once was.**
>
> - Apostle Bruce R. McConkie, *The Joseph Smith Translation,* pp. 12, 13

  As indicated by many other examples,[78] this is indeed the formal belief system embraced by the frontrunner for the 2012 Republican Party nomination.

- Mormon - Muslim parallels are already being drawn,[79] just as the bellicose LDS prophet Joseph Smith himself drew them:

---

[75] See page 75 and forward.

[76] See pages 23-25 for details. Googling "Mormon Racism" yields about 2.16 million results, including: LDS Mormon Church Racism Doctrine and Teaching (www.i4m.com/think/history/mormon_racism.htm); Racism in The Church of Jesus Christ of Latter-day Saints (Mormons) (www.religioustolerance.org/lds_race.htm); Mormon Racism (www.truthandgrace.com/Racism.html). The Mormon Curtain - MORMON RACISM (www.mormoncurtain.com/topic_racism.html); Mormon Church and racism: a new controversy about old teachings ...(www.slate.com/.../mormon_church_and_racism_a_new_controversy_about).

[77] See also "Mormon Bishop Mitt Romney's Anti-Christian Religion" (http://defendchristians.org/commentary/mormon-bishop-mitt-romneys-anti-christian-religion/). In this official LDS video (http://www.youtube.com/watch?v=A12bybW2doc) shot in the "sacred grove" in upstate New York where Smith allegedly received his visions, LDS president and holy prophet Gordon Hinckley declares Mormonism "the only true and living church on the face of the earth."

[78] See, e.g., http://www.i4m.com/think/history/mormon_christians.htm

During Missouri's "Mormon War" of 1838, Smith said, "I will be to this generation a second Mohammed, whose motto in treating for peace was 'the Alcoran [Koran] or the Sword.' So shall it eventually be with us—'Joseph Smith or the Sword!' "[80]

[M]y rational faculties would compel me to admit that the Mahometan history and Mahometan doctrine was a standard raised against the most corrupt and abominable idolatry that ever perverted our earth, found in the creeds and worship of Christians, falsely so named.

- Apostle Parley P. Pratt, **[Mitt Romney's great-great grandfather]**
Journal of Discourses, Vol. 3, p.40

So far as that one point is concerned, of worshipping the one true God under the name of Mahometanism, together with many moral precepts, and in war only acting on the defensive, I think they have exceeded in righteousness and truthfulness of religion, the idolatrous and corrupt church that has borne the name of Christianity.

- Apostle Parley P. Pratt, **[Mitt Romney's great-great grandfather]**
Journal of Discourses, Vol. 3, p.41

- Mormon polytheism[81] is akin to Greco-Roman mythology and heretical by ancient standards of Jewish and Christian orthodoxy; it honors a unitary, "greatest god" over *this* world (as with Islam) yet holds that there are many other finite gods of similar, perhaps superior stature, over other worlds. An important recent document co-signed by Christian theologian-apologists including Norman Geisler, R.C. Sproul, John Ankerberg and Kerby Anderson succinctly puts it this way:

  The Mormon Church teaches that God the Father, whom they call "Heavenly Father," was once a flesh and blood man from a planet (near a Star) called Kolob. Through his obedience to the same teaching espoused by Latter-day Saints, he was elevated to godhood sometime after his death. In fact, according to the Mormon Church, there are many such gods like "Heavenly Father" throughout the universe. According to Mormonism, God had a father and his father had a father and his father had a father *ad infinitum.*[82]

  Who would deny a core conflict with the broad, basic monotheism of moderate swing-state voters from Pennsylvania to Colorado, from North Carolina to Iowa?

- As with Islam, Mormonism evidences a *modern* history of violence, threatening and executing "Blood Atonement" against its leakers, dissenters, challengers, apostates and uppity women.[83] Which GOP analyst fancies that none of this will leak to the Purple States by November?

- Mormonism and Islam are two latter-day revelations which bear an anti-Semitic[84] knife-edge. Consider this sacred Mormon text:

  Wherefore, as I said unto you, it must needs be expedient that Christ ... should come among the Jews, among those who are the more wicked part of the world; and they shall crucify him ... and there is none other nation on earth that would crucify their God.... But because of priestcrafts and iniquities, they at Jerusalem will stiffen their necks against him, that he be crucified. Wherefore, because of their iniquities, destructions, famines, pestilences, and bloodshed shall come upon them; and they who shall not be destroyed shall be scattered among all nations.

  -- *The Book of Mormon*, 2 Nephi 10:3 – 6[85]

---

[79] Googling "Mormon Muslim" yields about 10.6 million results, including: Joseph Smith - The Second Muhammad? | Mormonism Research ...; BYU Muslims focus on Mormonism-Islam similarities | Deseret News; Similarities Between Mormonism and Islam; Similarities: Mormons and Muslims share much in their religion!; Joseph Smith and Muhammad.. - In Plain Site; Joseph Smith vs Muhammad: Who was the better liar? - Yahoo! Answers; "Are Mormons and Muslims Apples and Oranges?" (http://www.equip.org/articles/are-mormons-and-muslims-apples-and-oranges/), etc.

[80] Smith said it on October 14, 1838, according to Fawn M. Brodie's, *No Man Knows My History,* second edition, (New York: Alfred A. Knopf, 1971), p. 230–231, which in a footnote adds, "Except where noted, all the details of this chapter [16] are taken from the History of the [Mormon] Church. This speech, however, was not recorded there, and the report given here is based upon the accounts of seven men. See the affidavits of T.B. Marsh, Orson Hyde, George M. Hinkle, John Corrill, W.W. Phelps, Samson Avard, and Reed Peck in Correspondence, Orders, etc., pp. 57–9, 97–129. The Marsh and Hyde account, which was made on October 24, is particularly important. Part of it was reproduced in History of the [Mormon] Church, Vol. III, p. 167. See also the Peck manuscript, p. 80. Joseph himself barely mentioned the speech in his history; see Vol. III, p. 162."

[81] Joseph Smith taught, "You have got to learn to become Gods yourselves, the same as all Gods before you have done." Googling "Many Mormon Gods" yields about 30.6 million results.

[82] See "Mitt Romney, Mormonism and the Christian Vote: A Biblical Call to Christian Ministers and Leaders," (http://forthesakeofthegospel.com/document/)

[83] See, e.g., http://www.ldsvideo.org/2011/07/blood-atonement-and-mountain-meadows.html; "What is Blood Atonement?"(http://www.youtube.com/watch?v=kcOszCVeclw)

[84] Googling "Mormon Anti-Semitism" yields about 1.3 million results.

By sharp contrast, official Christianity teaches that *all* humans are deeply sinful: Because God so loved the world, he sent a Suffering Servant – first to be condemned in substitutionary atonement for humanity's sins (like Abraham's ram, a Passover lamb, a scapegoat or a blood sacrifice at Solomon's Temple), ultimately to rescue Israel and all humanity as their Davidic Messiah.

We all like sheep have gone astray, official Christianity holds, and we're *all* culpable in the unjust of death the Jewish Savior.[86] As an elemental matter of the Gospel and Josephus accounts, furthermore, it was pagan Rome which exercised ultimate earthly authority over the crucifixion of Jesus (and thousands of other Jews and Gentiles) during the reigns of Pontius Pilate, the Herods, and others. Indisputably, it was authoritarian, anti-Semite polytheism – not Jewish-rooted Christianity – which flattened Jerusalem in 586 BCE, 70 CE and during the 130's CE.

And yet now, for the first time ever, the Republican Party and the USA are lurching away from monotheism, indeed *aiming* to install a polytheist into the White House and world power.

Why Romney is no JFK

Romney can no more separate his candidacy from the extremes of LDS dogma[87] (by the broad American standards of Judeo-Christian monotheism) than he can from his own extreme record as governor of Massachusetts[88] (by the broad political standards of the US swing states).

And, he shows no signs of doing so. In 2007, Romney strongly affirmed his Mormonism to the Houston Ministerial Association, the same group before which John F. Kennedy spoke a half century earlier, seeking to ease concerns about his religion. Romney said,

> **Almost 50 years ago another candidate from Massachusetts explained that he was an American running for President, not a Catholic running for President. Like him, I am an American running for President. I do not define my candidacy by my religion. A person should not be elected because of his faith nor should he be rejected because of his faith.** [89]

But, c'mon, let's be real: What if a candidate embraces a nutty "faith" like Scientology, the Comet Cult, or Gaia? What if he rejects the monotheism of the Declaration of Independence and the American Founders in favor of a polytheistic pantheon of gods, akin to the ancient pagans?

What if his holy prophets are better remembered for their pedophilia than their piety? What if the candidate's sacred book is just as riddled with anachronisms[90] as were other men's wives with seed sown by the book's adulterous author? What if his religion, like that of Islam, systematically rationalizes the practice of lying and deception?[91] What if the candidate's silly prophets believed in lunar and solar residents?[92]

For four very good reasons, Mitt Romney is no JFK: First, self-identified Roman Catholics comprise about 24% of the U.S. population and their faith is a widely "known quantity"; Mormonism's share is less than 2% (coincidentally, about the same as the USA's self-identified gay and atheist populations, respectively).[93]

In contrast to Catholicism, LDS dogma and history represents a volatile "unknown quantity" to most of "Purple-State" America (as the surprising facts herein about Mormonism will attest to most readers). Once aware of such facts – many of them suppressed as a function of lazy media, cash-induced endorsements,[94] and the acquiescent

---

[85] http://www.lds.org/scriptures/bofm/2-ne/10?lang=eng

[86] This is the historic Christian understanding and summation of Bible passages like Isaiah 53, Isaiah 9, Isaiah 11, John 3:16 etc.

[87] Another brief, accurate video description of Mormon cosmology and metaphysics can be found here: http://carm.org/mormonism.

[88] See, e.g., http://www.massresistance.org/romney/

[89] "Romney's Faith in America address," (http://www.nytimes.com/2007/12/06/us/politics/06text-romney.html?pagewanted=print).

[90] "Book of Mormon Anachronisms" (http://www.youtube.com/watch?v=PqRT7VCwO2c).

[91] "LDS Honesty: Lying for the Lord" (http://www.mormonthink.com/lying.htm).

[92] http://en.wikipedia.org/wiki/Mormon_cosmology

[93] See, e.g., The Pew Forum on Religion and Public Life (http://religions.pewforum.org/reports/) and Peter *Sprigg's The Top 10 Myths about Homosexuality,* ("Myth 4: Ten Percent of the Population is Gay," Family Research Council, http://downloads.frc.org/EF/EF10F01.pdf). For a contrasting sense of scale, Pew indicates that the USA's combined, self-identified population of Catholics, Evangelicals, Orthodox Christians and tradition-oriented Jews exceeds 50% of the population.

[94] See, e.g., "35 Romney endorsers received contributions first" (http://www.salon.com/2012/01/07/35_romney_endorsers_received_contributions_first/); "Conservatives Challenge *National Review* to Come Clean on Romney "(http://www.massresistance.com/romney/press_release_071007.html); "Romney's Buyoffs" (http://massresistance.org/romney/#buyoff).

silence of countless bought-off GOP officials and compromised religious leaders – thoughtful *republicans* tend to concur that the GOP's Massachusetts Messiah is about as false a prophet as they come.[95]

Second, JFK was recognized as a World War hero, as the son of a diplomat who had given him a global geo-political perspective. Romney, by contrast, has pursued the post of Commander-in-Chief with no military or foreign policy experience (apart from proselytizing France as a Mormon missionary and presiding over Utah's 2002 Olympic Games; recent "gold metal gaffes" at London's summer games suggest he's already in way over his head).[96] JFK's religious heritage, moreover, gave him a worldwide purview; Romney's is vastly more parochialized, vastly more strange to citizens of the world who live beyond the canyons of Utah and the American southwest.

The third reason Romney's 2012 try is unlike Kennedy's of a half-century ago: JFK was a nominal, naughty, secularized Catholic who was in no way a clerical leader; Romney, by contrast, is a true-believing Mormon priest, missionary, BYU alum, Stake President and Bishop.[97] In 2008, Barack Obama had his "Pastor Problem," his connectivity to radical Chicago cleric Jeremiah Wright, with whom he eventually cut ties. In 2012, Mitt Romney *IS Jeremiah Wright* – a Mormon Bishop[98] tied not just to a local parish but overseeing *the entire Boston diocese* (to put the LDS organization in Catholic terms). As head of the Boston Stake, Romney was to Bay State Mormons what Cardinal Law was to Roman Catholics.

Fourth, Romney's relationship to Salt Lake City is *not* aptly analogized to JFK's relationship to Vatican City. The Pope does not claim a direct line to Heaven for the dictation of wholly new, divine revelations contradictory of the past; yet Romney's Mormon prophets seem to, *including those living in Utah today.*[99] Mormonism requires submission to an authoritarian hierarchy of "living prophets," today's links in an historic chain of domineering males and sexual predators which extends back into the 19th Century.[100]

At least in *that* rakish respect, as we'll see, JFK (and Joe, Bobby, Teddy, etc.) had a *lot* in common with the skirt-chasing founders of Mormonism, if not with Romney himself. Additional common ground between Romney and Kennedy, of course, is Massachusetts: Secularized and collectivized, beyond all recognition by the likes of Adams, Hancock, Revere and other Sons of Liberty, that commonwealth turned out – weirdly – to be the perfect place for Salt Lake City's favorite son to incubate the nationalization of government-controlled medicine, economy-steering CO_2 regulation… and perhaps, the end of the Institution of Marriage as we've known it.

Again, Romney declares: "I believe in my Mormon faith and I endeavor to live by it. My faith is the faith of my fathers – I will be true to them and to my beliefs."[101] By this, Tampa's GOP delegates and all American citizens stand duly warned: Their would-be President embraces the incredible teachings of Joseph Smith, Brigham Young and all other Mormon prophets… and takes them very seriously.

Mitt Romney is, of course, entitled to his own religion – yet *not* to *any* swing-state majority. Nor is he entitled to his own special ethics, logic or reality;[102] he aims to lead the USA and the entire world, not just his own private Idaho. Yet, this man's remarkable ability to reconcile objective reality with Joseph Smith's tall tales and tail-chasing (as non-LDS voters tend to see the libidinous Mormon prophet-god), presents us with three choices:

1. Romney's capacity to somehow integrate LDS racism, anti-Semitism, polytheism, polyamorous sexual pioneering, and its abundant contradictions, anachronisms and kooky cosmological claims without some kind of mind-melting, short-circuiting cognitive dissonance bespeaks an intellect *vastly superior* to that of average earth-bound voters; or
2. Romney is fully "in on the joke" that Joseph Smith, Brigham Young and their horny cohorts foisted on millions of gullible human beings, darkly embracing it; or

---

[95] In fairness to Gov. Romney, traditional Jews, Catholics, Protestants, Evangelicals and their clerical leaders generally regard latter-day visionaries like Muhammed and Joseph Smith, the respective founders of the Muslim and Mormon religions, to rank among history's most deceptive and dangerous false guides. Perhaps optimistically, it may be that Romney is merely a duped disciple, a naïve and credulous soul, as a function of a lifetime of programming.

[96] See, e.g., "Karl Rove: 'You have to shake your head' at Romney's Olympics gaffe," Boston Herald, July 27, 2012 (http://www.bostonherald.com/news/us_politics/view/20120727karl_rove_you_have_to_shake_your_head_at_romneys_olympic_gaffe/srvc=home&position=recent).

[97] http://en.wikipedia.org/wiki/Mitt_Romney

[98] Anyone on the right who ever doubted whether the candidacies of Christian clerics like Mike Huckabee or Pat Robertson would play to swing state America should be that much more concerned about the salability of "Bishop Romney".

[99] See, e.g., http://mormon.org/faq/present-day-prophet/; http://en.wikipedia.org/wiki/History_of_The_Church_of_Jesus_Christ_of_Latter-day_Saints

[100] We make no claims herein with regard to the personal lives or practices of any living links in that historic chain.

[101] "Romney's Faith in America address," (http://www.nytimes.com/2007/12/06/us/politics/06text-romney.html?pagewanted=print).

[102] Logical contradictions perceived in Mormon doctrine – and in Romney's relativist, ever-changing "Etch-a-Sketch" ethics and reality – will undoubtedly (and ironically) be on the receiving end of ever-more-withering treatment from a post-modern Left which largely dominates U.S. media and entertainment. One fine example: "A Quantum Theory of Mitt Romney,"(http://www.nytimes.com/2012/04/01/opinion/sunday/a-quantum-theory-of-mitt-romney.html?_r=2). The latter-day logical contradictions and cognitive dissonance of belief systems like Mormonism, Islam and Scientology can be aptly compared with those of post-modern materialism.

3. Romney, while reaching harder for nuclear access than Achmadinejad, harbors an astounding, Jonestown-like credulity which should terrify any rational U.S. citizen.

Romney can drink the Kool-Aid, but *should we?*

Abandoning Monotheism?

Will the G_P abandon G_D?

LDS Mormon doctrine to which Romney subscribes holds that, less than two centuries ago, an angel named Moroni – what remained of an ancient Israelite warrior whose tribe had migrated to the Americas – appeared to Joseph Smith, Jr. on a hill in upstate New York, not too far from Niagara Falls, so as to empower Smith to correct the errors of the Jewish and Christian scriptures. From Wikipedia:

> Mormonism .... was founded by Joseph Smith, Jr. ... [and] today represents the new, non-Protestant faith taught by Smith in the 1840s. After Smith's death, most Mormons followed Brigham Young to the Rocky Mountains as The Church of Jesus Christ of Latter-day Saints (LDS Church).... [T]he faith drew its first converts while Smith was dictating the text of the Book of Mormon. This book described itself as a chronicle of early indigenous peoples of the Americas, portraying them as believing Israelites, who had a belief in Christ many hundred years before his birth....
>
> Smith told his followers that he had seen a vision of God the Father and Jesus Christ in spring 1820 in answer to his question of which sect... he should join.... Smith further claimed that in answer to his prayer: **"I was answered [by Jesus] that I must join none of them, for they were all wrong; and the Personage who addressed me said that all their creeds were an abomination in his sight; that those professors were all corrupt"**.... By 1830, Smith reported that he had been instructed that God would use him to re-establish the true Christian church and that the *Book of Mormon* would be the means of establishing correct doctrine for the restored church....
>
> [After settling in Nauvoo, Illinois] In 1844, Smith was killed by members of the Illinois militia, precipitating a succession crisis. The largest group of Mormons accepted Brigham Young as the new prophet/leader and emigrated to what became the Utah Territory, where they incorporated The Church of Jesus Christ of Latter-day Saints. The church began to openly practice plural marriage, a form of polygamy that Smith had instituted in Nauvoo. Plural marriage became the faith's most sensational characteristic during the 19th century, but vigorous opposition by the United States Congress threatened the church's existence as a legal institution. In his 1890 Manifesto, church president Wilford Woodruff announced the official end of plural marriage, though the practice continued unofficially until the early 20th century. Several smaller groups of Mormons broke with the LDS Church over the issue of plural marriage, forming several denominations of Mormon fundamentalism....
>
> Mormons believe that their church is the "only true and living church" because of the divine authority restored through Smith, and that Smith and his successors are modern prophets who receive revelation from God to guide the church.... Mormon cosmology presents a unique view of God and the universe....[Mormons believe that the Bible] is incomplete and contains errors. In Mormon theology, many of these lost truths are restored in the *Book of Mormon*, which Mormons hold to be divine scripture and equal in authority to the Bible. The Mormon scriptural canon also includes a collection of revelations and writings contained in the *Doctrine and Covenants* and *Pearl of Great Price* ....
>
> Mormons believe the people of the Book of Mormon lived in the western hemisphere, that Christ appeared in the western hemisphere after his death and resurrection, that the true faith was restored in upstate New York by Joseph Smith, and that the Garden of Eden and location of Christ's second coming were and will be in the state of Missouri.[103]

Yet, swing-state voters in Missouri and elsewhere – most of whom are Catholic, Protestant or Evangelical – have been taught very differently from their pulpits for all the collective, cumulative Sundays of their lifetimes.

As if foreseeing latter-day figures like Muhammad, Smith and their enlightening angels, St. Paul, author of most of the New Testament, wrote that "there are some who trouble you and want to distort the gospel of Christ." Paul, the Jewish Pharisee, Roman citizen, disciple of Jesus, "Apostle to the Gentiles" and "Pillar of the Church" goes on in Galatians 1:

---

[103] http://en.wikipedia.org/wiki/Mormonism

"But even if we or an angel from heaven should preach to you a gospel contrary to the one we preached to you, let him be accursed. As we have said before, so now I say again: If anyone is preaching to you a gospel contrary to the one you received, let him be accursed."

Paul also wrote in 2 Corinthians 11 of

"false apostles, deceitful workmen, disguising themselves as apostles of Christ. And no wonder, for even Satan disguises himself as an angel of light."

(English Standard Version, emphases added).

As we'll soon see, it's quite safe to say that Purple-State voters even mildly literate in Judeo-Christianity (and *especially* those who lean agnostic, atheist, secular or non-aligned) could *never* become sufficiently comfortable with so squirrelly a scoundrel as Joseph Smith to elect him President of the United States:

Imagine a marital cheat of JFK or Clintonian proportions, add some pedophilia and homoeroticism, then add some cultic mind control and charlatanism. Replete with his magic tricks, latter-day sex doctrines, a nouveau gospel bestowed by an angel of light and abundant dubious proofs of his divine authority – plus all the charismatic, dictatorial charms of a Muhammad or Rev. Jim Jones – it's pretty tough to imagine how Joseph Smith could carry Ohio, Virginia, Florida or the "show-me" state of Missouri.

Big Love: Joseph Smith, Jr., the frisky founder of the Mormon religion and 1844 U.S. Presidential candidate, challenged the Jewish-Christian monotheism and hetero-monogamy of the American Founders. So too has his disciple and 2008-2012 emulator, Mormon Bishop Mitt Romney, especially through his history-making role as America's Founding Father of Gay Marriage.[104] Romney's sexual pioneering in Massachusetts – which he made the USA's first gay wedlock state (see page 43) – has been a necessary legal precursor to the reinstatement, and possible nationalization, of Utah-style polygamy as practiced by Romney's LDS ancestors and thousands of other Mormons well into the 20th Century.

Yet if that's a fair call, then why would Tampa's GOP delegates delude themselves into believing that swing-state voters may elect one of Smith's duped disciples, Mitt Romney? Why should they join the wagon train of True Believing Mormons in their truly bizarre beliefs? Why should any sane GOP delegate even *wish* to bet the ranch on a candidate, theoretically a President, who is under submission to a Living Prophet and his inspired apostles in Salt Lake City?

---

[104] See, page 47 and forward, and e.g., http://massresistance.org/romney/#SSM

Let's think about this carefully. Who's nuttier: Iran's Islamist Holocaust denier... or the top American affirmer of Prophet Smith's whoppers? Do we *really* want the Republican Party to put up someone who's in close competition? Do we really want to offset Achmadinejad, a believer in the apocalyptic Twelfth Imam, with Salt Lake City's anticipated fulfillment of The White Horse Prophecy?

> The disputed prophecy was recorded in a diary entry of a Mormon who had heard the tale from two men who were with Joseph Smith in Nauvoo, Ill. when he supposedly declared the prophecy."You will see the Constitution of the United States almost destroyed," the diary entry quotes Smith as saying. "It will hang like a thread as fine as a silk fiber."
>
> Not only will the Mormons save the Constitution, under the prediction, but the prophecy goes further, insinuating that Mormons will control the government."Power will be given to the White Horse to rebuke the nations afar off, and you obey it, for the laws go forth from Zion," the prophecy says. The LDS Church denounces the premonition, which was recorded 10 years after Smith's death.
>
> A church spokesman pointed to a quote from the faith's sixth president, Joseph F. Smith, who called the prophecy "ridiculous.""It is simply false; that is all there is to it," the church prophet was quoted saying. Joseph Smith, who Mormons believe found ancient gold plates and transcribed them into the Book of Mormon, ran for president in 1844, a year after he supposedly told of the White Horse Prophecy. Smith was murdered by a mob shortly thereafter. [105]

So, although one of the less-laughable pieces of Mormon folklore, it's one that LDS officials deny – perhaps because unlike all the *other* ridiculous components of Mormonism, this one could remind American voters to be wary of Mormon politicians.

> Romney avoids mentioning it, but Smith ran for president in 1844 as an independent commander in chief of an "army of God" advocating the overthrow of the U.S. government in favor of a Mormon-ruled theocracy. Challenging Democrat James Polk and Whig Henry Clay, Smith prophesied that if the U.S. Congress did not accede to his demands that "they shall be broken up as a government and God shall damn them." Smith viewed capturing the presidency as part of the mission of the church. He had predicted the emergence of "the one Mighty and Strong" — a leader who would "set in order the house of God" — and became the first of many prominent Mormon men to claim the mantle....But his candidacy was cut short when he was shot to death by an anti-Mormon vigilante mob. Out of Smith's national political ambitions grew what would become known in Mormon circles as the "White Horse Prophecy" — a belief ingrained in Mormon culture and passed down through generations by church leaders..." [106]

How the heck can brainy Karl Rove "the Architect"— albeit of massive GOP spending and debt hikes during the Bush 43 years[107] – possibly bet that Joseph Smith's and Romney's special version of reality (the racism, anti-Semitism, spooky prophecies, belligerent religious chauvinism and sci-fi polytheism of the Mormon holy texts, prophets and founding culture) somehow *won't* get broad play in heavily Jewish, heavily Hispanic Catholic, heavily evangelical Florida, mother of all U.S. swing states?

Do our friends Reince, Rove and other brilliant GOP quants – who can perhaps count every tree without seeing the forest? – *really* fancy that persisting Mormon proxy baptisms for dead Holocaust victims will play well in Miami?[108] Do they *seriously* believe that DNA-denying LDS claims (e.g., *that Native American Indians are descended from ancient, immigrant Israelites*) will just somehow get ignored?[109]

Whatever the suits wish to argue, Tampa's GOP delegates would be foolish to bet on *that.* The safer wager is that all such oddities of Mormonism – and many, many more – will soon be subject to withering fire from left-tilting media materialists in their relentless effort to take down the GOP; to tar the ancient Biblical faiths; and to win over U.S. young people to their bleak worldview, all in one fell swoop.[110]

---

[105] Thomas Burr, "Romney candidacy has resurrected last days prophecy of Mormon saving the Constitution," Salt Lake City Tribune, June 4, 2007 (http://www.sltrib.com/lds/ci_6055090)

[106] Sally Denton, "Romney and the White Horse Prophecy" (http://www.salon.com/2012/01/29/mitt_and_the_white_horse_prophecy/); see also Diane Tanner, "Joseph Smith's 'White Horse' Prophecy,"(http://www.utlm.org/onlineresources/whitehorseprophecy.htm); Sally Denton, "Romney and the White Horse Prophecy" (http://www.salon.com/2012/01/29/mitt_and_the_white_horse_prophecy/).

[107] Arthur Laffer and Stephen Moore, "Obama's Real Spending Record: Under Presidents Bush and Obama, Government Spending Exploded as a share of the Economy" (http://online.wsj.com/article/SB10001424052702303753904577450910257188398.html)

[108] See, e.g., "Elie Wiesel calls on Mitt Romney to make Mormon Church stop proxy baptisms of Jews" (http://www.washingtonpost.com/politics/elie-wiesel-calls-on-mitt-romney-to-make-mormon-church-stop-proxy-baptisms-of-jews/2012/02/14/gIQAZK6bER_story.html)

[109] See, e.g., Bill McKeever, "DNA Science Challenges LDS History," (http://www.equip.org/articles/dna-science-challenges-lds-history/).

[110] See, e.g., Bill Maher's discussion of Mormonism here: http://www.youtube.com/watch?v=aKqqGX0DEMM&feature=related

Mormon Racism and the Hispanic Vote

Here's sufficient reason why no faithful Jew, Christian or GOP delegate should associate himself or herself with the nomination of Mitt Romney – and why it must be averted: The holy texts and prophets of Romney's LDS Mormonism absolutely reek with racism.

African-American voters are as likely to vote overwhelmingly for Obama as the tiny but overwhelmingly-white Mormon population is likely to vote for Romney (if the GOP foolishly nominates him at Tampa). Yet crucial Hispanic voters – already wary of the GOP frontrunner as a function of deportation threats he made against illegal immigrants during the primaries – have yet to hear Mormon Bishop Mitt Romney repudiate the overt racism of his holy Mormon prophets and his holy scriptures from *The Book of Mormon:*

- **Alma 3:6 And the skins of the Lamanites were dark, according to the mark which was set upon their fathers, which was a curse upon them because of their transgression and their rebellion against their brethren, who consisted of Nephi, Jacob, and Joseph, and Sam, who were just and holy men.**

- **1 Nephi 12:23 And it came to pass that I beheld, after they had dwindled in unbelief they became a dark, and loathsome, and a filthy people, full of idleness and all manner of abominations.**

- **2 Nephi 5:21 For behold, they had hardened their hearts against him, that they had become like unto a flint; wherefore, as they were white, and exceedingly fair and delightsome, that they might not be enticing unto my people the Lord God did cause a skin of blackness to come upon them.**

- **1 Nephi 11:13 And I beheld the city of Nazareth; and in the city of Nazareth I beheld a virgin, and she was exceedingly fair and white.**

- **1 Nephi 13:15 And I beheld the Spirit of the Lord, that it was upon the Gentiles, and they did prosper and obtain the land for their inheritance; and I beheld that they were white, and exceedingly fair and beautiful, like unto my people before they were slain.**

- **2 Nephi 30:6 And then shall they rejoice; for they shall know that it is a blessing unto them from the hand of God; and their scales of darkness shall begin to fall from their eyes; and many generations shall not pass away among them, save they shall be a pure white (1830 edition) and a delightsome people.**

- **Jacob 3:8 O my brethren, I fear that unless ye shall repent of your sins that their skins will be whiter than yours, when ye shall be brought with them before the throne of God.**

- **3 Nephi 2:15 And their curse was taken from them, and their skin became white like unto the Nephites.**

- **Mormon 5:15 And also that the seed of this people may more fully believe his gospel, which shall go forth unto them from the Gentiles; for this people shall be scattered, and shall become a dark, a filthy, and a loathsome people, beyond the description of that which ever hath been amongst us, yea, even that which hath been among the Lamanites, and this because of their unbelief and idolatry.**

- **2 Nephi 10:3 – 6 Wherefore, as I said unto you, it must needs be expedient that Christ ... should come among the Jews, among those who are the more wicked part of the world; and they shall crucify him ... and there is none other nation on earth that would crucify their God.... But because of priestcrafts and iniquities, they at Jerusalem will stiffen their necks against him, that he be crucified. Wherefore, because of their iniquities, destructions, famines, pestilences, and bloodshed shall come upon them; and they who shall not be destroyed shall be scattered among all nations."**

How can Republicans capture sufficient Electoral College numbers in the battleground states if they nominate a Mormon missionary, Stake President and Bishop who has yet to repudiate such heinous, yet supposedly *sacred racist words,* from the *Book of Mormon*?

Because Romney believes these words are holy scripture – the divinely-revealed Word of (one of) Mormonism's (many) god(s) handed down on golden plates to Joseph Smith by an angel on hill near Palmyra, New York – the media has absolutely every right and duty to be sure that swing-state voters know it. And, to expect Romney to repudiate and distance himself from such filth in much the same way Fox News demanded Obama distance himself from the outrageous rhetoric of his pastor, the Rev. Jeremiah Wright.

If descended in any manner from peoples whom Europeans saw as the Indians of the Americas – as indeed are many swing-staters of Mexican, Cuban, Native American or Central American ancestry – then Mormonism, without a shred of scientific DNA evidence, generally holds such voters to be of "Lamanite" derivation.

> According to the *Book of Mormon*, a Lamanite ... is a member of a dark-skinned nation of indigenous Americans that battled with the light-skinned Nephite nation. Although mainstream archaeologists, geneticists, and historians do not recognize the existence of Lamanites, adherents of the Latter Day Saint movement typically believe that the Lamanites comprise some part, if not the entirety, of the indigenous peoples of the Americas and the Polynesian people.
>
> The *Book of Mormon* describes the Lamanites as descendants of Laman and Lemuel, two rebellious brothers of a family of Israelites who crossed the ocean in a boat around 600 BC. Their brother Nephi founded the Nephite nation.
>
> The Lamanites reputedly gained their dark skin as a sign of the curse for their rebelliousness (the curse was the withdrawal of the Spirit of God), and warred with the Nephites over a period of centuries. The book says that Jesus appeared [in the Americas] and converted all the Lamanites to Christianity; however, after about two centuries, the Lamanites fell away and eventually exterminated all the Nephites....
>
> The non-canonical introduction to the 1981 LDS Church edition of the Book of Mormon stated, "the Lamanites are the principal ancestors of the American Indians." The wording was changed in the 2006 Doubleday edition and subsequent editions published by the LDS Church, stating only that the Lamanites "are among the ancestors of the American Indians." Many Latter Day Saints also consider Polynesian peoples and the other indigenous peoples of the Americas to be Lamanites. A 1971 church magazine article referred to Lamanites as "consist[ing] of the Indians of all the Americas as well as the islanders of the Pacific."
>
> The existence of a Lamanite nation has received no support within mainstream science or archaeology. Genetic studies indicate that the indigenous Americans are primarily related to present-day populations in Mongolia and its environs, and the Polynesians to those in southeast Asia....
>
> In the *Book of Mormon,* Lamanites are described as having a "skin of blackness" caused by God's curse on the descendants of Laman for their wickedness and corruption: "And he had caused the cursing to come upon [the Lamanites], yea, even a sore cursing, because of their iniquity. For behold, they had hardened their hearts against him, and they had become like unto a flint; wherefore, as they were white, and exceedingly fair and delightsome, that they might not be enticing unto my people the Lord God did cause a skin of blackness to come upon them." [2 Nephi 5:21]....
>
> Several *Book of Mormon* passages have been interpreted by some Latter Day Saints as indicating that Lamanites would revert to a lighter skin tone upon accepting the gospel. For example, early editions of the *Book of Mormon* contained the passage: "[T]heir scales of darkness shall begin to fall from their eyes; and many generations shall not pass away among them, save they shall be a white and a delightsome people".
>
> In 1840, with the third edition of the *Book of Mormon,* the wording was changed to "a pure and a delightsome people" by Joseph Smith, Jr., who claimed to be the translator of the book. However, all future LDS Church printings of the Book of Mormon until 1981 continued from the second edition, saying the Lamanites would become "a white and delightsome people". In 1960, LDS Church apostle Spencer W. Kimball suggested that the skin of Latter-day Saint Native Americans was gradually turning lighter:
>
> > I saw a striking contrast in the progress of the Indian people today .... The day of the Lamanites is nigh. For years they have been growing delightsome, and they are now becoming white and delightsome, as they were promised. In this picture of the twenty Lamanite missionaries, fifteen of the twenty were as light as Anglos, five were darker but equally delightsome. The children in the home placement program in Utah are often lighter than their brothers and sisters in the hogans on the reservation. At one meeting a father and mother and their sixteen-year-old daughter we represent, the little member girl—sixteen—sitting between the dark father and mother, and it was evident she was several shades lighter than her parents—on the same reservation, in the same hogan, subject to the same sun and wind and weather.... These young members of the Church are changing to whiteness and to delightsomeness. One white elder jokingly said that he and his companion were donating blood regularly to the hospital in the hope that the process might be accelerated.[111]

But wait, there's more: Mormon Bishop Romney's holy prophet Brigham Young – the man for whom Romney's alma mater is named – said:

> **You see some classes of the human family that are black, uncouth, uncomely, disagreeable and low in their habits, wild, and seemingly deprived of nearly all the blessings of the intelligence that is generally bestowed**

[111] http://en.wikipedia.org/wiki/Lamanite

upon mankind. The first man that committed the odious crime of killing one of his brethren will be cursed the longest of any one of the children of Adam. Cain slew his brother. Cain might have been killed, and that would have put a termination to that line of human beings. This was not to be, and the Lord put a mark upon him, which is the flat nose and black skin.

Trace mankind down to after the flood, and then another curse is pronounced upon the same race-that they should be the "servant of servants;" and they will be, until that curse is removed; and the Abolitionists cannot help it, nor in the least alter that decree. How long is that race to endure the dreadful curse that is upon them? That curse will remain upon them, and they never can hold the Priesthood or share in it until all the other descendants of Adam have received the promises and enjoyed the blessings of the Priesthood and the keys thereof. Until the last ones of the residue of Adam's children are brought up to that favourable position, the children of Cain cannot receive the first ordinances of the Priesthood."

LDS President and Prophet Brigham Young, delivered in the Tabernacle,
Great Salt Lake City, October 9, 1859, *Journal of Discourses,* 26 vols., 7:, p.291

Shall I tell you the law of God in regard to the African race? If the white man who belongs to the chosen seed mixes his blood with the seed of Cain, the penalty, under the law of God, is death on the spot. This will always be so.

LDS President and Prophet Brigham Young, *Journal of Discourses,* vol. 10, p. 110).

Rationalizing the ban on black LDS priests that persisted almost into the 1980's, LDS authority Bruce R. McConkie writes,

As a result of his rebellion, Cain was cursed with a dark skin; he became the father of the Negroes, and those spirits who are not worthy to receive the priesthood are born through this lineage. Noah's son Ham married Egyptus ,a descendant of Cain, thus preserving the Negro lineage through the flood. ...in a broad general sense, caste systems have their origin in the gospel itself, and when they operate according to the divine decree, the resultant restrictions and segregation are right and proper and have the approval of the lord. To illustrate: Cain, Ham, and the whole negro race have been cursed with a black skin, the mark of Cain, so they can be identified as a caste apart, a people with whom the other descendants of Adam should not intermarry.

LDS Apostle Bruce R. McConkie, *Mormon Doctrine,* 1958 edition, pages 102, 477, 107-108

Mitt Romney has described his emotions (he "wept") when he heard that the segregationist LDS ban on black priests ended in 1978. (Because of Romney's long record of misleading statements, it is not entirely clear if these were tears of joy or tears of regret).

In any case, neither the LDS nor Romney has ever repudiated the *doctrinal basis* – the holy words of the *Book of Mormon* and Mormonism's latter-day "living prophets" – for that ban. Here, therefore, are the questions the media (quite properly) will be asking this fall:

- Does Romney hold *The Book of Mormon* to be authoritative, to be divinely-revealed holy scripture?
- If so, does he believe, per the scriptural passages above, that the darker skin of Hispanic Americans, Native Americans, Pacific Islanders or African-Americans is indeed a sign of their accursedness and that of their Lamanite ancestors, by (one of) his god(s)?
- Does Romney believe the prophetic words of LDS President Brigham Young, for whom his college was named, that the mark of a divine curse upon the descendants of Cain is "the flat nose and black skin"?
- Why doesn't Romney accept the scientific DNA evidence against the descent of the original Americans from ancient Israelites?

Let's be real: Is there any GOP political consultant who imagines that potentially winnable Hispanic voters in New Mexico, Nevada and Florida won't care what Romney has to say – or not say – on these matters? For that matter, is there any GOP suit who believes that college-educated women in the suburbs of Des Moines, Philadelphia, and Arlington won't care?

The Manhattan Declaration

Who are we? We're Jewish and Christian Americans among 525,000 souls who have signed *The Manhattan Declaration* (or affirmed that within it which is consistent with Judaism and personal conviction) and/or among the listed **Swing-State Speakers Bureau Invitees** (see Appendix), many heading for Tampa. We stand, determined and united, to uphold:

- The essential American idea to which Jefferson and the USA's Founders assented in our nation's *Declaration of Independence*, that all human beings are designedly "Created equal" by the One G_d of the Bible and are "endowed by their Creator with certain unalienable rights" such as Life and Liberty;
- The underlying Judeo-Christian agreement on Natural Law, those commonalities of human experience and inference from design upon which American Society and the Republic itself are predicated;
- Our longstanding Judeo-Christian agreement on the Rule of Law; Constitutionalism; Individual Freedom; Religious Liberty and Tolerance; Minimalist Government; Equality in the sight of G_d and under the Law; and the U.S.- Israel Alliance;
- The self-evident truth that *Creator-endowed* men and women, subject to "the Laws of Nature and of Nature's God,"[112] are necessarily non-random, non-accidental and *physically designed* beings who are unavoidably accountable to their Creator for their conduct;
- The nomination and election of a Republican Presidential ticket which can truly weld and unite the GOP's conservative, libertarian, Judeo-Christian traditionalist and Tea Party wings;
- The nomination and election of a 2012 Republican ticket endowed with military experience, knowing war well enough to strive to avoid it, yet fully ready to execute the first duties of the President as Commander-in-Chief: To defend Americans, and universal American liberties as Jefferson and the Founders defined them, in a very dangerous world – while prudently avoiding American bloodshed in foolish or unconstitutional entanglements;
- The nomination and election of a next President and Vice President who, recognizing the truths of 1776 to be just as valid today as in 1776 -- and therefore embracing the core concerns of *The Manhattan Declaration* on Marriage, Life and Religious Liberty – will sign before witnesses *The Manhattan Declaration,*[113] *The Marriage Vow, The Pro-Life Presidential Leadership Pledge*, *The Personhood Pledge* and *The Repeal ObamaCare Pledge.*

Tellingly, Romney has rejected or entirely avoided *all five* of these written pledges.[114]

As we've said, he has no military or foreign policy experience. And, as a grown-up LDS Bishop and polytheist, he simply *cannot mean* what the Declaration's monotheistic signers affirmed when, with a "firm reliance on the protection of divine Providence" they appealed "to the Supreme Judge of the world for the rectitude" of their intentions;[115] Mormonism, as we'll see below, has more gods than Homer's *Iliad* or Stan Lee's *The Avengers.*

---

[112] From *The Declaration of Independence.*

[113] Or, if Jewish, affirm that within *The Manhattan Declaration* which is consistent with Judaism.

[114] As of June 22, 2012, Romney has signed NONE of these pledges, while Santorum – who seemed to be leading non-Romney alternative up to his withdrawal – had signed ALL of them. Santorum, Bachmann and Perry signed *The Marriage Vow*, a national pledge document which has been described as a policy-oriented "Manhattan Declaration with teeth." (For the full original text, go to https://motherjones.com/files/marriagevow.pdf). For the text of *The Repeal ObamaCare Pledge* from Independent Women's Voice, go to http://www.therepealpledge.com/. That pledge – signed by virtually every GOP contender EXCEPT Romney, today more clearly than ever represents not only a cry for market-based health care, but also a tangible stand for religious liberty against the coercive anti-faith, anti-life aspects of RomneyCare/ObamaCare. For the texts of the Susan B. Anthony List *Pro-Life Presidential Leadership Pledge* and the *The Personhood Pledge,* go to http://www.sba-list.org/2012pledge and http://www.personhoodusa.com/blog/personhood-republican-presidential-candidate-pledge, respectively. Again, virtually all 2012 contenders signed those pledges EXCEPT Romney.

[115] From *The Declaration of Independence.* University of Baltimore law professor Michael B. Meyerson in "Was the Declaration of Independence Christian?," The Wall Street Journal, July 6, 2012 (http://online.wsj.com/article/SB10001424052702304211804577504923449570972.html?mod=googlenews_wsj) writes that,

> [T]he language of the Declaration wasn't limited to a particular faith. Deliberately designed to be as inclusive as possible, it was a quintessentially American achievement—specific enough to be embraceable by those with orthodox religious views but broad enough to permit each American to feel fully included and equally respected. George Washington maintained this adroit balance when he became president. In his first inaugural address, written with the assistance of James Madison, Washington declared that it would be "peculiarly improper to omit in this first official Act, my fervent supplications to that Almighty Being who rules over the Universe." Even Jefferson and Madison, often described as believing in a total separation of religion and government, continued the practice of using inclusive religious language. Jefferson urged in his first inaugural, "May that infinite power, which rules the destinies of the universe, lead our councils to what is best," while Madison stated that, "my confidence will under every difficulty be best placed . . . in the guardianship and guidance of that Almighty Being whose power regulates the destiny of nations." The Framers didn't see such nondenominational language as divisive. They believed it was possible—in fact desirable—to have a public expression of religion that is devout, as long as it recognizes and affirms the variety of belief systems that exist in our pluralistic nation.

Indeed, the endowing, designing Creator of our 1776 Declaration and national charter is not boxed-in by Anglican, Catholic, Protestant or Jewish denominational details, yet is described, in unifying fashion, as the infinite, personal and caring monotheistic power in whom the American Founders recognized universal human rights to be anchored. A half century later, Joseph Smith, Brigham Young and their Mormon disciples (including Mitt Romney's great, great grandfather, Miles Romney), would seek to supplant American monotheism and hetero-monogamy with polytheism, polygamy and other forms of sexuality more frequently found in pagan or Islamic portions of the world and world history.

The Sci-Fi President

To our friend Reince and all of our fellow RNC delegates whom Romney has jammed into this tight spot: Is there any disputing that the GOP frontrunner is about as white, rich and Mormon as he possibly could be? Do we *really* suppose that the racially-explosive language[116] of sacred LDS texts and oracular prophets like Brigham Young – so far entirely unrepudiated by Romney – somehow *won't* receive wide exposure in the Trayvon age?

If the inherent racism of Romney's Mormon scriptures and prophets isn't quite alienating enough to battleground voters in states like New Mexico, Nevada and Florida – especially to crucial Hispanic voters already wary of Romney on illegal immigration and deportation issues – then *another* sort of alien will doubtless seal the GOP's celestial fate:

Romney's Mormonism holds that earth's (main) god is a physical being who comes from, or near, a star called "Kolob."[117] Mormonism's first two divine prophets, Joseph Smith and Brigham Young, proclaimed the moon, sun or both to be inhabited.[118] According to Wikipedia:

> LDS Church leaders have espoused opinions that demonstrate their personal beliefs in other life in the universe. According to Oliver B. Huntington, Joseph Smith, Jr. taught that there was life on the Moon:
>
>> "As far back as 1837, I know that he said the moon was inhabited by men and women the same as this earth, and that they live to a greater age than we do—that they generally live to near the age of 1000 years. He described the men as averaging near six feet in height, and dressing quite uniformly in something near the Quaker style. In my Patriarchal blessing, given by the father of Joseph the Prophet [Joseph Smith, Sr.], in Kirtland, 1837, I was told that I should preach the gospel before I was 21 years of age; that I should preach the gospel to the inhabitants upon the islands of the sea, and—to the inhabitants of the moon, even the planet you can now see with your eyes."
>
> ....In a sermon given on July 24, 1870, LDS Church President Brigham Young discussed the inhabitation of that the moon and the sun as well as other astronomical ideas:
>
>> ....I will tell you who the real fanatics are: they are they who adopt false principles and ideas as facts, and try to establish a superstructure upon a false foundation. They are the fanatics; and however ardent and zealous they may be, they may reason or argue on false premises till doomsday, and the result will be false. ...Who can tell us of the inhabitants of this little planet that shines of an evening, called the moon? When we view its face we may see what is termed "the man in the moon," and what some philosophers declare are the shadows of mountains. But these sayings are very vague, and amount to nothing; and when you inquire about the inhabitants of that sphere you find that the most learned are as ignorant in regard to them as the most ignorant of their fellows.
>>
>> So it is with regard to the inhabitants of the sun. Do you think it is inhabited? I rather think it is. Do you think there is any life there? No question of it; it was not made in vain.
>
> ....Some modern LDS Church leaders have taught that there are people living on other earths. For instance, apostle Joseph Fielding Smith wrote:
>
>> "We are not the only people that the Lord has created. We have brothers and sisters on other earths. They look like us because they, too, are the children of God and were created in his image, for they are also his offspring."
>
> Smith also wrote,
>
>> "...the great universe of stars has multiplied beyond the comprehension of men. Evidently each of these great systems is governed by divine law; with divine presiding Gods, for it would be unreasonable to assume that each was not so governed."

---

[116] See pages 23-25. Early tremors have been felt: "Dozier: Romney should denounce racist Mormon church" (http://www.sfltimes.com/index.php?option=com_content&task=view&id=9454&Itemid=199)

[117] See http://www.lds.org/scriptures/gs/kolob.t1?lang=eng&letter=k; http://en.wikipedia.org/wiki/Kolob;

[118] http://www.challengemin.org/moon.html

Apostle Neal A. Maxwell wrote, "we do not know how many inhabited worlds there are, or where they are. But certainly we are not alone."[119]

Secular prophet Newt Gingrich only envisioned *colonizing* the moon – not fraternizing with lunar natives – yet even *that* sounded loony enough to help crash his candidacy. It seems, however, that Gingrich, Santorum, Bachmann, Perry, Cain and possibly even Ron and Rand Paul may collectively jettison their conservative credibility[120] with moonstruck, on-stage Florida convention endorsements.

Planet Romney

But, before any Tampa delegates, fawning operatives or failed challengers immolate themselves to help launch such a fatally-flawed nominee, each may wish to recall the awful spectacle of NASA's *Challenger;* for all the reasons discussed herein, no GOP frontrunner in memory has been a more certain electoral crash-burn than this Rocket Man.

Rather than reduce their own brands and that of the entire GOP to ashes, Tampa's eager endorsers and entrusted delegates may wish to ponder how swing-state voters will react on learning that Mitt Romney believes not only is the U.S. Presidency within reach; *so too, literally, is his own planet:*

Romney's LDS Mormonism holds that God the Father in the Bible (Elohim) was once a man, and that just like Elohim, dutiful men like Joseph Smith and Mitt Romney can also become gods of their own worlds. From the official LDS Mormon website as of late July, 2012:

> **Is President Lorenzo Snow's oft-repeated statement—'As man now is, God once was; as God now is, man may be'—accepted as official doctrine by the Church?....The Prophet Joseph Smith himself publicly taught the doctrine the following year, 1844, during a funeral sermon of Elder King Follett: 'God himself was once as we are now, and is an exalted man, and sits enthroned in yonder heavens! ... It is the first principle of the Gospel to know for a certainty the Character of God, and to know that we may converse with him as one man converses with another, and that he was once a man like us; yea, that God himself, the Father of us all, dwelt on an earth....'**
>
> **Also: " 'Father Smith said to my brother that he would soon be convinced of the truth of the latter-day work, and be baptized; and he said: 'You will become as great as you can possibly wish—EVEN AS GREAT AS GOD, and you cannot wish to be greater.' .... It is clear that the teaching of President Lorenzo Snow is both acceptable and accepted doctrine in the Church today.[121]**

Spencer W. Kimball, the Twelfth LDS president, taught:

> **Brethren 225,000 of you are here tonight. I suppose 225, 000 of you may become gods. There seems to be plenty of space out there in the universe. And the Lord has proved that he knows how to do it. I think he could make, or probably have us help make, worlds for all of us, for every one of us 225,000** [122]

For that matter, dutiful LDS wives like Ann Romney can become divinized as well. There's little doubt that the governor's beautiful, well-spoken wife was regarded a campus goddess at BYU, where Romney met his First Lady (but not necessarily *only* lady, as LDS men may add spiritual wives in Mormonism's "Celestial Kingdom"). What will become clear this fall to the public, however, is that Mormons believe Ann Romney can, with any of Mitt's other celestial wives, become a *literal goddess* in the afterlife upon her exaltation/apotheosis with her husband. Joseph Fielding Smith Jr. taught, for example,

> **The Father has promised us that through our faithfulness we shall...have the privilege of becoming like him. To become like him we must have all the powers of godhood; thus a man and his wife when glorified will have**

---

[119] http://en.wikipedia.org/wiki/Mormon_cosmology

[120] Santorum and his top staffer disappointed conservatives by endorsing Romney in 2008. While competing in the 2012 primaries, Santorum reportedly told supporters that he would not have done so had he known of Romney's role as America's Founding Father of Gay Marriage (See, page 47 and forward, and e.g., http://massresistance.org/romney/#SSM). Yet now, despite that knowledge, it seems Santorum is in the process of repeating his 2008 error to, once again, "take one for the team." True, heroic loyalty to the Nation – and the Republican Party, its principles and well-being -- requires that aspiring future leaders like Santorum, Gingrich, Paul and all RNC delegates unite to STOP ROMinee in Tampa. To have any reasonable hope of defeating Barack Obama, RNC DELEGATES MUST EXERCISE THEIR RULES AUTHORITY TO NOMINATE ONE OF THOSE CONTENDERS OR AN ENTIRELY NEW NAME.

[121] The official LDS website, citing *Teachings of the Prophet Joseph Smith*, sel. Joseph Fielding Smith, Salt Lake City: Deseret Book, 1938, pp. 345–46; Eliza R. Snow, *Biography and Family Record of Lorenzo Snow*, Salt Lake City: Deseret News Co., 1884, pp. 9–10. (http://www.lds.org/ensign/1982/02/i-have-a-question/i-have-a-question?lang=eng).

[122] *The Ensign*, Nov. 1975, 80.

> **spirit children who eventually will go on an earth like this one we are on and pass through the same kind of experiences, being subject to mortal conditions, and if faithful, then they also will receive the fulness of exaltation and partake of the same blessings. There is no end to this development; it will go on forever. We will become gods and have jurisdiction over worlds, and these worlds will be peopled by our own offspring. We will have an endless eternity for this.**[123]

So, do Santorum, Gingrich, Ron, Rand and GOP Congressmen, Senators and Governors *really* wish to bet their brands and credibility on this quixotic quest: To win access to the Lincoln Bedroom for the favorite son of a historic sex cult which simmers with polytheism, polyamory, pedophilia,[124] child brides,[125] homoeroticism and naked temple rituals?[126] Hasn't that storied place been sullied enough by the likes of JFK, Bill Clinton and their overnight guests?

Even were *all* such GOP leaders to insist on doing so – as if joining Bishop Romney under the spell of Prophet Smith two centuries after the latter's self-divinization – why should any of the Republican Party's *thinking* Tampa delegates just mindlessly follow them, like lemmings or LDS Stepford Wives, over the cliff?

As noted upfront, Romney as of early August was losing the Electoral College in a rout which threatens GOP Senate prospects in the overlapping swing states. [127] One analyst writes,

> Given [the] data, if this election was just a referendum on Obama and nothing else Romney should be up by 5-10 points right now, simply by not being Obama. Romney has out-raised Obama in money, his name I.D. currently sits at about 95%, and a majority of Americans believe the country is headed in the wrong direction.
> To put the current poll numbers in perspective, a recent *New York Times* story found that on average the challenger in July held a 4-point lead over the incumbent going back to 1968, which is as far back as their database goes.[128]

As of early August, Intrade predictive markets – where knowledgeable people bet real cash on political outcomes – had Obama at 57, Romney at 40.[129] Analyst Nate Silver's *New York Times* forecast/now-cast was rating Romney's odds at about 30%.[130] While closer popular polling numbers based on samples from solid Red States and Blue States may make for good conversation, what ultimately counts is the Electoral College count which, even re-classing soft Obama states as toss-ups, Romney is losing badly.[131]

And all of this *before* the nation as a whole, and especially the swing states, comes to comprehend the creepy belief system to which Mitt Romney subscribes. Founded in rural New York less than two centuries ago, Joseph Smith's spectacularly successful experiment in creative writing and groupthink thrives today on the shore of this continent's Dead Sea, as did Sodom and Gomorrorah for a time on another.

Horny Prophets

From the start, "mainstream" LDS Mormonism has deeply concerned itself with male sexual gratification, particularly that of its founders. The coital appetites of Joseph Smith and Brigham Young (with over 80 child brides or "plural wives" between them) and many of their appointees, associates, relatives and other Mormon prophets (heterosexual, homosexual or incestuous) are a matter of historical record.[132] Examples: [133]

- Ten years [prior to his polygamous marriage to Nancy Marinda Hyde when she was 27], Smith had been tarred and feathered for supposedly seducing Nancy at age 16 while staying with her family. Nancy was likely taught polygamy by Joseph when her husband, Orson Hyde, was on his mission to Palestine. In 1841, Nancy was given a direct revelation through Joseph to "hearken to the counsel of my servant Joseph in all things whatsoever he shall teach unto her"

[123] *Doctrines of Salvation,* Vol.2, p.48
[124] See, e.g., http://www.exmormon.org/mormon/mormon216.htm
[125] See, e.g., http://helpthechildbrides.com/stories.htm
[126] See pages 53-55.
[127] Seehttp://www.realclearpolitics.com/epolls/2012/president/2012_elections_electoral_college_map_no_toss_ups.html; http://www.realclearpolitics.com/epolls/2012/president/2012_elections_electoral_college_map.html; http://www.realclearpolitics.com/epolls/2012/senate/2012_elections_senate_map.html.
[128] http://stevedeace.com/news/national-politics/why-romney-should-be-well-ahead/
[129] http://www.intrade.com/v4/home/
[130] http://fivethirtyeight.blogs.nytimes.com/.
[131] See http://www.realclearpolitics.com/epolls/2012/president/2012_elections_electoral_college_map.html
[132] See, e.g., "Mormon Polygamy" (http://www.ldsvideo.org/2011/06/polgamy.html); "Joseph Smith's Polygamy Chronology" with enhancements in bracksetrs. (http://www.i4m.com/think/polygamy/JS_Polygamy_Timeline.htm); "Mormonism and Polygamy" (http://en.wikipedia.org/wiki/Mormonism_and_polygamy);
[133] All are from "Joseph Smith's Polygamy Chronology" (http://www.i4m.com/think/polygamy/JS_Polygamy_Timeline.htm)

(History of the Church, vol. 4, pg. 467). In May 1844 Nancy would become pregnant with Smith's child while Hyde was on another mission (sent by Smith). She later divorced Hyde and voiced her disgust of polygamy....

- [On May 29, 1844] Three women testify that [LDS] Assistant President John C. Bennett and Apostle William Smith taught them that [William's older brother Joseph] Smith approved of "spiritual wifery" wherein several men have sexual relations with the same woman. The women testifying were Margaret and Matilda Nyman and Catherine Fuller Warren. The report of the Nymans was later printed in the 29 May 1844 *Nauvoo Neighbor.* The sisters said that Elder Chauncy Higbee had advised them that Smith approved of "spiritual wifery" but gave instructions to keep the matter a secret because "there was no sin when there is no accuser." Catherine Fuller Warren in her 20 May 1842 testimony responded to charges of "unchaste and unvirtuous conduct with John C. Bennett and others" by admitting to having intercourse not only with him but with Chauncy Higbee and the prophet's younger brother, Apostle William Smith. Speaking in her defense, however, she insisted that the men had "taught the doctrine that it was right to have free intercourse with women and that the heads of the Church also taught and practised it which things caused her to be led away thinking it to be right."....

- [On July 15, 1842] Thousands of Nauvoo Mormons search for Orson Pratt **[Romney's great-great uncle]** after discovering a suicide note. They find him distraught because Smith, according to Pratt's wife, had tried to seduce Pratt's wife Sarah....

- Joseph Smith's personal secretary and church patriarch, Elder Benjamin F. Johnson, wrote "His brother, Hyrum, said to me, 'Now, Brother Benjamin, you know that Brother Joseph would not sanction this if it was not from the Lord. The Lord revealed this to Brother Joseph long ago, and he put it off until the Angel of the Lord came to him with a drawn sword and told him that he would be slain if he did not go forth and fulfill the law." He told my sister to have no fears, and he there and then sealed my sister, Almira, to the Prophet....Soon after this he was at my house again, where he occupied my Sister Almira's room and bed, and also asked me for my youngest sister, Esther M."....

- Helen Mar Kimball writes of how she married Joseph Smith [at age 14, on May 1, 1843]: "Having a great desire to be connected with the Prophet, Joseph, he (my father) offered me to him; this I afterwards learned from the Prophet's own mouth. My father had but one Ewe Lamb, but willingly laid her upon the altar: how cruel this seemed to my mother whose heartstrings were already stretched until they were ready to snap asunder, for she had already taken Sarah Noon to wife and she thought she had made sufficient sacrifice but the Lord required more."…. The next morning, Joseph Smith finally appeared himself to explain the "law of Celestial Marriage" and claim his teen bride. In her memoir, Helen wrote, "After which he said to me, 'if you take this step, it will ensure your eternal salvation and exaltation and that of your father's household and all of your kindred.' This promise was so great that I willingly gave myself to purchase so glorious a reward."

- Helen also writes about her mother's reaction to all of this: "None but God and his angels could see my mother's bleeding heart - when Joseph asked her if she was willing, she replied 'If Helen is willing I have nothing more to say."...."She had witnessed the sufferings of others, who were older and who better understood the step they were taking, and to see her child, who had yet seen her fifteenth summer, following the same thorny path, in her mind she saw the misery which was as sure to come as the sun was to rise and set; but it was hidden from me."

- Helen thought her marriage to Joseph Smith was only dynastic. But to her surprise, it was more. Helen confided to a close friend in Nauvoo: "I would never have been sealed to Joseph had I known it was anything more than ceremony. I was young, and they deceived me, by saying the salvation of our whole family depended on it."....

- [On May 28, 1843], Joseph and Emma Smith are the first couple "sealed" in marriage for eternity. During the previous month, he had married as polygamous wives seventeen-year-old Lucy Walker, sixteen-year-old Flora Ann Woodworth, and fourteen-year-old Helen Mar Kimball who later testified that he had sexual relations with them....

- [On August 11, 1843], Smith performs a marriage for his brother Hyrum and his first plural wife and tells William Clayton, "you have a right to get all you can."....

- [On November 5, 1843], Smith becomes violently ill at dinner and assumes that his wife Emma of trying to poison him due to her opposition to polygamy. At the prayer circle meeting that evening Smith accuses her of poisoning his cup of coffee, and Brigham Young regards her shocked silence as proof of her guilt....

- William Law files a formal complaint with the Hancock County circuit court charging Smith was living "in an open state of adultery" with Maria Lawrence, Smith's foster daughter and polygamous wife. Maria Lawrence was a teenaged orphan who was living in the Smith household. In fact, Smith had secretly married both Maria, age 19 and her sister Sarah, age 17 on 11 May 1843 and was serving as executor of their $8,000 estate. William Law apparently hoped that disclosing Smith's relationship with the young girls might lead him to abandon polygamy, but Smith immediately excommunicated Law, had himself appointed the girls' legal guardian, and rejected the charge in front of a church congregation on 26 May 1844, denying that he had more than one wife....

- [About a month before his 1844 murder] Smith denies polygamy, boasts he has done more than Jesus Christ [saying] to a congregation "Come on! ye prosecutors! ye false swearers! All hell, boil over! Ye burning mountains, roll down your lava! for I will come out on the top at last.

> **I have more to boast of than ever any man had. I am the only man that has ever been able to keep a whole church together since the days of Adam. A large majority of the whole have stood by me. Neither Paul, John, Peter, nor Jesus ever did it. I boast that no man ever did such a work as I. The followers of Jesus ran away from Him; but the Latter-day Saints never ran away from me yet. You know my daily walk and conversation. I am in the bosom of a virtuous and good people.** "[134]

Indeed, our LDS friends and loved ones *are* by and large a virtuous and good people who, abundant evidence shows, have been cruelly deceived;[135] how can any honest Christian, Jew or GOP Tampa delegate further this deception by pretending that Mitt Romney – a disciple of deceivers, duped himself *yet maybe not* – is worthy of the nation's trust?

On May 14, 1843, Joseph Smith's brother, "Presiding Patriarch and Associate President Hyrum Smith assure[d] a [Nauvoo] citywide congregation that only the Devil would give a revelation approving [plural] 'wifes & concubines.'"[136] The truth, it seems, is that a horny, manipulative rake named Joseph Smith cleverly molded many gods (including the deity of the Bible) into his own, polyamorous image:

Smith's (and Romney's) doctrine contends that the Heavenly Father of the Bible has "a body of flesh and bones as tangible as man's"[137] for physical sex with, among others, our unnamed Heavenly Mother,[138] Eden's Eve and the Virgin Mary.[139]

Mormonism holds that Earth's god (Elohim, the Hebrew deity of the Bible) had amorous flesh-and-blood parents, grandparents and so on, in an eternal regression (and progression) of finite yet frisky divinized human beings or demi-gods.[140] It's easy to envision late-night TV labels for such a system: "AmWay Godhood," the multi-level marketing of male-dominated divinity. Instead of of cash, cars and vacation incentives, male recruits get planets and polygyny forever. It is Smith's new spin on misogynistic Muhammad's 70 virgins, a future status now available to male LDS adherents from Salt Lake City to Provo, from Boston to La Jolla.

Similarly to the LDS view of our Heavenly Father's love life, the GOP frontrunner's ever-fascinating faith holds that Jesus – Satan's brother – sexually, polygamously consorted with Mary, Martha and Mary Magdalene:[141]

> Apostle Orson Hyde repeated his propositions about the marital and parental status of the Son of God in a sermon in the Tabernacle on March 18, 1855. Hyde reasserted that Jesus Christ was the husband of the wedding at Cana, that Mary and Martha, among others, were his wives, and that the Son of God sired children in the flesh. He said,
>
> > I discover that some of the Eastern papers represent me as a great blasphemer, because I said, in my lecture on Marriage, at our last Conference, that Jesus Christ was married at Cana of Galilee, that Mary, Martha, and others were his wives, and that he begat children.
>
> ....The Son, according to Hyde, was merely following the practice of his own Father who physically sired him with Mary.... Apostle Hyde addressed the Saints in Great Salt Lake City on December 21, 1856 on a variety of subjects including polygamy, and the marriage and fatherhood of Christ. During his defense of polygamy he affirmed his consistent teaching that the Son was married to Mary and Martha and fathered children in the flesh....
>
> > It will be borne in mind that once on a time, there was a marriage in Cana of Galilee; and on a careful reading of that transaction, it will be discovered that no less a person than Jesus Christ was married on that occasion.

---

[134] "Joseph Smith's Polygamy Chronology" (http://www.i4m.com/think/polygamy/JS_Polygamy_Timeline.htm)
[135] Charges of gross deception by Mormon leaders, even very recent ones, come from center, left and right, e.g.: Ken Clark, "LDS Honesty: Lying for the Lord" (http://www.mormonthink.com/lying.htm);"Gordon B. Hinckley's Lies," (http://www.gaymormon.com/theology/policy/generalauthorities/byname/hinckley-gordon-b/lies.htm); Darrick B. Everson, "MORMONISM INSIDE-OUT:22 Shocking FACTS the Mormon Church Does NOT Want YOU to Know!" (http://www.angelfire.com/planet/lds/22.html); Darrick B. Evenson, "Gordon B. Hinckley: The Lying Prophet," (http://www.angelfire.com/planet/lds/Hinckley.html);
[136] "Joseph Smith's Polygamy Chronology" (http://www.i4m.com/think/polygamy/JS_Polygamy_Timeline.htm)
[137] http://www.lds.org/scriptures/dc-testament/dc/130.22?lang=eng;
[138] http://en.wikipedia.org/wiki/Heavenly_Mother_(Latter_Day_Saints)
[139] See, e.g., "Was the LDS Jesus born of the Virgin Mary?" (http://carm.org/was-lds-jesus-born-of-virgin-mary).
[140] See note 2, "LDS Video Encyclopedia: Pre-existence and Afterlife" (http://www.ldsvideo.org/2011/06/preexistance-and-afterlife.html).
[141] "[F]ive high-ranking LDS authorities affirmed the plural marriage of the Son. The five include Orson Hyde, Orson Pratt, Jedediah M. Grant, Joseph F. Smith and Joseph Fielding Smith. Four of the five were apostles at the time of their remarks and two of the five ascended to the presidency of the Church," per Cky J. Carrigan in "Did Jesus Christ Marry and Father Children?" (http://www.emnr.org/papers/jesusmarry.htm). See also, e.g., "Mormon vs. Biblical Teaching about Jesus," (http://wri.leaderu.com/mormonism/jesus-refs.html).

> If he was never married, his intimacy with Mary and Martha, and the other Mary also whom Jesus loved, must have been highly unbecoming and improper to say the best of it.[142]

As an LDS Bishop, Romney would hold that Jesus polygamously sired children and that Joseph Smith, the now-divinized LDS founder, is of Jesus' family line.[143] Mormon authorities teach, furthermore, that Jesus was crucified for his commitment to polygamy:

> The earliest known official remark by an LDS authority on the marital status of the Son of God was by Jedediah M. Grant (appointed to the Seventy in 1845). On August 7, 1853, Grant addressed the Saints in the Tabernacle in Great Salt Lake City. Grant, a polygamist himself, taught that the chief reason for the persecution of Christ was his polygamy….
>
> > **The grand reason of the burst of public sentiment in anathemas upon Christ and his disciples, causing his crucifixion, was evidently based upon polygamy, according to the testimony of the philosophers who rose in that age. A belief in the doctrine of a plurality of wives caused the persecution of Jesus and his followers. We might almost think they were Mormons.**[144]

This, too would seem to be an instance of LDS officials fashioning a god in their own image, especially that of their founder, Joseph Smith. The official LDS story is that Smith died a martyr's death in Nauvoo, Illinois, today a Mormon shrine site not too far from the homes of Lincoln, Grant and Reagan.

The Martyred Molester

The truth, however, is a bit earthier. As former Mormon missionary Darrick B. Everson colorfully tells it, and concurred by numerous sources and accounts, Smith's decision to have sex with his foster daughters Maria and Sarah Lawrence (see above) pushed the pedophile and polygamy envelopes a little too far:

> The REAL Reason Joseph Smith was killed in 1844: Mormons are told from birth that Joseph Smith was a martyr, that he voluntarily went to Carthage Jail in June of 1844 to surrender his life for the truth "as a lamb to the slaughter"; knowing he would die for the truth. They are not told the "reason" he was arrested. Most Church teachers simply tell young Mormons that Joseph Smith was arrested on "trumped up charges"; not telling them what the charges are. Mormons youth believe this, without question, that Joseph Smith was arrested and killed merely because he was the head of an unpopular religion. The truth is this:
>
> In 1844 a Mormon named Lawrence dies. He has two orphaned daughters, Sarah and Maria, ages 14 and 16. Before his death, Lawrence names the two leaders of the Church at that time, Joseph Smith, and his first counselor in the First Presidency, William Law, to be the Guardians (i.e. Foster-Fathers) of the two girls. Who better men to trust than the two closest men to God on earth? Lawrence leaves his daughters about $1800 in cash and holdings, a huge sum at that time.
>
> William Law, the first counselor in the First Presidency of the Mormon Church, then claims …. that Joseph Smith "married" both the daughters to himself (Joseph), who were living the Smith home at the time. That's right! **Joseph Smith married his own foster-daughters!** Law also claims that Joseph Smith appropriated their inheritance money for himself. William Law then discovers that Joseph Smith has many more secret "wives". He concludes that Joseph has "fallen". He privately confronts Joseph Smith, who tells him polygamy is of God and that Law just had to accept that. This is at the same time Joseph Smith is publicly denying he is a polygamist, and also excommunicating anyone who publicly teaches polygamy.
>
> William Law then forms a cabal with some other apostate Mormons to depose Joseph Smith and take over the Church (Law is First Counselor, the second highest Mormon Church office). Members of this cabal include some of the highest men in the Church at that time. Most of the Apostles were away on missions to England. The cabal plan[s] to either get Joseph Smith arrested and sent away, or publicly disgraced so that Joseph Smith would resign as Prophet. There is no evidence they plan to kill him, or that any of them had anything to do with his assassination. They plan to appoint David Whitmer as the new Prophet of the Church.

---

[142] Cky J. Carrigan, "Did Jesus Christ Marry and Father Children?" (http://www.emnr.org/papers/jesusmarry.htm).
[143] See, e.g., http://www.ldschurchnews.com/articles/60264/Joseph-Smith-a-witness-of-Christ.html and http://www.i4m.com/think/bible/mormon-jesus-married.htm
[144] Cky J. Carrigan, "Did Jesus Christ Marry and Father Children?" (http://www.emnr.org/papers/jesusmarry.htm).

> David Whitmer was one of the "Three Witnesses" to The Book of Mormon. It was on a Whitmer farm that the Book of Mormon was translated. It was at another Whitmer farm that the Church was founded in 1830. Whitmer left the Church in 1838, claiming that Joseph Smith and Oliver Cowdery had a "band of Danites" who were stealing from Gentiles (non-mormons) and that Cowdery had threatened his life for revealing that fact. Whitmer left and settled in Richmond, Missouri. He tried to start another "Church of Christ" but his efforts proved fruitless. The cabal in Nauvoo decided to wrest the Church away from Joseph Smith, and have Whitmer appointed the new Prophet. The group decide[d] to publish a newspaper called "The Nauvoo Expositor" which will, in a few issues, expose Joseph Smith as a secret polygamist, thief, liar, tyrant, and "fallen" prophet (not false, but "fallen"). They buy a printing press, and issue the first edition of *The Nauvoo Expositor.*
>
> Joseph Smith, as mayor of Nauvoo, immediately orders the *Nauvoo Expositor* to be closed, and orders the Town Marshall to take the plates for the publication into the street and destroy them. The Marshall obeys, and the type and printing press is carried out into the street and destroyed with large hammers. William Law and the other members of the cabal (all of them Mormons in high Church positions) say they they received many death threats, and had to leave Nauvoo for their own safety.
>
> The governor of Illinois then issues an arrest warrant for Joseph Smith, because he has illegally shut down an opposition newspaper. Joseph Smith does not go quietly. He first calls up the 3,000 strong Nauvoo Legion, and asks them to prevent his arrest at all costs. The Governor issues a new arrest warrent for treason against the State, because only HE (the Governor) can call up a State Militia for action, and the Nauvoo Legion is part of the State Militia of Illinois. He issues a direct order for the Nauvoo Legion to stand-down. Joseph Smith then flees to the Territory of Iowa, but a number of close friends of his accuse of him of being a coward. Joseph Smith reluctantly returns to Nauvoo and surrenders himself to the Sheriff of Hancock County, who takes him to Carthage, the county seat. At Carthage Jail, Joseph Smith procures a smuggled-in firearm, and also writes letters asking the Nauvoo Legion to come to Carthage and rescue him from jail.
>
> On June 22nd, 1844, a mob painted in black face gathers outside of the jail, then storms it. They kill Hyrum Smith [Joseph's brother], and wound John Taylor, a Mormon apostle. Joseph Smith fires at the mob with his gun, wounding two. When he is out of bullets, he gives the Masonic sign of distress (raising both arms into squares and saying, "O Lord My God! Is there no help for the widow's son?" Masons promise to come to the aid of other Masons whenever they hear this). Joseph Smith gets out "O Lord My God..." but is shot before he can finish saying the rest. Even though there are Masons in the mob, none come to his aid. He tries to escape out a window, but is shot from the ground. He falls out the window to the ground, and is shot again repeatedly until he is dead.
>
> Joseph Smith had NO intention of dying in Carthage. He did everything to try to prevent that. He tried escaping to Iowa, but was called a "coward" by his closest friends and supporters. He tried calling up the Nauvoo Legion to prevent his arrest. He then wrote to Nauvoo from the jail asking the legion and Marshall of Nauvoo to come get him out of jail! At first he thought the "mob" outside was his rescue party. As the mob stormed the jail, he shot two of the mob members with a "12 shooter" designed by a Mormon named Browning, father of the famous gunsmith. The reason why Joseph Smith was arrested is because he illegal[ly] shut down a newspaper which was revealing that he was secretly a polygamist; [which] the Mormon Church has admitted as FACT since 1852.

While Mormon polygamy mostly cuts one way – polygyny, but not too much polyandry[145] – LDS women willing to share one man among multiple celestial sex partners do enjoy some special compensations; as we've already seen, they can become goddesses. This is Mormon "Celestial Marriage," a dogma Mitt Romney embraces today just as surely as his great grandfather, Miles Park Romney embraced all five of his wives, and an earthier kind of group sex, until his death in 1904.[146]

But, Mitt Romney's neutered, spiritualized kind of polyamory has a dark – and *living* – history. As a thoughtful commentator at exmormon.org writes,

> Polygamy and Mormonism are inseparably entwined. One of the most offensive aspects of Mormon-based polygamy is the rampant practice of taking underage girls as polygamous wives. This is precisely what Brian David Mitchell did when he abducted Elizabeth Smart. In the western United States, there are at least 30,000 people involved in the practice of Mormon-based polygamy. In these polygamous groups, the compulsion for underage girls to marry polygamists--usually men much older than themselves--is a part of everyday life. In these communities, girls as young as 12 or 13 are often married off to priesthood leaders. The most powerful and influential of these priesthood holders have first pick of the girls. Parents of the young girls submit their daughters willingly into these unions with the hope of being blessed by God in their afterlife.

---

[145] See, e.g., http://www.ldsfreedom.org/node/7
[146] http://en.wikipedia.org/wiki/Miles_Park_Romney

One asks, where did this practice come from? Why do these offenders take such young girls as wives? What does Mormon doctrine have to do with this? These are indeed puzzling questions, but the answers are simple. The founder of Mormonism, Joseph Smith Jr. set the precedent for this behavior.

Smith married several underage girls himself. The most notorious example of this is in the case of Helen Mar Kimball. Young Helen married Smith in May, 1843. She was 14 years old; the same age as Elizabeth Smart was at the time of her abduction. Helen's father, Heber Chase Kimball gave his daughter to Smith as a token of his unquestioning devotion. In return, Smith promised that this union would seal up the salvation of the Kimball family. Smith didn't use a knife to coerce this young girl, he used the weapon he was most adept at using, psychological manipulation....

There is profound ignorance of these facts among the rank-and-file members of the LDS Church. The leaders of this church actively pretend that polygamy never existed. Today they provide educational pamphlets for their members that portray Smith, Brigham Young, and several other early presidents of the Church of Jesus Christ of Latter-day Saints as monogamous. Many members of the LDS Church don't even believe that the founder of their church was a polygamist, let alone a man who filled his harem with underage girls as young as 14.

The LDS Church discontinued the practice of polygamy in 1890, but this was only a move to relieve pressure that was placed on them by the US Government. It was also a move toward the goal of establishing statehood for Utah. The practice was discontinued, but the doctrine is still in place and can be found in the Doctrine and Covenants, Section 132. This is canonized LDS scripture. I recommend that anyone interested in this phenomenon read this piece of LDS scripture. Here is the link to *Doctrine and Covenants,* Section 132: http://scriptures.lds.org/dc/132 [147]

Today, in the age of Warren Jeffs, Jerry Sandusky, Brian David Mitchell (Elizabeth Smart's abductor) and countless other pedophiles, the exmormon.org commentator raises a crucial question for LDS leaders, like Mitt Romney. Just as they should with the racist and anti-Semitic statements laced throughout Mormon scripture, are they willing to repudiate the Mormon doctrinal basis for child brides?

Yes, the LDS has abandoned earth-bound polygamy (for the time being) and yes, the LDS began accepting black priests in 1978. However, it seems neither Romney nor his prophets in Salt Lake City have ever repudiated the supposedly revealed, holy dogma upon which Mormon pedophilia and racism are based. Peterson writes,

The LDS Church finds itself in a serious dilemma by refusing to repudiate this doctrine, an act that would seriously undermine the alleged divine calling of their founder and expose him for the sexual predator he really was. But by allowing this doctrine to remain in canonized form within their holy scriptures, they are allowing a hideous practice to continue unchallenged. Extremely devout members find themselves very troubled when they study the practice of polygamy according to Joseph Smith, the founder of Mormonism, who was also the man who established the precedent for not only practicing polygamy, but taking underage girls as polygamous wives.

These devout members find themselves in serious trouble with the LDS Church hierarchy when they start looking into this doctrine. Expressing a belief in this doctrine is a sure-fire way to get oneself excommunicated. After finding themselves excommunicated, inevitably these devout Mormons get involved in Mormon Fundamentalism, the current religious movement in which Mormon-based polygamy is held to be a sacred doctrine. The ranks of Mormon Fundamentalist groups are swelling rapidly as a result of their inherent fecundity, and also because of the steady stream of devout, but disaffected Mormons who are leaving the LDS Church to join with them[148]

Great grandpa Romney was there in Nauvoo and in Utah, a fundamentalist Mormon who soaked it all in and passed it all down to the handsome candidate, Mormon priest, missionary, BYU alum, Stake President and LDS Bishop who now expects pliant GOP delegates to nominate him for the Presidency.

But if Tampa's delegates do that, how will it play with monogamous soccer moms in suburban Cincinnati, Sarasota and Sioux City? How about with those not just personally repulsed by the institutionalized misogyny of polygamy (see, "Muslim World"), but who rightly fear for their own sons and daughters in a society in which the pedophile predations of men like Sandusky, NAMBLA, Brian David Mitchell and too many priests, pastors and schoolteachers have thrived?

Also: Doesn't the picture of slavish, heavenly harems – forever birthing "spirit babies" for eternally-erect Mormon men – play quite nicely into the Obama-MSM narrative that in Mitt Romney's America, women are second-class citizens? Joseph Smith's Celestial Cialis, his Viagra-from-Niagara, may *alone* suffice to take the Republican Party over the falls this fall.

---

[147] http://www.exmormon.org/mormon/mormon216.htm
[148] http://www.exmormon.org/mormon/mormon216.htm

All martyrdoms created equal? Left: Joseph Smith, Jr. fell to his death at the Carthage, Illinois jail on June 22, 1844, after his top Mormon lieutenants publicly exposed him for having sex with his foster daughters – and for other polygynous acts which Smith had publicly denied. Right: According to LDS authorities, the flesh-and-bone Heavenly Father had sired Jesus via natural sex with the Virgin Mary. After Jesus himself was wed at Cana, and after being polygynously joined to Mary, Martha and Mary Magdalene, he was crucified because, in the words of LDS official Jedediah M. Grant, of "belief in the doctrine of a plurality of wives."

So, would *we* be the crazy ones to anticipate media depictions of Mitt Romney as the credulous dupe, or malevolent heir, of sex-crazed charlatans?[149] Do cheerleading blond FOX News faces *really* contend that the issue of what's inside Mitt's head –racist, pagan-ish, polyamorous Mormon polytheism – is *irrelevant?* That the un-deprogrammed mental state, the credulity and gullibility of the Republican nominee, is *irrelevant? Seriously?*

To voters in the toss-up states, won't the GOP look as if it's being piloted by a Space Cadet?

Mormons, Multiversers and Bill Maher

Bright minds like that of Bill Maher, Christopher Hitchens,[150] Richard Dawkins and other aggressive materialists of our time (whether icons of media or the academy) might predictably chide back with something snarky like: "Well, it's just as loony to believe the Bible's Passover stories, that the Hebrew divinity actually parted the Red Sea for Moses and the Children of Israel… or that Heaven could raise one of them from the dead a few days after his last Seder."

Two responses come to mind, the pertinence of which to the American Presidency in 2012, we believe, should be clear in a moment. First, mock it as we may please, such nonetheless *are* the narratives which most U.S. citizens, swing-state voters especially, accept at one level or another; the USA *is in fact* largely populated by Jewish-Christian monotheists who, as a matter of the nation's Protestant-Catholic-Jewish European heritage and widespread current belief, more or less acknowledge the one, absolute G_d of Abraham, Isaac and Jacob.

---

[149] See, e.g., "Amorous Advances by the Mormon Prophet" (http://www.mrm.org/amorous-advances); "Mormonism Disproved in less than 3 minutes" (http://www.youtube.com/watch?v=D0u6clxJmI8&feature=related); "Book of Mormon Anachronisms" (http://www.ldsvideo.org/2011/03/book-of-mormon-anachronisms.html); *The God Makers* (http://www.youtube.com/watch?v=zfz6pG5JRQY&feature=related); "Joseph Smith's False Prophecies"(http://www.ldsvideo.org/2011/06/joseph-smiths-false-prophecies.html)

[150] For the always-entertaining take of the late Hitchens, see "Romney's Mormon Problem; Mitt Romney and the weird and sinister beliefs of Mormonism" (http://www.slate.com/articles/news_and_politics/fighting_words/2011/10/is_mormonism_a_cult_who_cares_it_s_their_weird_and_sinister_beli.html); those of us who respected Christopher's intellect and felt affection for him will miss debating him on his devoutly atheistic faith. We pray, furthermore, that he has been welcomed by his merciful and loving Creator, upon whom the American Founders bet everything as they cited the unalienable human rights with which Hitchens, and all of us lesser-gifteds, have been endowed.

Second, cocksure materialists, those who postulate *a priori* that Matter precedes Mind – those who as an article of blind faith simply deny that Design precedes Production – would seem to bear the greater burden of explaining such brute facts as the intricately-balanced organization of the solar system, this planet, the biosphere and human beings. From butterflies to baby girls, from the microcosm of a living cell to the macrocosm of the empirical universe, no probability math allows for random physical forces and blind natural selection to generate all the apparent design we see, especially within the 14 billion years or so implied by current cosmic expansion rates running backward to the Big Bang.[151]

So, dogmatic skeptics, devout materialists and assorted accomodationists have posited their own latter-day revelation to somehow explain it all: Not a "Book of Mormon," but a "Book of Multiverse," the entirely speculative, unscientific and thoroughly faith-based notion that there simply *must* be millions or billions of universes; how *else,* they ask, could we possibly have arrived here in our finely-tuned, life-supporting spot without supernatural aid and, literally, against all odds? Once we've ruled-out the Jewish-Christian monotheism and Natural Law premises of the American Founders upfront, well, we simply *must* be living in a lucky universe among a billion or trillion lifeless, unlucky ones we just can't see![152]

Similarly, in ruling-out the One, Infinite, Omnipotent G_d of Moses and Jesus, Romney's polytheism favors a multi-world reality somewhat akin to the materialist multiverse of the neo-atheists: Each metaphysic excludes the absolute G_d (and valuing standard) of the Torah and Christian Scriptures; each effectively or actually divinizes Man as the finite measure of all things; each rejects the Judeo-Christian premises of Washington, Adams and Jefferson; each dissolves monogamy along with monotheism, sanctioning polyamorous gratification (hetero-, homo-, bisex, incestuous, transgender, group, serial, etc) above the nuclear family and the needs of children; and *neither* metaphysic is, even remotely, based upon empirical science and general observation.

From the ancient standpoint of Jewish-Christian monotheism as well as that of modernity's American Founders,[153] embracing an entirely accidental yet life-yielding multiverse requires about the same degree of faith as that held by Joseph Smith's disciples in his occultic seer stones, dowsing rods and magical powers.[154] It represents about the same level of speculative fantasy as does the latter-day revelation – by the LDS prophet-scholar for whom Romney's alma mater, Brigham Young University is named – of persons inhabiting the moon, sun and "Kolob."[155]

So, in his defense, GOP frontrunner Mitt Romney isn't really that far out of step with the materialist Left. That their Multiversism is almost as unscientific, if not quite as silly, as Mormonism is made clear by the following physicist:

> **For a start, how is the existence of the other universes to be tested? To be sure, all cosmologists accept that there are some regions of the universe that lie beyond the reach of our telescopes, but somewhere on the slippery slope between that and the idea that there are an infinite number of universes, credibility reaches a limit. As one slips down that slope, more and more must be accepted on faith, and less and less is open to scientific verification. Extreme multiverse explanations are therefore reminiscent of theological discussions. Indeed, invoking an infinity of unseen universes to explain the unusual features of the one we do see is just as ad hoc as invoking an unseen Creator. The multiverse theory may be dressed up in scientific language, but in essence it requires the same leap of faith.**
>
> — Paul Davies, *A Brief History of the Multiverse*

Yet, himself a leader in the empirical search for extraterrestrial intelligence, Davis seems to recognize that presupposing a law-governed universe originated by an infinite, intelligent and orderly deity was essential to the rise of modern science in the first place.[156]

---

[151] No scholarly think tank has done better work than Seattle's Discovery Institute, an ensemble of Jewish, Christian and secular scientists, to repudiate the manifestly non-empirical, unscientific notion of an entirely random, accidental, mindless and un-designed descent of all life on earth (plant, fungus, bacterial, animal and human) from a common, single-celled ancestor (http://www.discovery.org/csc/). That premise, essentially at the root of Darwinian materialism as well as many polytheistic and pantheistic depictions of reality, has been at war for generations with the Natural Law monotheism of America's founding charter and her Founders, as expressed in *The Declaration of Independence* – on which our Creator-endowed rights of Life and Liberty (and Property, Procreation, Self-Defense, Religion, Association, Speech, etc.) hang.

[152] See, e.g., http://en.wikipedia.org/wiki/Multiverse#Anthropic_principle

[153] Judaism and Christianity are monotheistic, but Judaism is unitarian (one personal G_d) while Christianity is trinitarian (one G_d in three persons). Mormonism, by contrast, is radically polytheistic: Finite gods and goddesses ruling over countless other planetary worlds, and at least 3-5 distinct and separate deities or demigods for this world: Elohim, the flesh-and-blood Heavenly Father; a Heavenly Mother or "Queen of Heaven"; Yahweh/Jesus, Elohim's physical son; the Holy Spirit (a non-physical deity); and possibly Lucifer (the brother of Jesus).

[154] See, e.g.,D. Michael Quinn, *Early Mormonism and the Magic World View;* http://en.wikipedia.org/wiki/D._Michael_Quinn#Early_Mormonism_and_the_Magic_World_View

[155] See http://www.lds.org/scriptures/gs/kolob.t1?lang=eng&letter=k; http://en.wikipedia.org/wiki/Kolob;

[156] Claiming today's scientific enterprise "to be free of faith is manifestly bogus," Paul Davies wrote in "Taking Science on Faith," *The New York Times,* November 24, 2007 (http://www.nytimes.com/2007/11/24/opinion/24davies.html?pagewanted=2&_r=1).

The summer sci-fi film *Prometheus*, not to mention *2001: A Space Odyssey* and many others, shows that Mormons and Multiversers aren't the only folks to envision physical, god-like aliens sowing life on earth. Yet in each case, even Hollywooders realize that *it's only a movie...* while TBM-LDS Bishop Romney, the frontrunner for the GOP nomination, is required to believe that Joseph Smith's inventive script depicts a *literal reality.*

Although openness to life on other worlds doesn't inherently contradict Judaism or Christianity, it seems that Mormonism, Multiverse-ism and most movies these days strive to avoid the American Founders' premise of One Ultimate Designer whom, monotheists from Genesis to Jesus, from Moses to Maimonides, from Newton to Washington have held, purposefully made us male and female, in the *Imago Dei.*

2012 Space Odyssey: Maybe the reason RomneyCare's $0 co-pay abortions, Romney's avoided pro-life pledges and his dubious pro-life conversion[157] just don't add up is because Mormonism contends that bodies are unnecessary to the survival of pre-existent "spirit-babies" spawned by physical sex between our finite Heavenly Father and Mother on or near the star "Kolob."[158]

[B]oth religion and science are founded on faith — namely, on belief in the existence of something outside the universe, like an unexplained God or an unexplained set of physical laws, maybe even a huge ensemble of unseen universes, too. For that reason, both monotheistic religion and orthodox science fail to provide a complete account of physical existence. This shared failing is no surprise, because the very notion of physical law is a theological one in the first place, a fact that makes many scientists squirm. Isaac Newton first got the idea of absolute, universal, perfect, immutable laws from the Christian doctrine that God created the world and ordered it in a rational way. Christians envisage God as upholding the natural order from beyond the universe, while physicists think of their laws as inhabiting an abstract transcendent realm of perfect mathematical relationships. And just as Christians claim that the world depends utterly on God for its existence, while the converse is not the case, so physicists declare a similar asymmetry: the universe is governed by eternal laws (or meta-laws), but the laws are completely impervious to what happens in the universe.

[157] See "Romney's Abortion Record: Spin vs. Truth" (http://www.slatev.com/video/romneys-abortion-record-spin-vs-truth/) and "The Conversion" (http://www.slate.com/articles/news_and_politics/the_conversion/2012/02/mitt_romney_s_abortion_record_flip_flop_or_conversion_.html

[158] Bruce R. McConkie, *Mormon Doctrine,* p. 516;

And yet, despite our self-evident design for heterosex and offspring, for fidelity to mate and Maker – GOP delegates are now being asked to nominate America's Founding Father of Gay Marriage[159] – a polytheistic relativist who's been just about as comfy with abortion, and every coital inversion of the GLBT-confused, as were his American ancestors with polygamy: Romney has embraced gay adoption and childrearing, the imposition of open homosexuality and bisexuality into U.S. military barracks and platoons, ENDA, "Gay/Straight Youth Pride" Rainbow Days and a scientifically-groundless moral equivalence between racial traits and sexual proclivities.[160]

Particularly obnoxious – and weirdly reminiscent of Joseph Smith's polygamy cover-ups – has been Romney's feigning to oppose the same-sex unions which he himself brought about in Massachusetts![161] If the GLBT's capture the GOP through Romney, if the Party of Lincoln is held hostage by the Log Cabin sodomy club, who doubts we'll soon see chilling effects on national Republican leaders, churches, synagogues and hetero-monogamy itself? It's already happening now, as some spine-free pols and pulpits collude to hide the ugly truth about Mitt Romney from the sheep they've been entrusted to lead.

Yet Mormonism, Multiverse-ism and most science fiction is alien to the Jewish-Christian Natural Law monotheism of the American Founders. The Mosaic *Shema* of Deuteronomy 6:4 says:

"Hear, O Israel: the Lord is our God, the Lord is one."

Moses declares in Deuteronomy 4:39: *"know this day, and lay it to thy heart, that HaShem, He is G-d in heaven above and upon the earth beneath; there is none else."*[162] Citing Deuteronomy 6:19 and Leviticus 19:18, Jesus said that Heaven's greatest command is to *"'Love the Lord your God with all your heart and with all your soul and with all your strength and with all your mind' and, 'Love your neighbor as yourself.'"*

We do not wish, therefore, to meanly pick on Mormons, Multiversers or GLBTers, nor on any human beings who may embrace science-free cosmological narratives which envision infinite gods, the infinite malleability of logic or an infinite variety of socio-sexual confusions. Of necessity, faithful Jews and Christians must contest the sci-fi narratives of such latter-day religions (all of them incompatible with traditional Judaism and Christianity). Our central challenge, however, is to *the political science fiction* which holds that any Republican delegate is actually *bound* to violate his or her own conscience, faith or common sense by backing any given wing-nut or sure swing-state loser for the U.S. Presidency. In fact, Mr. Romney has no more legal or RNC Rules-based entitlement to any Tampa delegate's support than does a street person who fancies himself Maimonides, Jesus or E.T.[163]

Conservatives would be facing similar political risks were the GOP frontrunner a Branch Davidian, Sunni Muslim or survivor of the Heaven's Gate "Comet Cult." John Travolta and Tom Cruise are gloriously free in the USA, of course, to follow frauds like L. Ron Hubbard, the founder of the Scientology.[164] That sci-fi writer famously said, "Writing for a penny a word is ridiculous.... If a man really wanted to make a million dollars, the best way to do it would be start his own religion."[165]

To push an ardent, official leader of a sci-fi cult for the Presidency of the United States, however, is not such a light thing; rather, it is a watershed moment for our nation. Romney's creed – and the particular ways he has chosen to live it out in public life – understandably alarms the well-informed. Formally intolerant, we repeat, LDS Mormon dogma regards all religious competitors to be "abominations."

---

[159] See, page 47 and forward, and e.g., http://massresistance.org/romney/#SSM

[160] See, e.g., http://massresistance.org/romney/

[161] See page 47 and forward.

[162] See also Isaiah 44:6,8 and 45:5,6 and 18; and Psalm 86:10.

[163] For the very real potential event that Presidential primaries may yield a presumptive nominee discovered to have a fatal political problem – e.g., a history of mental illness, suicide attempts, pedophilia, incest, spousal abuse, bisexuality, Satanism, embezzlement, emailing lewd photographs of himself, involvement in a kooky cult, etc.. – RNC Rules ultimately empower delegates to vote their consciences, in entirely unbound fashion, on every ballot – *including, necessarily,* the First Ballot. In this manner, the Republican Party protects the nation and its brand by upholding "small-r" republicanism, by empowering elected delegates to dutifully exercise their good judgment and wisdom, rather than binding them to "small d" democratic or "mobocratic" election results which can be unduly influenced by money, mass hysteria, misleading advertising, bad journalism, foreign interests, extortion, etc. See www.thereal2012delegatecount.com; Response to "A Rogue Convention?" (http://www.fairvote.org/response-to-a-rogue-convention-how-gop-party-rules-may-surprise-in-201); "A Rogue Convention? How GOP party rules may surprise in 2012"(http://www.politico.com/news/stories/1111/69048_Page2.html); Reality Check: Republican Delegates "Unbound"? (http://www.youtube.com/watch?v=anWsU93fFsk&feature=relmfu); http://www.examiner.com/article/rnc-delegates-not-bound-to-any-candidate-on-first-ballot; and pages 75 forward.

[164] http://en.wikipedia.org/wiki/Scientology

[165] http://www.don-lindsay-archive.org/scientology/start.a.religion.html

Mitt's multi-world sci-fi polytheism, in turn, is not regarded as remotely Christian (or Jewish) by Catholic, Protestant, Evangelical pastors and rabbis within "Purple-State America." [166] Can there be any sociological doubt that for informed clerics and their flocks, the curious visions and dogmas of Romney's LDS… smack of LSD?[167]

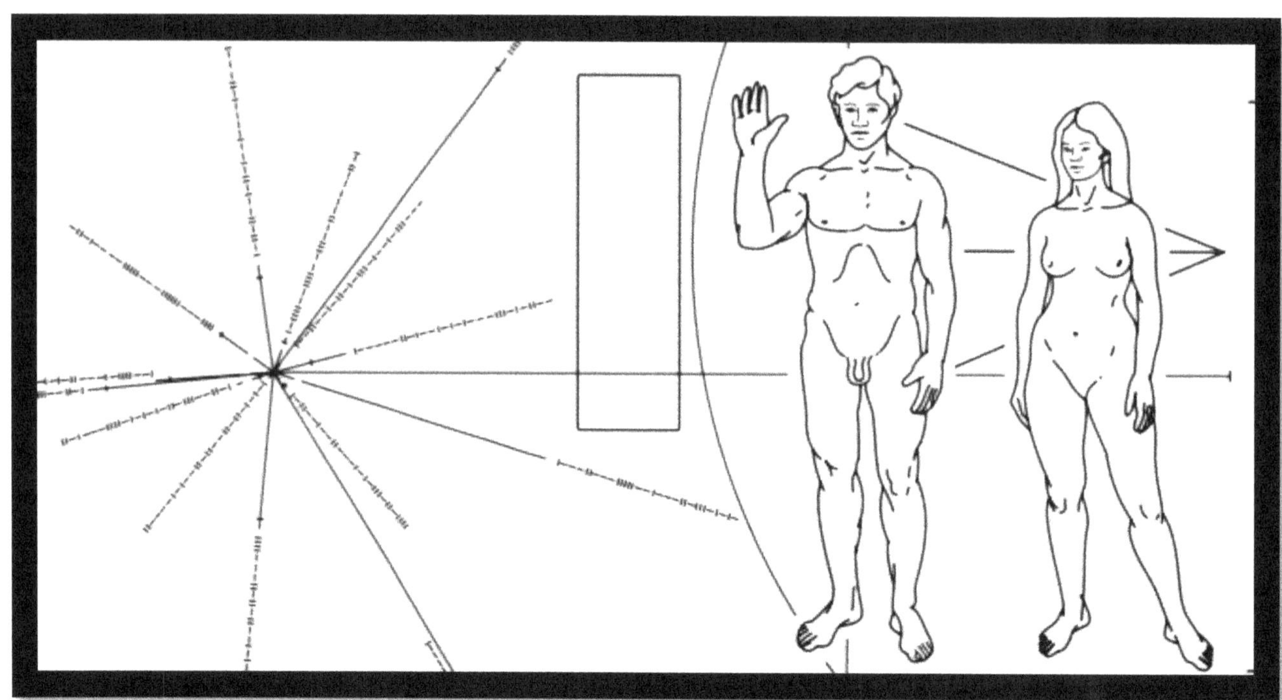

We hold this truth to be self-evident: That if indeed all human beings are "created equal" and "endowed by their Creator," "Nature's God" and "the Supreme Judge of the world" with unalienable rights such as to Life and Liberty – exactly as America's monotheistic Founders claimed in our national charter, The Declaration of Independence – then we must also, manifestly, be *designed* for heterosexuality and reproduction. And, if our transcendent human rights are contingent upon the intelligent design of humanity, as the Founders claimed, then we might well predict, as indeed the empirical science shows, that no one is "born gay."[168] (Diagram from plaques of the 1972 Pioneer 10 and 1973 Pioneer 11 spacecraft, the first manufactured objects to exit our solar system, wishfully designed for communication with extraterrestrial life from this or another universe).

Again: Such practical, dry-eyed, tough-love political observations herein aren't meant to be personally hurtful to Mssrs. Cruise, Travolta, Romney nor any alumnus of BYU; rather, they are meant to *protect* the Republican Party, its brand, and the nation itself from a Tampa Tragedy that is all but certain to result in the re-election of Barack Obama.

While Bibliocentric Jews and Christians may not agree on the nature and identity of the Jewish Messiah,[169] we can all recognize (if we have eyes to see it) that our nation's leadership now teeters on the brink of the gaping, cosmic chasm which divides Western monotheism from relativist, authoritarian polytheism[170] – and that by his record, a fluid, poll-driven and *demonstrably lawless*[171] Mr. Romney embodies the latter.

Although the Left undoubtedly will do what it can't resist through November (mocking most non-materialist creeds, but *especially* Romney's), grassroots faithful on the right and center will be doing what *we* can't resist, namely,

---

[166] See, e.g., "Is Mormonism Christian?" (http://carm.org/is-mormonism-christian); http://catholiclane.com/politics-and-theology-the-mormon-implications/

[167] See, e.g., http://www.i4m.com/think/history/holy-ghost.htm

[168] See page 70 and forward.

[169] See Daniel 7, Psalm 22 and Isaiah 9, 11 and 53 for pertinent Jewish Scriptures which are taken in differing ways by the two ancient Messianic traditions. Jews and Christians do agree, however, that there is but one absolute and infinite G_d over the universe, not a plurality of gods and goddesses over this and many worlds.

[170] Next February could find two polytheists, as President and Senate Majority Leader, atop the world's most powerful government. Without being too alarmist, we would also observe that from 586 BCE through 70 CE and the 1940's CE, things have tended not to go well for Biblical monotheists when polytheism has reigned. Greek polytheism, and the sacrifice of pigs to an image of Zeus erected by Antiochus Epiphanes in the Second Jewish Temple, fueled the Maccabbean Revolt of 167-164 BCE to which the Jewish holiday of Hanukah is tied. Roman polytheism and plans to build a temple to Jupiter upon the leveled Temple Mount in Jerusalem led to the Bar Kokhba revolt of 132-136 CE; indeed Hadrian built that pagan temple, renamed Jerusalem "Aelia Capitolina," and renamed Judea as "Syria Palaestina" (after the ancient Philistines whom David had fought). See, e.g., http://en.wikipedia.org/wiki/Bar_Kokhba_revolt#Outcome_of_the_war. Pagan and occult practices within the National Socialists and the SS is well documented.

[171] See, for example, page 9-14; Romney became "America's Founding Father of Gay Marriage" by a cynical act of lawlessness. See, page 47 and forward, and e.g., http://massresistance.org/romney/#SSM

defending our children and brethren from an essentially pagan, DC-decreed syncretism. Do Reince, Rove, FOX News and other GOP oracles *simply not get it* that Bibliocentric leaders are driven by *an affirmative Scriptural duty* to expose idolatry, polytheism, paganism and occultism within their societies?

Can't they see that faithful Jews and Christians are obligated to incline toward the friendly, neighborly and prayerful hope that all – from Scientologists to Mormons, from Muslims and Multiversers – may one day come to know the one, loving and gracious Creator G_d of Abraham, Isaac and Jacob?

Gov. Moonbeam, President Sunbeam

Bought-and-paid-for players in the GOP Establishment and some subsidiary, sadly co-opted "Religious Right" leaders – who perhaps abandoned their first love long ago or redefined it into an irrelevant, otherworldly private sphere – are now colluding against RNC delegates in the expectation that Tampa's potential patriotic heroes, just 236 years from the founding of our Republic, will cooperate in Romney's coronation.

The reality, nonetheless, is this: If Romney becomes Tampa's "ROMinee," more than enough affirmers of *The Manhattan Declaration*, ex-Mormons and grassroots swing-state pastors will feel compelled by love of G_d, their flocks, their neighbors and Truth itself to expose Mormonism – as well as the troubling record and mindset of the particular LDS Bishop who so fervently aspires to preach to all of us from the Presidential Bully Pulpit.

For three millennia, good teachers have taught from Solomon's Proverbs, "As a man thinketh, so he is."[172] Are we not thus obligated to carefully scrutinize Romney's deeds, dodging and dogmas, as does this video,[173] and as do these 32 videos? [174] Are we not thus obligated to let all our countrymen know that this[175] is the swill that's swirling around inside Bishop Romney's head?

To "political pragmatists" who say, "Look at the man's *policies,* not his personal religion," we must impatiently answer: Either way, Romney is an unacceptable Tampa choice. His private Idaho, his strange mental reality seems inextricably connected to his statist public policy record. The swing states don't want a "President Sunbeam"; they want a Commander-in-Chief who's grounded in *real* reality. A first-ballot nomination for Romney is a GOP death wish: Californians may be comfy with their "Gov. Moonbeam," but swing-state voters – religious and secular – will *never, ever* get comfy with the idea of a President whose horny holy prophets envision lunar and solar residents.

Meanwhile multiversers and other materialists – despite a paucity of empirical evidence and at contradictory odds with the American Declaration of 1776 – deeply embrace the dogma that humanity accidentally descended from an entirely random, uni-celled common ancestor of apes, insects and mushrooms. This is the fervent, atheistic faith of the Left (and a minority of the libertarian Right), the free exercise of which is protected by the First Amendment – yet not from skeptical challenge by empirical science[176] and logicians adept at detecting buried premises.

What TBM's (True Believing Multiversers and Mormons) have in common at their core, it seems, is a shared antipathy to the Jewish-Christian monotheism and hetero-monogamy of the American Founders. Thus, Romney pushed harder and earlier than Obama to advance the GLBT agenda, from his support of open homosexuality in the U.S. military to his gutting of one-man, one-woman marriage as public policy.[177]

Assuming he's just as duped as millions of other disciples of Joseph Smith and Brigham Young, it would be difficult (and quite wrong) to hate Mitt Romney; for the same reason, however, we just don't believe that he can or should be elected President of the United States. We would especially seek to remind all Tampa delegates, activists and *Manhattan Declaration* signatories/affirmers of this:

> **Our republic was founded, and is entirely predicated, upon the premises of Jewish-Christian monotheism and Natural Law. Because Romney and Obama respectively stand at *de jure* and *de facto* odds with those premises in their evolving, overwhelmingly statist ethical relativism, this document calls all faithful Jews,**

---

[172] Proverbs 23:7

[173] http://www.youtube.com/watch?v=fGAhiVutAx4&ytsession=Al8C1pf7s66iYxcy64fiCNCW9syd3_-WMdri6g3WJQ4w81-GFeMFkmGSZnilNM3Z4Wn-FqhY14O9GFUOUhKbN5wV-xjetoZIp2_3GMLSIko3x8AKoC0bnRh4o2mDar0n1H2KFLu_ZPkTFN9Ti-meDDhqYuzEh2VXtJHU-aT4se7S2pkcv7RPTIU-tJnSK00m8MerVQNatwg

[174] http://www.youtube.com/playlist?list=PLEC087120FC7B1DA3&feature=plcp

[175] "What do Mormons Really Believe?" (http://www.youtube.com/watch?v=3HSlbuli7HM).

[176] See, e.g., Ann Gauger, Douglas Axe and Casey Luskin, *Science & Human Origins,* Discovery Institute Press, 2012.

[177] See, e.g., http://www.boston.com/news/daily/11/romneyletterbaywindows.pdf and page 47 forward.

Christians and "small-r" *republican*[178] RNC delegates to their manifest *duty* to *demand* a better choice, a genuine choice, for their nation at Tampa.

Romney is NOT inevitable;[179] if he is, then so too is Republican defeat.[180]

Like LDS Stepford Wives

With this paradoxical man, the GOP gets the worst of all LDS worlds[181]: Romney's past policies as well as his *current* ones defy the standards of swing-state voters (and those of decent, ordinary rank-and-file Mormons with weaker connectivity than Romney to Nauvoo) on issues such as homosexuality, government mandates and authoritarianism. Like LDS Stepford Wives, however, some of Romney's "Harem Delegates" not only keep glossing-over that; they ignore the giant distinction between his polytheism and the monotheism of the Founders.[182]

Can they grasp that swing-state voters will soon be learning that the LDS pantheon is populated by divinized demi-gods (or demagogues?) like Joseph Smith, Brigham Young and one day... by Mitt Romney himself? Once again: The Republican Party's frontrunner not only believes in many gods, as all Mormon bishops must; Romney believes that he and his wife (and added "spiritual wives") can, upon their exaltation/apotheoses, *literally become god and goddesses of their own planet!*[183]

To declare themselves divine was the hubris of the Caesars. Even born-and-bred Mormons, however, perceive similar inclinations in Salt Lake City. As we've noted, one native Mormon writes that "LDS culture — along with the institutional LDS church — is the most authoritarian, controlling culture on the face of the earth."[184] This tendency manifests hard in Romney himself, the favorite political son of the LDS:

After arriving at the Massachusetts State House, Romney ... set up two of the country's first fusion centers, the controversial data-mining hubs that vacuum up and share intelligence from local, state and federal agencies and the private sector to detect terrorist plots. To some, the fusion centers suggest a Big Brother surveillance state. Romney also pushed for them as chairman of a federal task force on intelligence sharing. "He was definitely instrumental in laying the intellectual framework for fusion centers, and the role of state and local law enforcement in domestic counter terrorism and the need for clear guidelines concerning state and local domestic intelligence gathering," [A Homeland Security director] said. There are now 77 fusion centers nationwide. But, as in other areas of governance where he tended to go it alone, Romney did not confer with state legislators or the public to address concerns about how the centers would affect privacy and civil liberties. He simply issued an executive order.[185]

---

[178] Auburn University's Prof. Paul Johnson defines a republic as "a form of government (a.k.a. 'representative democracy') in which ultimate political power is theoretically vested in the people but in which popular control is exercised only intermittently and indirectly through the popular election of government officials and/or delegates..." (http://www.auburn.edu/~johnspm/gloss/republic). Distinguishing a republic from majoritarian democracy and other sorts of tyranny, George Mason University Prof. Walter Williams says, "John Adams captured the essence of the difference when he said, 'You have rights antecedent to all earthly governments; rights that cannot be repealed or restrained by human laws; rights derived from the Great Legislator of the Universe'.... Adams said, 'Remember, democracy never lasts long. It soon wastes, exhausts, and murders itself. There was never a democracy yet that did not commit suicide.'" (http://www.thefreemanonline.org/columns/the-pursuit-of-happiness-democracy-or-republic/) . A *republic* – and a truly *Republican* Party – relies upon thoughtful elected representatives who, rather than mirroring majoritarian or mobocratic impulses of manipulable electorates, dutifully exercises sober judgment concerning the unalienable Creator-endowed natural rights of the People, and concerning the records of aspiring leaders who, like Romney, have so clearly demonstrated their willingness to trample those rights.

[179] See http://www.thereal2012delegatecount.com/.

[180] See, e.g., Joseph Farah, "Why Romney Can't Win" (http://www.wnd.com/2012/03/why-romney-cant-win/); "Mormon Bishop Romney Cannot Beat Obama" http://mormonromney.blogspot.com/2012/04/t-he-media-destroyed-sarah-palin-and.html; Steve Deace, "Something Wicked this Way Comes" (http://stevedeace.com/news/videos/something-wicked-this-way-comes/).

[181] This is not an idle turn of phrase. LDS Mormon polytheism holds that there are countless planets like earth with human life on them, overseen by countless procreating god-and-godess couples who once were human themselves: The G_d of the Bible, Elohim, also was once an ordinary human who now is our sexually-active and polygamous Father in Heaven. LDS Mormon couples like Mitt and Ann Romney, if celestially married for eternity in a Mormon Temple, have the hope of becoming gods and goddesses of their own worlds. See notes 5 and 10.

[182] While LDS Mormon culture during Romney's lifetime has in many ways mirrored traditional Judeo-Christian norms, Romney's public policies, especially with regard to abortion, homosexuality and environmentalism (e.g., Climate regulation), have had rough correspondence with the pagan mores of Greco-Roman polytheistic societies – and certain elite LDS circles -- in which earth/nature/celestial worship, child sacrifice and sodomy were normative. For evidence that citizens of the 2012 swing states reject the normalization of homosexuality, see table on page __. Additional congruence between Mormon polytheism and Greco-Roman polytheism has arguably included: Polygamy/polygyny, demi-gods, racism, relativism, authoritarianism, anti-semitism (or anti-Judaism), and opposition to orthodox Christianity.

[183] LDS Apostle Bruce R. McConkie declared, for example: "Exaltation grows out of the eternal union of a man and his wife. Of those whose marriage endures in eternity, the Lord says, "Then shall they be gods" (D. & C. 132:20); that is, each of them, the man and the woman, will be a god. As such they will rule over their dominions forever (*Mormon Doctrine,* 613; cf. 257)."
For more examples, see http://www.christiandefense.org/mor_exaltation.htm#ldsex3 and many other sources available under such Google search terms as "Mormon Polytheism" or "Mormon Exaltation."

[184] "Understanding Mitt's Mormon Culture" (http://www.renewamerica.com/romney_mormon.htm)

[185] http://www.huffingtonpost.com/2012/05/04/mitt-romney-homeland-security-massachusetts_n_1467940.html?ref=topbar

As we'll see, that too is essentially how Romney brought gay marriage to Massachusetts. Not only do swing-state voters expect procedural integrity and basic soundness of mind in a GOP nominee; they demonstrably oppose Romney's offenses to the core moral and humanitarian concerns shared by our fellow signer/affirmers of *The Manhattan Declaration* – on Life, Marriage and Religious Liberty – especially the man's obsequious embrace of a broadly coercive GLBT Agenda, and plenty of other stuff on the left.

Not long ago, the Club for Growth declared, "Romney supports big government solutions to health care and opposes pro-growth tax code reform – positions that are simply opposite to those supported by true economic conservatives." On economics, he rated a gubernatorial C from the Cato Institute.[186]

On climate regulation, "Romney boasts that 'Massachusetts is the first and only state to set CO2 emissions limits on power plants'.... Romney did more than any Democrat governor to dramatically advance three of the Left's more important policies: Cap-and-Trade, gay marriage, and government control of health care."[187] The same writer, the former head of the Council on National Policy, reports:

> **[M]ore evidence has surfaced that Romney will govern as a global warming zealot. It turns out that one of Romney's largest donors is Julian Robertson Jr., who has given $1.3 million to the pro-Romney Super Pac, Restore our Future. Robertson serves on the board of the Environmental Defense Fund and was a big cheerleader for Obama's 2009 Cap-and-Trade bill. When Robertson's office was questioned about Romney's views on global warming, a spokesperson responded that, "he [Robertson] has confidence that Romney, once he's in there, will do the right thing." Can you spell SELL-OUT?**
>
> **But that's not all. A number of other global warming zealots are backing Romney including billionaire Trammel Crow and Rob Sisson, who heads up a group called Republicans for Environmental Protection. And one of Romney's economic advisors is Greg Mankiw, who has spent much of his career pushing for a carbon tax to finance all the wacky global warming programs of the type Mitt pushed in Massachusetts. Also advising Romney on environmental issues are James Connaughton, a cap-and-trader who headed up Bush's Council of Environmental Quality, and Jeff Holmstead, a Bush EPA official known for his extreme global warming views. But this isn't surprising given the fact Romney hired hard-Left environmentalist John Holdren – now Obama's science advisor – to be a key advisor while Governor of Massachusetts.**[188]

A Choice, Not an Echo

Because Team Obama will certainly bring it all out by November anyway, our coalitional DUMP ROMNEY effort has already been documenting in the swing states – with generous anonymous backing from pro-industry, pro-liberty and pro-monotheism camps – the reality which every thinking Tampa delegate now, or one day, will rightly rue:

> **Romney has been, and remains, a nice, handsome and coifed statist. He would, by far, be the most lawlessly anti-liberty, anti-family and anti-constitutional authoritarian[189] GOP nominee in US history. How bitterly ironic it would be if, three years after the rise of a movement which hearkens back to the Boston Tea Party, an awkward liberal from Boston should be the herald of its demise?**
>
> **Sons of Liberty disguised as Indians brought on the American Revolution; could an authoritarian Son of the LDS (which fancies aboriginal Indians as disguised Israelites!) mark the end of American liberty as the swing states go with the devil they know? Truly *republican* convention delegates should *never, ever* permit Romney to destroy their brand, and our opportunity to end Obama's reign, by making him the 2012 GOP standard bearer**

---

[186] http://www.factcheck.org/2012/02/romneys-fiscal-conservative-whopper/

[187] Steve Baldwin, "Do voters know Romney's views on Global Warming?" (http://www.freerepublic.com/focus/f-bloggers/2867770/posts).

[188] Baldwin, "Why Is Romney Being Supported By The Global Warming Crowd?" (http://www.westernjournalism.com/why-is-romney-being-supported-by-the-global-warming-crowd/). The writer adds:

> Robertson, Crow, Sisson, etc. must know something we don't. That's right, we're being set up folks. We're being screwed by the RINO wing of the GOP. Yet conservatives by the thousands continue to vote for Romney like lemmings crawling to water. Part of the reason why this is happening is that many of America's leading conservatives have remained silent or neutral in this race. Many leaders are tied to groups that took money from one of Romney's six PACS over the last six years and so they either cheerlead for Romney or stay silent. And then there are many conservatives supporting Romney in hopes of receiving a position in his administration. You know, the "career first, America last" types.

[189] We are *not* here referring to Romney's Mormon religion, the Church of Jesus Christ and Latter-Day Saints, which is indeed authoritarian in structure and run by a council of Twelve Apostles and a president in Salt Lake City, Utah. Rather, we are here referring to Romney's proven tendency to behave as a *secular authoritarian,* in violation of constitutional Rule of Law and in service to *the cult of statism*. To grasp the distinction, see Who is Mitt Romney by native Mormon Stephen Stone (http://www.renewamerica.com/romney.htm).

Liberty's enemies have two horses in this race, an LDS-GLBT "White Horse" and a Left-GLBT horse of a different color (who's no "Dark Horse," but rather is already winning by a wide margin on the Electoral College map). To suppose that the GOP frontrunner's judicial appointments would be significantly better than Obama's is to ignore the ugly record of his picks in Massachusetts.[190] In fact, Romney and Obama are two sides of the same statist, relativist coin: *Heads they win; tails they win.* This YouTube from Ron Paul's camp helps make the point.[191]

To lamely argue that Romney is better than Obama is like saying Pol Pot wasn't as bad as Mao, or that Prophet Smith did less damage than Prophet Muhammad; it makes the point that Tampa's totally unbound delegates simply *must* strive to give the nation something better at the end of August: A *new name,* neither Romney nor Obama, yet a proven leader capable of protecting Americans and liberty itself in a dangerous world.

RNC leaders, religious "leaders" and failed 2012 candidates who argue for our collective submission to the lesser evil – and by the Jewish-Christian standards of *The Manhattan Declaration*, Romney's record and polytheistic belief system are rife with evil – have accepted the *false choice* represented by the *demonstrably false notion* of Romney's Tampa inevitability.[192] Exemplary of, and driving, the bad journalism:

> **The Associated Press count, source for most news media, has consistently presented inflated, misleading and inaccurate figures. The "AP Delegate Tracker" ... betrays a casual disregard for precision, e.g., with this clearly false statement: "Former Massachusetts Gov. Mitt Romney became the Republican party's presidential nominee by crossing the threshold of 1,144 delegates to the GOP national convention this summer." This is simply false.[193]**

By ignoring such brainwashing media, LDS or GOP Establishment masters who hold no authority over the elected *republican* representatives of the *Republican* Party, Tampa's unbound delegates would wisely do everything in their power to delay any Romney nomination past the first ballot in favor of more careful consideration on a second, third or later ballot, just as has occurred in Republican National Conventions past.

By so doing, "enlightened" delegates who accurately recognize their free status and true, first-ballot power can help their fellow delegates realize, at least by the second ballot, that in fact, no GOP delegates are married to Mitt Romney on *any* round of balloting. Again: We are *not* plural Mormon wives, and we *do* have a duty to derail this devil's choice[194] which voters will otherwise face in November.

Romney backs Gay Childrearing...

If indeed there are devout Mormon souls who know him but cannot in good conscience vote for Romney –

---

[190] Amy Contrada, "Romney's Judiciary" (http://www.amycontrada.com/Romney_s_Judiciary.html)

[191] http://www.youtube.com/watch?v=IWDJEc92d38

[192] For the very real potential event that Presidential primaries may yield a presumptive nominee discovered to have a fatal political problem – e.g., a history of mental illness, suicide attempts, pedophilia, incest, spousal abuse, bisexuality, Satanism, embezzlement, emailing lewd photographs of himself, involvement in a kooky cult, etc.. – RNC Rules ultimately empower delegates to vote their consciences, in entirely unbound fashion, on every ballot – *including, necessarily,* the First Ballot. In this manner, the Republican Party protects the nation and its brand by upholding "small-r" republicanism, by empowering elected delegates to dutifully exercise their good judgment and wisdom, rather than binding them to "small d" democratic or "mobocratic" election results which can be unduly influenced by money, mass hysteria, misleading advertising, bad journalism, foreign interests, extortion, etc. See www.thereal2012delegatecount.com; Response to "A Rogue Convention?" (http://www.fairvote.org/response-to-a-rogue-convention-how-gop-party-rules-may-surprise-in-201); "A Rogue Convention? How GOP party rules may surprise in 2012"(http://www.politico.com/news/stories/1111/69048_Page2.html); Reality Check: Republican Delegates "Unbound"? (http://www.youtube.com/watch?v=anWsU93fFsk&feature=relmfu); http://www.examiner.com/article/rnc-delegates-not-bound-to-any-candidate-on-first-ballot; and pages 75 and forward.

[193] http://www.thereal2012delegatecount.com/

[194] Some traditionalists note that an Obama-Romney choice is not unlike dilemmas which faced ancient Israelites (in *Israel,* not the LDS Americas!) after the deaths of David and Solomon – and which, according to the Jewish Scriptures, ultimately resulted in the devastation of of the Northern Kingdom, the Southern Kingdom and Jerusalem itself. Who, knowing their respective hostility to hetero-monogamy and human life, can deny that both Obama and Romney echo the child-sacrificing and Sodom-inclined idolatrous kings of the Original Testament? As if chiding us for all of our latter-day apostasies, the Jewish Prophet Jeremiah says in chapter 7,

> Will ye steal, murder, and commit adultery, and swear falsely,[194] and offer unto Baal, and ...other gods whom ye have not known...that ye may do all these abominations?... The children gather wood, and the fathers kindle the fire, and the women knead the dough, to make cakes to the Queen of Heaven, and to pour out drink-offerings unto other gods, that they may provoke Me....Therefore thou shalt say unto them: This is the nation that hath not hearkened to the voice of HaShem their G-d, nor received correction; faithfulness is perished, and is cut off from their mouth....For the children of Judah have done that which is evil in My sight, saith HaShem; they have set their detestable things in the house whereon My name is called, to defile it. And they have built the high places of Topheth, which is in the valley of the son of Hinnom, to burn their sons and their daughters in the fire; which I commanded not, neither came it into My mind. Therefore, behold, the days come, saith HaShem, that it shall no more be called Topheth, nor The valley of the son of Hinnom, but The valley of slaughter; for they shall bury in Topheth, for lack of room. And the carcasses of this people shall be food for the fowls of the heaven, and for the beasts of the earth; and none shall frighten them away. Then will I cause to cease from the cities of Judah, and from the streets of Jerusalem, the voice of mirth and the voice of gladness, the voice of the bridegroom and the voice of the bride; for the land shall be desolate.

In I Kings 18, Elijah puts things rather more starkly, " 'How long halt ye between two opinions? If HaShem be G_d, follow Him; but if Baal, follow him.' And the people answered him not a word."

and there are [195] – why would *any* devout Jews, Christians, Tampa delegates or signatories/affirmers of *The Manhattan Declaration* weakly go whoring themselves over to this false prophet (and follower of false prophets), especially given that no Tampa delegate is bound to him, even on the first ballot?[196]

Yet, what else can one call it when Liberty University, the world's largest Christian school at nearly 100,000 enrollees, slavishly lauds an engineer of gay wedlock, child sacrifice and Anti-Liberty with an honorary doctorate? As if mimicking Notre Dame when it sullied its own name (by awarding doctoral honors to a new President who had proven himself not only the enemy of unborn babies, but of those who had *survived* abortion), why would Jerry Falwell's school cozy-up so to a sodomy proponent, to a polytheist?[197]

Will podia at both schools remain wide open to such men, like the thirsty thighs of a fallen woman? Do the trustees at Liberty and Notre Dame (which today is suing their honorary Ph.D in connection with ObamaCare's so-called "contraceptive mandate") even realize that, long before Obama decreed the distribution of abortifacients by religious institutions under ObamaCare, Romney had done similarly in Massachusetts?[198]

Do they get it that the Pell Grants and USDE student loans which fuel their schools will, very likely and relatively soon, be conditioned on *each school's surrender* and submission in the war against human life, hetero-monogamy and Judeo-Christianity itself which Obama *and* Romney have been waging for so long?

Did they catch it that his Liberty University doctoral acceptance speech simply *described* what to swing-state voters is normal and obvious: "Marriage is a relationship between a man and a woman." Romney did *not* say at Liberty, "Legal marriage in America *ought* to be only between one man and one woman." LDS Prophet Joseph Smith didn't believe that, nor did Prophet Brigham Young. Nor did Romney's great grandfather Miles Park Romney, born into Mormonism at Nauvoo, eventually to have five wives.

Nor does Romney who, as we'll see below, begat the USA's first homosexual marriages. Just after Obama embraced gay marriage, Romney came out of the closet for gay childrearing:

> **Romney told Fox News host Neil Cavuto, "I know many gay couples that are able to adopt children. That's fine. But my preference is that we ... continue to define marriage as the relationship between a man and a woman." The statement seemed to put Romney in the position of condoning same-sex families with children as long as the parents do not marry.**
>
> **Later in the interview, he said, "I believe that my record as a person who has supported civil rights is strong and powerful.... if two people of the same gender want to live together, want to have a loving relationship, or even to adopt a child -- in my state individuals of the same sex were able to adopt children. In my view, that's something that people have a right to do."[199]**

A day later, Romney attempted to walk-back his support for GLBT childrearing into a merely descriptive statement: "Actually, I think all states but one allow gay adoption. So that's a position which has been decided by most of the state legislatures, including the one in my state some time ago. So I simply acknowledge the fact that gay adoption is legal" – although Romney has been proclaiming, from as early as 2006, that he substantively supports such policy.[200]

Frequently, Romney describes what "is" to avoid indicating what he feels "ought" to be. He sometimes also fudges what "is" to be what he'd *like it to be:* His statement that all states but one permit homo/bisex adoption is simply false.[201] Most states do not allow homosexual couples to adopt children, and as a matter of social science, that

---

[195] Stephen Stone, http://www.renewamerica.com/romney_obama.htm

[196] For the very real potential event that Presidential primaries may yield a presumptive nominee discovered to have a fatal political problem – e.g., a history of mental illness, suicide attempts, pedophilia, incest, spousal abuse, bisexuality, Satanism, embezzlement, emailing lewd photographs of himself, involvement in a kooky cult, etc.. – RNC Rules ultimately empower delegates to vote their consciences, in entirely unbound fashion, on every ballot – *including, necessarily,* the First Ballot. In this manner, the Republican Party protects the nation and its brand by upholding "small-r" republicanism, by empowering elected delegates to dutifully exercise their good judgment and wisdom, rather than binding them to "small d" democratic or "mobocratic" election results which can be unduly influenced by money, mass hysteria, misleading advertising, bad journalism, foreign interests, extortion, etc. See www.thereal2012delegatecount.com; Response to "A Rogue Convention?" (http://www.fairvote.org/response-to-a-rogue-convention-how-gop-party-rules-may-surprise-in-201); "A Rogue Convention? How GOP party rules may surprise in 2012"(http://www.politico.com/news/stories/1111/69048_Page2.html); Reality Check: Republican Delegates "Unbound"? (http://www.youtube.com/watch?v=anWsU93fFsk&feature=relmfu); http://www.examiner.com/article/rnc-delegates-not-bound-to-any-candidate-on-first-ballot; and page 75 forward.

[197] See, e.g., http://www.youtube.com/watch?v=BYRplf2F9NA and Links to Barack Obama's votes on Illinois' Born Alive Infant - Jill Stanek

[198] http://www.amycontrada.com/Romney_s_CPAC_Speech.html

[199] "Romney says he's 'Fine" with gay couples adopting children" (http://nationaljournal.com/2012-presidential-campaign/romney-says-he-s-fine-with-gay-couples-adopting-children-20120510).

[200] "Romney: States Should Be Permitted To Legalize Same-Sex Adoptions" (http://thinkprogress.org/lgbt/2011/10/14/344328/romney-states-should-be-permitted-to-legalize-same-sex-adoptions/).

[201] http://thinkprogress.org/lgbt/2012/05/12/483187/romney-now-only-acknowledges-same-sex-adoption-days-after-supporting-it/

seems to be a good thing; a blizzard of studies decisively indicate that children do much better if raised by a mother and father.[202]

… While ignoring GLBT Child Sexual Abuse

Social science indicates, furthermore, that it's a monstrous myth that homo/bisexuals are no more likely to sexually sexually abuse children than straight people. In *The Top 10 Myths about Homosexuality,* Sprigg writes that "The percentage of child sexual abuse cases in which men molest boys is many times higher than the percentage of adult males who are homosexual, and most men who molest boys self-identify as homosexual or bisexual." If the contrary were true, "it would support the notion that homosexuals should be allowed to work with children as schoolteachers, Boy Scout leaders and Big Brothers or Big Sisters," [and foster parents, adoptive parents, etc.]

> However, it is not true. The research clearly shows that same-sex child sexual abuse (mostly men molesting boys) occurs at rates far higher, proportionally, than adult homosexual behavior, and it strongly suggests that many of those abusers are homosexual in their adult orientation as well.
>
> As this is perhaps the most explosive claim about homosexuals, a couple of clarifications are in order. This does not mean that all homosexuals are child molesters—no one has ever claimed that. It does not even mean that most homosexuals are child molesters—there is no evidence to support that. But there is evidence that the relative rate of child sexual abuse among homosexuals is far higher than it is among heterosexuals. This conclusion rests on three key facts:
>
> - **Pedophiles are [almost] invariably males:** A report by the *American Professional Society on the Abuse of Children* states: "In both clinical and non-clinical samples, the vast majority of offenders are male."59 The book Sexual Offending Against Children reports that only 12 of 3,000 incarcerated pedophiles in England were women."60
> - **Significant numbers of victims are males:** A study of 457 male sex offenders against children in *Journal of Sex & Marital Therapy* found that "approximately one-third of these sexual offenders directed their sexual activity against males."61 A study in the *Journal of Sex Research* found that although heterosexuals outnumber homosexuals by a ratio of at least 20 to 1, homosexual pedophiles commit about one-third of the total number of child sex offenses.62
> - **Many pedophiles consider themselves to be homosexual:** Many people who write about the issue of pedophilia argue that most men who molest boys are merely attracted to children, not to adult males, but they do not cite any specific data to support that assertion. In fact, a study of 229 convicted child molesters in *Archives of Sexual Behavior* found that "eighty-six percent of offenders against males described themselves as homosexual or bisexual."63
>
> Since almost thirty percent of child sexual abuse is committed by homosexual or bisexual men (one-third male-on-male abuse times 86% identifying as homosexual or bisexual), but less than 3% of American men identify themselves as homosexual or bisexual,64 we can infer that homosexual or bisexual men are approximately ten times more likely to molest children than heterosexual men.
>
> In addition to the actual data on elevated rates of homosexual child abuse, there is clearly a sub-culture among homosexual men that openly celebrates the idea of sexual relationships between adult men and underage boys, whether pre-pubescent or adolescent. Such relationships are referred to in some research literature using neutral-sounding euphemisms such as "age-discrepant sexual relations (ADSRs)"65 or "intergenerational intimacy."66
>
> Lesbian writer Paula Martinac summarized this phenomenon:
>
> > **. . . [S]ome gay men still maintain that an adult who has same-sex relations with someone under the legal age of consent is on some level doing the kid a favor by helping to bring him or her "out." . . . [A]dult-youth sex is viewed as an important aspect of gay culture, with a history dating back to "Greek love" of ancient times. This romanticized vision of adult-youth sexual relations has been a staple of gay literature and has made appearances, too, in gay-themed films. . . . Last summer, I attended a reading in which a gay poet read a long piece about being aroused by a flirtatious young boy in his charge. In response, the man went into the boy's bedroom and [sexually abused the boy as he] slept. . . . Disturbingly, most of the gay audience gave the poet an appreciative round of applause. . . The lesbian and gay community will never be successful in fighting the pedophile stereotype until we all stop condoning sex with young people**.[67][203]

---

[202] See Peter Sprigg, *The Top 10 Myths about Homosexuality,* (Family Research Council, http://downloads.frc.org/EF/EF10F01.pdf), at 30-39; 44-47

[203] Peter Sprigg, *The Top 10 Myths about Homosexuality* (Family Research Council, http://downloads.frc.org/EF/EF10F01.pdf). His "Myth 8" footnotes are as follows:

59 John Briere, et al., eds., The APSAC Handbook on Child Maltreatment (Thousand Oaks, California: Sage Publications, 1996), pp. 52, 53.

60 Dawn Fisher, "Adult Sex Offenders: Who are They? Why and How Do They Do It?" in Tony Morrison, et al., eds., Sexual Offending Against Children (London: Routledge, 1994), p. 11.

That such predatory recruiting activity thrives in gay youth and sex clubs linked to schools and neighborhoods in Massachusetts and across the nation pursuant to "Romney's Gubernatorial Gay Youth Pride Proclamation" is made clear here.[204] And, if indeed the institution of marriage, traditional hetero-monogamy, exists especially for the sake of children, isn't Romney's embrace of homo/bisex childrearing (along with almost all the rest of the GLBT agenda) even worse than Obama's wish to solemnize anal intercourse from coast to coast?

Conveniently, there's no need to weigh who's the lesser evil on these fronts because long before Obama formally embraced homosexual wedlock, Romney had already made himself America's Founding Father of Gay Marriage.[205] Mitt Romney has rejected *The Marriage Vow, The Pro-Life Presidential Leadership Pledge*, *The Personhood Pledge* and *The Repeal ObamaCare Pledge* throughout all of 2011-2012 because, we suspect, they run counter to the relativist, statist premises upon which he and Obama have built their careers. For example, ObamaCare and its model, RomneyCare, hold Jeffersonian, Creator-endowed rights of life and liberty in low regard:

- Both rely on coerced insurance purchasing, the liberty-defying Individual Mandate recently upheld by the U.S. Supreme Court (by ridiculously construing the compulsion as a "tax" rather a "penalty," in any case common features of RomneyCare and ObamaCare). According to a June 5, 2012 issue of *The Wall Street Journal,*

  When Mitt Romney left office as Massachusetts governor, his aides removed all emails from a server computer in the governor's office.... But a small cache of emails survived, including some that .... [show that] Mr. Romney and his aides... strongly defended the so-called individual mandate, a requirement that everyone in Massachusetts have or buy health insurance. And they privately discussed ideas that might be anathema to today's GOP – including publicly shaming companies that didn't provide enough health insurance to employees.

  Indeed, when ObamaCare was upheld by the Supreme Court's late June ruling, the President gloated that even "the current Republican nominee" had supported the Individual Mandate. Obama wasn't lying.

- Both RomneyCare and ObamaCare force employers, insurers and premium-paying individuals to violate their religious convictions and rights of conscience (via mandated contraceptives, sterilization, etc);

- And, both forcibly subsidize the killing of tiny Americans while laying the groundwork for medical rationing and euthanasia. ObamaCare's so-called "contraceptive mandate" is in fact an "abortion mandate" for collectively-funded abortion drugs (and is just one Executive Order away from surgical abortion coverage). Yet RomneyCare, even more horrifically, fully subsidizes elective chemical *and* surgical abortions, with $0 co-pay.[206] From the *National Catholic Reporter:*

  During the 2008 campaign, some pro-life Republicans charged that Obama was "the most pro-abortion candidate" in history and they have repeated the charge now that he is in the White House. But, there is no comparison between the way Obama handled abortion coverage in his health care reform and the way Romney handled it in his. A judge in Ohio ruled this year that Obama's reform does not include federal funding of abortion. Judge Timothy Black held that the "express language of the PPACA [Patient Protection and Affordable Care Act, aka Obamacare] does not provide for tax-payer funding of abortion. That is a fact, and it is

---

61 Kurt Freund, et al., "Pedophilia and Heterosexuality vs. Homosexuality," Journal of Sex & Marital Therapy 10 (1984): 197.
62 Kurt Freund, Robin Watson, and Douglas Rienzo, "Heterosexuality, Homosexuality, and Erotic Age Preference," The Journal of Sex Research 26, No. 1 (February, 1989): 107.
63 W. D. Erickson, "Behavior Patterns of Child Molesters," Archives of Sexual Behavior 17 (1988): 83.
64 Edward O. Laumann, John H. Gagnon, Robert T. Michael, and Stuart Michaels, The Social Organization of Sexuality: Sexual Practices in the United States (Chicago: University of Chicago Press, 1994), p. 293—"Altogether, 2.8 percent of the men and 1.4 percent of the women reported some level of homosexual (or bisexual) identity."
65 See Bruce Rind, "Gay and bisexual adolescent boys' sexual experiences with men: An empirical examination of psychological correlates in a nonclinical sample," Archives of Sexual Behavior Vol. 30, Issue 4, August 1, 2001; also Jessica L. Stanley, Kim Bartholomew, Doug Oram, "Gay and Bisexual Men's Age-Discrepant Childhood Sexual Experiences," The Journal of Sex Research, Vol. 41, Number 4, November, 2004: pp. 381-389: online at: http://findarticles.com/p/articles/mi_m2372/is_4_41/ai_n9488757/
66 Gerald P. Jones, "The Study of Intergenerational Intimacy in North America: Beyond Politics and Pedophilia," Journal of Homosexuality, Vol. 20, Issue 1 & 2 (February 1990), pp. 275 – 295. This entire journal of the Journal of Homosexuality—at least nineteen articles—was devoted to this topic.
67 Paula Martinac, "Do We Condone Pedophilia," PlanetOut.com, February 27, 2002.

[204] http://www.massresistance.org/docs/gen2/12c/Flanders_lawsuit/index.html
[205] See page 47 and forward.
[206] See "RomneyCare Now Funding FREE Abortions: A Disqualifier for Mitt Romney's Candidacy," by Amy L. Contrada, (http://www.amycontrada.com/Romney_s_FREE_Abortions.html).

clear on its face." On its face, Romneycare does provide for taxpayer funding of abortion. So, will GOP pro-lifers admit that Romney has now succeeded to the title of "most pro-abortion candidate" in history?[207]

Indeed, RomneyCare's individual insurance and abortion mandates; its author's authoritarian embrace of GLBT aims; and his anti-science, earth-worshiping collectivism with regard to Climate regulation have been statist hallmarks of the GOP frontrunner's public career. So, why ever would Jews, Christians or religious/secular libertarians of any stripe have expected Romney – who makes "no apologies" for RomneyCare – to have joined most other 2012 POTUS candidates in signing *The Repeal ObamaCare Pledge*?

Mormon "Truth"

Why has Romney chosen fellow Mormon, former Utah governor and *pro-ObamaCare* lobbyist Mike Leavitt to head Romney's Transition Team? And now, with "RomneyCare writ large" upheld by the U.S. Supreme Court, why would any sane Tampa delegate actually *trust* Mitt Romney to repeal a giant new entitlement which is modeled, as he hoped, on his socialist pioneering in Massachusetts?

U.S. Senate President Harry Reid, Romney's across-the-aisle LDS fellow and crucial to the enactment of ObamaCare has for decades artfully practiced deception on the Nevada and national stages as Romney's forerunner; Reid, however, may not even be worthy to untie the sandals of Mormonism's Golden Boy. Were swing-state voters to shrug-off Romney's record and eccentric beliefs, these three– "Big Government" Mormons – Romney, Reid and Leavitt – would represent a triumvirate in Washington, D.C. – and perhaps, a triumph for polytheism over the monotheism of America's founders.

Americans correctly perceive that something is very, very off with the GOP frontrunner, with the LDS White Horse. Perhaps they grasp that he is a card-carrying member of a cult which treats truth as something infinitely malleable, which rationalizes lying at every turn. And, a small industry has been launched – from the right, left and center, to catalog the GOP frontrunner's whoppers.[208]

Sure, we're used to lying Democrats in the Oval Office – Think: Clinton, Monica, Obama, Ayres – but it now seems, as a function of his religious exemplars – that Mitt Romney is muddying the comparably cleaner Republican Party brand by taking falsehood to a whole new, systemic level. That, it seems, is what he has been doing in connection with his phony exit from Bain Capital in 1999.[209] And, in misrepresenting his record to gullible conservatives.[210] And, on pretty much everything else.

But again, consider his exemplars: Joseph Smith was the ultimate con man, trading heavenly salvation for big money and little girls. Brigham Young too, was a creep. One of their latest successors, Gordon B. Hinckley, beloved President and "Living Prophet" of the Church of Jesus Christ of Latter-day Saints, with his son was plausibly accused, before his 2008 death, of covering up bisexual orgies, phony religious documents and financial scandals which tarred their family name and church.[211]

After working full time for 27 years as Coordinator of the LDS Church Education System (CES) and serving as a Mormon Bishop, Ken Clark (whose story can be found here) wrote about the LDS habit of "Lying for the Lord" at the 2008 ExMormon Foundation Conference in Salt Lake City.

> Noted LDS historians D. Michael Quinn and B. Carmon Hardy have written compassionately and humanely as they describe the history of Mormonism, and the use of deception as a useful tool to manage the minds of its adherents and public perception.
>
> Hardy, recognizing that LDS public discourse routinely used fake denials and deception called it "pretzeled language." He quoted Apostle Matthias Cowley who said, "I am not dishonest and not a liar and have always been true to the work and to the brethren." Cowley later admitted, "We have always been taught that when the brethren were in a tight place that it would not be amiss to lie to help them out." (Hardy, *Solemn Covenant,* 373,374)

---

[207] Michael Sean Winters, "The Problem with RomneyCare" (http://ncronline.org/blogs/distinctly-catholic/problem-romneycare)
[208] See, e.g., http://romneytheliar.blogspot.com/
[209] Christopher Rowland, "Mitt Romney Stayed at Bain 3 years longer than he stated," The Boston Globe (http://articles.boston.com/2012-07-12/politics/32633322_1_bain-capital-mitt-romney-financial-disclosure); see also http://talkingpointsmemo.com/archives/2012/07/no_romney_didnt_leave_bain_in_1999.php
[210] See, e.g., http://www.amycontrada.com/Romney_s_CPAC_Speech.html
[211] See, e.g., Darrick B. Evenson, "Gordon B. Hinckley: The Lying Prophet," (http://www.angelfire.com/planet/lds/Hinckley.html).

> In my effort to defend the church from detractors I learned that ironically, members get excommunicated precisely because they publish the truth, and refuse to adopt lying, deception, or suppression of facts as an ethical standard. Loyalty is more important in the LDS church than honesty. I found this out the hard way while teaching for the Church Education System. Honesty was referred to as undermining the testimonies of the youth, or undermining the authority of the prophets.
>
> D. Michael Quinn, excommunicated in 1993 said, "The tragic reality is that there have been occasions when Church leaders, teachers, and writers have not told the truth they knew about difficulties of the Mormon past, but have offered to the Saints instead a mixture of platitudes, half-truths, omissions, and plausible denials.[212]

Perhaps, in their evaluation of the favorite son of the LDS, regular swing-state voters have begun to intuitively perceive what Romney's collaborating allies in Salt Lake City, the GOP Establishment and Log Cabin/GOProud circles have known for years:

Romney spawned Gay Wedlock

As a matter of full disclosure and informed consent, all RNC delegates and all Americans deserve to know, *right now,* ahead of Tampa and ahead of November, this hard fact:

Mitt Romney truly is "America's Founding Father of Gay Marriage"[213] – as much the USA's pioneer of homosexual wedlock as Joseph Smith and Brigham Young were pioneers of polygamy and pedophilia. Just as RomneyCare modeled and foreshadowed ObamaCare, so Romney's reign in Masssachusetts will – if GOP delegates do not rescue their nation in Tampa – foreshadow the nationalization of gay marriage, the GLBT agenda and very likely polygamy as well.

In his famous 2003 dissent in *Lawrence v. Texas,*[214] Supreme Court Justice Antonin Scalia argued that laws against prostitution, bestiality, incest and bigamy/polygamy must fail under the logic of a jurisprudence that invalidates Western Civilization's, and the USA's, public policy of hetero-monogamy.[215] The *Lawrence* ruling came down less than a year ahead of Romney's decision to make Massachusetts the beachhead for the solemnization of sodomy – same-sex-as-Sandusky – in legal matrimony.

How did Gov. Romney embrace and enshrine such logic in Massachusetts? Answer: In violation of the Commonwealth's John Adams constitution of 1780; no original Boston Tea Partier nor any self-respecting descendant in today's contemporary Tea Party movement could ever, in knowledgeable good conscience, have any part in the elevation of this lawless authoritarian, this wily emulator of false prophets past, to the U.S. Presidency.

Romney's assault on one-man, one-woman marriage by way of Massachusetts – once a Yankee evangelical anti-slavery, anti-polygamy hotbed – can be seen as a rich form of payback for the abolition of Mormon polygamy, and the emancipation of LDS child brides, by the abolitionist Republican Party of the 1800's. From Wikipedia:

> America was both fascinated and horrified by the practice of polygamy, with the Republican platform at one time referencing "the twin relics of barbarism - polygamy and slavery."... The private practice of polygamy, or more accurately, polygyny, was instituted in the 1830s by founder Joseph Smith, Jr. The public practice of polygamy ("plural marriage") by the church was announced and defended in 1852 by one of the Council of the Twelve Apostles, Elder Orson Pratt **[Romney's great-great uncle]** by the request of the church President at that time, Brigham Young....

---

[212] Ken Clark, "LDS Honesty: Lying for the Lord" (http://www.mormonthink.com/lying.htm)

[213] See, e.g., "The Governor's New Clothes; How Mitt Romney Brought Same-Sex Marriage To America," (http://robertpaine.blogspot.com/2006/06/governors-new-clothes-how-mitt-romney_17.html); http://en.wikipedia.org/wiki/Same-sex_marriage_in_Massachusetts);The Mitt Romney Report: "Gay Marriage" in Massachusetts (http://massresistance.org/romney/#SSM); 'Gay' marriages put on Romney's shoulders (http://www.wnd.com/2012/01/gay-marriages-put-on-romneys-shoulders/) and "Manifest Mormon Destiny," http://www.renewamerica.com/mormon_destiny.htm. Scathing critiques, "Open Letter" rebukes, and other records of Romney's Leftism list fellow Mormons, a former Massachusetts assistant U.S. attorney, law professors, a state judge and lawmaker, clerics, independent scholars, lawyers, physicians, activists and media professionals among Romney's thoughtful detractors. See, e.g., "An Open Letter to Mitt Romney," (http://theinteramerican.org/blogs/law-and-government/324-letter-to-governor-romney-by-john-haskins.html), ""An Open Letter to Rush Limbaugh" (http://www.rushtellthetruth.blogspot.com/); "A Warning to the 'Conservative Elites' about Mitt Romney" (http://theinteramerican.org/commentary/322-a-stern-warning-to-the-qconservative-elitesq-about-mitt-romney.html); Although none of his underfunded GOP opponents effectively exploited this treasure trove of negative material, the media will have no such challenge undermining Romney in the swing states this fall if RNC delegates are foolish enough to nominate him in Tampa.

[214] http://www.law.cornell.edu/supct/html/02--102.ZD.html

[215] For an argument in the affirmative for hetero-monogamy, see Sherif Girgis, Robert P. George and Ryan T. Anderson, "What is Marriage?", *Harvard Journal of Law and Public Policy,* Vol. 34, No. 1, pp. 245-287, Winter 2010. (http://www.harvard-jlpp.com/wp-content/uploads/2011/08/GeorgeFinal.pdf).

> Joseph Smith publicly condemned the practice, denying the fact that he was involved in it, and participants were being excommunicated, as church records and publications reflect. But church leaders nevertheless began practicing polygamy in the 1840s, particularly members of the Quorum of the Twelve. Sidney Rigdon, during a period when he was apostate from the church, wrote a letter in backlash to the *Messenger and Advocate* in 1844 condemning the church's Quorum of the Twelve and their alleged connection to polygamy:
>
> > " It is a fact so well known that the Twelve and their adherents have endeavored to carry on this spiritual wife business ... and have gone to the most shameful and desperate lengths to keep from the public. First, insulting innocent females, and when they resented the insult, these monsters in human shape would assail their characters by lying, and perjuries, with a multitude of desperate men to help them effect the ruin of those whom they insulted, and all this to enable them to keep these corrupt practices from the world."
>
> At the time the practice was kept a secret from non-members, and many church members at large. Throughout his life, Smith publicly denied having multiple wives.
>
> However, John C. Bennett, a recent convert to the church and the first mayor of Nauvoo, used ideas of eternal and plural marriage to justify acts of seduction, adultery and, in some cases, the practice of abortion in the guise of spiritual wifery.... In April 1844, Joseph Smith referred to polygamy as "John C. Bennett's spiritual wife system" and warned "if any man writes to you, or preaches to you, doctrines contrary to the Bible, the Book of Mormon, or the book of Doctrine and Covenants, set him down as an imposter." Smith mused
>
> > " we cannot but express our surprise that any elder or priest who has been in Nauvoo, and has had an opportunity of hearing the principles of truth advanced, should for one moment give credence to the idea that any thing like iniquity is practised, much less taught or sanctioned, by the authorities of the Church of Jesus Christ of Latter Day Saints."
>
> The practice was publicly announced in Utah in 1852, some five years after the Mormons arrived in Utah, and eight years after Smith's death. The doctrine authorizing plural marriage was published in the 1876 version of Doctrine and Covenants.... It was not until 1904, under the leadership of President Joseph F. Smith, that the church completely banned new plural marriages worldwide.... Although the 1904 Manifesto ended the official practice of new plural marriages, existing plural marriages were not automatically dissolved. Many Mormons, including prominent church leaders, maintained existing plural marriages well into the 20th century.[216]

To all snobs who would dismiss history via Wikipedia, we say: You can readily confirm it all from abundant and more esoteric sources if you wish, but in any case realize this much: If these plain facts about Romney's religion and its frisky, prevaricating prophet are readily available to the American masses via Wikipedia – the go-to reference and *Encyclopedia Britannica* of this generation, one of the busiest websites on the planet – then *why* would any rational Tampa delegate imagine that a majority of swing-state voters will opt for one of Joseph Smith's disciples this fall?

Prophet, Priest, King ... and President.

In the spring of 1844 – while a candidate for the U.S. Presidency – Joseph Smith was anointed Mormonism's theocratic king.

> **The kingdom's clerk William Clayton wrote that during the 11 April 1844 meeting "was prest. Joseph chosen as our Prophet, Priest and King by Hosannas." William Marks, who was present at the coronation, later stated that the Council of Fifty performed an ordinance "in which Joseph suffered himself to be ordained a king, to reign over the house of Israel forever."**
>
> **A later revelation to the Council of Fifty affirmed that God called Smith "to be a Prophet, Seer and Revelator to my Church and Kingdom; and to be a King and Ruler over Israel." In detailed minutes of this same ceremony years later, the Council of Fifty's standing chairman, John Taylor [said Smith] was "anointed & set apart as a King, Priest and Ruler over Israel on the Earth."** [217]

Knowledgeable Jews and Christians will recognize that tri-partite title as an unveiled Messianic reference. Mormon Apostles Lyman Wight and Heber C. Kimball wrote to Smith 1844 that "you are already President Pro tem of the world." [218]

---

[216] http://en.wikipedia.org/wiki/Mormonism_and_polygamy, with added enhancements in brackets.
[217] "Joseph Smith's Polygamy Chronology" (http://www.i4m.com/think/polygamy/JS_Polygamy_Timeline.htm)
[218] "Joseph Smith's Polygamy Chronology" (http://www.i4m.com/think/polygamy/JS_Polygamy_Timeline.htm)

Reaching for similar stratospheric heights in 2012, Romney has proven himself on par with his holy prophet, priest and king when it comes to doubletalk on one-man, one-woman marriage. At the Conservative Political Action Conference (CPAC), Romney said in a speech, "Less than a year after I took office, the state's supreme court inexplicably found a right to same-sex marriage in our constitution. I pushed for a stay of the decision." Massachusetts Romney observer Amy Contrada, however, offers a helpful translation:

> Romney is right: The November 2003 finding was "inexplicable" because a "right to same-sex marriage" is not in the Constitution. The four judges simply invented it. So why did Governor Romney give it any credence? Why did he not just ignore this act of judicial overreach…?
>
> It was also "inexplicable" because the Court had no authority to act on marriage (an area the state Constitution reserves to the Governor and Legislature), or overturn the existing man-woman marriage law (which even the Court said it was not doing). The Legislature never changed the law as the Court suggested it do (since it had no power to order another branch to act). The Massachusetts Constitution states clearly that only the Legislature can make or overturn a law.
>
> Governor Romney had no order (even an illegitimate one) from the Court, and no authorization from the Legislature, to enact "gay marriage" through his executive departments. Yet he did just that in early 2004 – to the shock of many. Romney never once discussed the Constitution's clear separation of powers during the crisis. But he repeatedly called the Court ruling "law" that he had to obey….
>
> Why did he enforce this illegitimate ruling the Court could not have enforced on its own? Romney knew when running for Governor in 2002 that the Massachusetts Supreme Judicial Court would soon be issuing a pro-gay-marriage ruling. What did he have to say on the issue as a candidate? Plenty – at a meeting in a gay bar with the homosexual Log Cabin Republicans. Romney:
>
>> **… promised to obey the courts' [sic] ultimate ruling and not champion a fight on either side of the issue. "I'll keep my head low," he said, making a bobbing motion with his head like a boxer, one participant recalled…. [Romney] promised the Log Cabin members that he would not champion a fight against same-sex marriage…. And, in the aftermath of the Massachusetts court decision, Mr. Romney, though aligning himself with the supporters of a constitutional amendment, did order town clerks to begin issuing marriage licenses to same-sex couples. Some members of Log Cabin Republicans say that in doing so, he ultimately fulfilled his promise to them….**
>>
>> – *The New York Times,* September 8, 2007
>
> ….What happened when the Massachusetts Court opinion was announced on November 18, 2003? [Romney] delivered [a] brief, tepid statement – which failed to make any argument for either constitutional government or traditional marriage….He never expanded on the reasons for traditional marriage other than noting its long history and every child's need for a mother and a father. (That is, except when the "parents" are "gay," and then he thinks their adoptive "rights" should be acknowledged.)
>
> How can he be called a champion for marriage?….Romney [bowed to the Court as] supreme arbiter of the law with final authority over the other two branches, no matter how absurd their opinion. But that directly contradicts the Massachusetts Constitution's separation of powers clauses (written by John Adams)…. [Rather than ignore the Court's overreach or challenge it], Romney's Chief Legal Counsel, Daniel Winslow, helped guide the way. Later, Winslow was thanked by the Massachusetts homosexual-transgender lobby for his support implementing the "gay marriage" ruling.

Wikipedia timeline excerpts below hint at what is, perhaps, the most ignored political news story of the last decade:

- **November 18, 2003:** The Massachusetts Supreme Judicial Court rules 4 to 3 in *Goodridge v. Department of Public Health* that the state's ban on same-sex marriage is unconstitutional and gives the state legislature 180 days to change the law….
- **April 16, 2004:** Legislative action to change the laws still has not occurred. "He [Romney] placed the blame for the confusion on the Legislature, which has yet to follow a directive from the SJC to change the state's marriage laws to reflect the legalization of same-sex matrimony." "I believe the reason that the court gave 180 days to the Legislature was to allow the Legislature the chance to look through the laws developed over the centuries and see how they should be adjusted or clarified for purposes of same-sex marriage; the Legislature didn't do that," Romney said….
- **May 17, 2004:** Gov. Romney ordered town clerks to issue marriage licenses to same-sex couples as per the Supreme Judicial Court's ruling, 180 days after it was issued, ***without the legislative action called for by the actual ruling.*** The city of Cambridge began processing applications at one minute past midnight, cheered on by a crowd of five thousand gathered outside City Hall…. [emphasis added].[219]

[219] http://en.wikipedia.org/wiki/Same-sex_marriage_in_Massachusetts

In short: A bare majority of four Massachusetts Supreme Judicial Court judges *requested* that the co-equal Legislative Branch of the Massachusetts government pass a law to facilitate the homosexual marriage right which the Court somehow, amazingly, discovered within the John Adams constitution. The four judges wrote in pertinent part:

> We declare that barring an individual from the protections, benefits, and obligations of civil marriage solely because that person would marry a person of the same sex violates the Massachusetts Constitution....Entry of judgment shall be stayed for 180 days ***to permit the Legislature to take such action as it may deem appropriate in light of this opinion***.[220] [emphasis added].

Meanwhile, Gov. Mitt Romney – aided and abetted by his pro-GLBT chief legal counsel Winslow[221] – eagerly offered his unilateral submission to a remarkably gentle piece of judicial activism, a ruling which neither ordered, nor commanded, *nor even named* the governor!

Romney, in other words, submissively surrendered his co-equal Executive Branch, his governmental manhood, to an absurd ruling which asked no such thing of him. The court had (vainly) sought help *from the legislature* to enact a statute around the homosexual marriage right it had "discovered" in the Commonwealth's 1780 constitution. And yet, it was Romney, the unmentioned governor who sprang to attention, like an unspayed lapdog, at this spectacular opportunity to solemnize sodomy, to deliver for the Log Cabinistas and make Massachusetts the USA's first gay marriage state.

On the very day that Mitt Romney brought gay marriage to the USA, Amherst Law Professor Hadley Arkes wrote in *National Review:* "Romney could have invoked the Massachusetts constitution (Part 2, ch. III, art. V): 'All causes of marriage, divorce, and alimony, and all appeals from the Judges of probate shall be heard and determined by the Governor and Council, until the Legislature shall, by law, make other provision.'"[222] Instead, *under orders from Romney himself,* Justices of the Peace were threatened and Massachusetts began issuing wedding licenses altered from "Bride and Groom" to read "Party A and Party B."[223]

Even by way of (dubious) judicial supremacist construction, Romney had no legal duty to submit to an activist ruling which named the legislature, *not the governor,* in an implied *request* to pass the USA's first homosexual marriage legislation. Yet Romney's meek, weak submission to the desires of a leftist Court and GLBT lobby[224] was, in retrospect, about as sure as that of a frightened youth to a Penn State chickenhawk – or a young missionary to an LDS groper in a naked Temple ritual.[225]

Had the court actually named the governor, he could have invoked his own oath to uphold the Massachusetts Constitution, in which John Adams Left no trace, in word or concept, of gay marriage. Instead, and despite the fact

---

[220] *Goodridge vs. Dept. of Public Health* (http://weblinks.westlaw.com/result/default.aspx?action=Search&cnt=DOC&db=MA%2DORCS%2DWEB&eq=search&fmqv=c&fn=%5Ftop&method=TNC&mt=Westlaw&n=2&origin=Search&query=CO%28SJCF+SJCRES+SJCOPJ+APPF+APPRES%29+%26+TI%28GOODRIDGE%29&rlt=CLID%5FQRYRLT60672165413174&rltdb=CLID%5FDB52157165413174&rlti=1&rp=%2Fsearch%2Fdefault%2Ewl&rs=MACS1%2E0&service=Search&sp=MassOF%2D1001&srch=TRUE&ss=CNT&sskey=CLID%5FSSSA61157165413174&sv=Split&vr=1%2E0)

[221] In a September 16, 2010 press release titled "Massachusetts Gay Lobby Endorses Mitt Romney's Attorney for 2010 House Seat," Winslow received these glowing words of praise: "But what makes this endorsement very unusual in LGBT politics is that Dan Winslow was Governor Mitt Romney's Chief Legal Counsel during Massachusetts fight for Marriage Equality (2002-2005).... Arline Isaacson touted Republican Dan Winslow for his support of The Goodridge Decision, his zero tolerance of hate crimes and told the Caucus gathering, 'Winslow is what we need,' in terms of a Republican that understands LGBT issues. Isaacson also gave a bit of insight into Winslow's history as the Romney attorney that changed our state's marriage license wording from 'Bride and Groom' to 'Party A and Party B'." Treating journalists, the public, and conservatives as if naïve fools, the release add, "Romney as we all remember worked with the bigots at the Massachusetts Family Institute as well as the Catholic Church, Black Ministerial Alliance and various and sundry other anti-gay organizations to redact the Goodridge Decision, stop same-sex marriages, and leave gays and lesbian couples, their families and children unprotected in the Commonwealth." This, however, is ridiculous on its face: Winslow worked for Romney and was the instrument of Romney's unconstitutional, illegal and entirely non-obligatory implementation of a liberal court's holding that male-male and female-female matrimony should commence in the Bay State. Romney's legal duty, in fact, was to do nothing. (http://www.freerepublic.com/focus/f-news/2868503/posts).

[222] Arkes wrote in "The Missing Governor: Have Republican leaders lost their confidence on basic moral matters?" (http://old.nationalreview.com/arkes/arkes200405170901.asp).

> May 17, 2004, 9:01 a.m.: Since 12 A.M. this morning, clerks in liberal enclaves in Massachusetts have been issuing marriage licenses for couples of the same sex and perhaps even pronouncing them married.... Romney could have invoked the Massachusetts constitution (Part 2, ch. III, art. V): "All causes of marriage, divorce, and alimony, and all appeals from the Judges of probate shall be heard and determined by the Governor and Council, until the Legislature shall, by law, make other provision."....Romney could have pointed out here that the Supreme Judicial Court had actually violated the constitution by taking jurisdiction in a class of cases that the constitution had explicitly withheld from the courts.... He could invoke his powers under the constitution; cite the error of the court in seizing jurisdiction wrongfully for itself; and order all licenses of marriage to be sent on to Boston, to his office, until the legislature, in the fullness of time, settled its policy on marriage.... [T]he court could be compelled now to face precisely the issue that the judges had skirted: whether the majority of four had themselves violated the constitution of Massachusetts. Faced with a tension of that kind, it was even conceivable that one of the wavering judges of the four might peel away, and in peeling away, leave the issue back where it belonged — in the political arena, with the governor and the legislators.... [W]hy not finally take his stand on the constitution itself, where his own authority on matters of marriage is clearly spelled out? And in taking his stand on the constitutional question, he would move to higher ground, with the burden of challenge shifted to the courts.... [Romney is at risk of conveying that Republicans] lose their confidence to speak when it comes to addressing the questions of deepest moral consequence, the questions that establish the terms of principle on which we live.

[223] "Justices of the peace warned not to discriminate against same sex couples" Associated Press, April 25, 2004, (http://massresistance.org/romney/articles/AP_042504.html)

[224] Romney had in 1994 written to gays in the Massachusetts Log Cabin Republican Club, "If we are to achieve the goals we share, we must make equality for gays and lesbians a mainstream concern." (http://www.nytimes.com/2006/12/09/us/politics/09romney.html?_r=1).

[225] See pages 53-55.

that the Court *did not* name the governor, it would seem Romney bent over (forwards) to receive from the court what "the laws of Nature and of Nature's God"[226] does not permit.[227]

This is the kind of leader whom some Tampa delegates wish to nominate for the Presidency? *This* is a leader who can check judicial or U.N. overreach? *This* is a man who can stand up to federal deficits and debt-financing by the Dems and RINOs of Capitol Hill? If he can't even stand up to GLBT jihadis, how can we expect Romney – with no military or foreign policy experience whatsoever – to resist Iranian, multilateral or stateless Islamist jihadis who lust for the destruction of Jews, Christians, Israel and the USA?

In truth, we can't know *what* to expect from Romney, because even what might charitably be spun as a cave-in by a craven pol without a core or compass was, in fact, a lawless, authoritarian act: It was Gov. Romney – not his aide Mr. Winslow nor the GLBT lobby nor the Court – who brought gay marriage to the USA by way of Plymouth Rock, Boston Harbor, Bunker Hill and the Old North Church.

This wasn't exactly akin to John Roberts reading the word "penalty" as "tax" in his tortured interpretation of the Affordable Care Act; it was, rather, an LDS relativist reading lesbianism, male-male anal sex, and (coming soon) polygamy into an 18th Century constitution. Romney's coercive GLBT mandates, health mandates, climate mandates and others typify the practical contempt which he has demonstrated toward American liberty and constitutionalism.

Romney has deep personal roots in an extreme-outlier form of authoritarian religion[228] (as does Obama) relative to the USA's historic Judeo-Christian mainstream. Inclined either to submit themselves to tyrannical pronouncements (such as may flow from the high priests of activist courts, imams or sacred Salt Lake City councils) or to assert their own demagogic, demi-god like authority over constitutional constraints, both Romney and Obama seem, at core, to be lawless men.

Therefore why, with our Republic at stake, would we settle for *either* at Tampa?

Gay Soldiers, Diplomats, ENDA: Romney's GLBT agenda

The Family Research Council shows Romney as the only 2012 GOP Presidential contender to join Obama in support of ENDA, proposed "non-discrimination" legislation "that adds sexual orientation as a protected class."[229] ENDA would:

- Make it illegal fire a man who shows up to work wearing a dress, pantyhose and high heels – even if he's your son's kindergarten teacher.

---

[226] Those are the words of the Declaration which Adams crafted with Jefferson, but they unmistakably echo Genesis, the entire Torah and the Christian texts, especially St. Paul in Romans 1.

[227] David French, an evangelical and fellow Harvard alum of Romney's, damns the governor with unavoidably faint praise at an embarrassingly-sycophantic "Evangelicals for Mitt" website: "Since the marriage laws had already been interpreted [by the Court] to include same-sex marriage, the legislature did not have to take any action at all for same-sex marriage to become legal. *It was already legal because of the court's decision.*" [Emphasis added]. The weakness of French's judicial supremacism is cleared-up by the following questions: If the Court had instead found a constitutional right to cannibalism, post-partum abortion of unwanted children, bestiality, coprophilia, or necrophilia in the John Adams constitution of 1780… would such a ridiculous declaration make it the law, or might not the other co-equal branches of Massachusetts have a say? French continues, "Frankly, it is sad that so many could be misled by something so simple–and simply wrong. When the Governor confronted the Massachusetts Supreme Court, he had two choices: (1) He could fight the decision using legal means; or (2) he could risk contempt citations and impeachment in an ineffectual, grandstanding attempt to block same-sex marriages. Rather than becoming the what the media would undoubtedly call the 'George Wallace of gay marriage' and hand homosexual activists a propaganda victory to go along with their court victory, Governor Romney fought using the law and using his enormous gifts of persuasion." (http://www.patheos.com/blogs/frenchrevolution/2011/12/15/did-gov-romney-choose-gay-marriage-santorum-misconstrues-romneys-record/). Ignoring arguments made by Arkes and others who argued for confrontation, leadership and spine from Romney, French essentially declares Romney a coward for his failure to "risk contempt citations and impeachment" by doing nothing to facilitate a facially outrageous declaration by the Court. Because Romney's polytheist relativism (and ambition) moves him to accept unscientific and unproven GLBT premises that homosexuality is innate, genetically determined and irresistible, however, French is being generous to imply cowardice on Romney's part. It seems such evangelicals and conservatives are becoming to Romney what Romney has always been to the GLBT lobby: Shameless brown-nosers.

[228] Obama's father was Muslim; Romney's father was Mormon. Each sect is predicated upon latter-day revelations from heaven (respectively, via Muhammad's Quran of 632 CE and Joseph Smith's more recent New York works of about 1,200 years later, especially the *Book of Mormon* and *Book of Moses* of1830 CE) and also upon authoritarian interpretation, in the case of Mormonism by 12 Apostles in Salt Lake City. These revelations augment, and often contradict, the Jewish and Christian Bibles. Muslims and Mormons, for one example, hold the Jewish Messiah to be a finite creature rather than uncreated and omnipotent. Each Presidential frontrunner, while growing up in a Judeo-Christian American milieu, was naturally and deeply imprinted by the faith of his father. It is historically indisputable, however, that each of those faiths are completely alien, to America's Founding Fathers. As with Islam relative to the hetero-monogamous norms of the rabbinical and Christian eras, Romney's LDS Mormon heritage has been both sexually liberal (with polygamy commonplace until 1890) as well as conformist (regarding both abortion and homosexuality as sin). Romney's public policy record, however, has been hostile to normative hetero-monogamy while promotional toward abortion and homosexuality. At least these regards, therefore, Romney has been just as out-of-step with the faith of his fathers as has Obama.

[229] *The Wall Street Journal* reported on April 12 that Obama "won't issue an executive order anytime soon banning discrimination against gay and lesbian workers by federal contractors"; meanwhile, A 2012 voter guide from Family Research Council shows Romney as the only GOP Presidential contender in support of ENDA, the proposed federal Employment Non-Discrimination Act "that adds sexual orientation as a protected class"

- Protect workplace bisexuality.
- Establish homosexuality as a protected behavior, just like immutable traits like race and gender.[230]

In May 2012, while Romney was still contending in the GOP primaries, a pro-GLBT news site clarified that – as we've seen with regard to RomneyCare/ObamaCare and his own inauguration of gay marriage – Romney as a Presidential aspirant modally favors state coercion over federal coercion:

> In 1994, Romney infamously pandered to the Log Cabin Republicans of Massachusetts in a failed U.S. Senate run, promising to co-sponsor the Employment Non-Discrimination Act (ENDA) and broaden it to include protections for housing and credit. He added that preventing discrimination against gays and lesbians should be a "mainstream concern." In his coordination of the 2002 Olympics in Salt Lake City, he even followed through on this commitment by approving a nondiscrimination policy with sexual orientation protections and working with the local gay community to "enhance diversity in the Olympic workforce." [As he was fixing his sights on the Presidency in]... 2007, however, Romney told Tim Russert on *Meet The Press* that he had changed his position on ENDA:
>
>> RUSSERT: You said that you would sponsor the Employment Nondiscrimination Act. Do you still support it?
>>
>> ROMNEY: At the state level. I think it makes sense at the state level for states to put in provision of this.
>>
>> RUSSERT: Now, you said you would sponsor it at the federal level.
>>
>> ROMNEY: I would not support at the federal level, and I changed in that regard because I think that policy makes more sense to be evaluated or to be implemented at the state level.[231]

Both Romney and Obama support open homosexuality in the U.S. Armed Forces.[232] In the same "infamously pandering" letter to the Log Cabin Republicans mentioned above (the club's name itself is a giggling reference to anal sex), Romney wrote that

> **President Clinton's gay military efforts are "the first of a number of steps that will ultimately lead to gays and lesbians being able to serve openly and honestly in our nation's military. That goal will only be reached when preventing discrimination against gays and lesbians is a mainstream concern, which is a goal we share."**

To be clear, this would mean, under a Romney Administration, the ongoing, thoroughgoing institutional integration of open, politically-protected same-sex attracteds (and behaviors) within the intimate confines of U.S. military platoons, barracks, tents, subs, aircraft, armored vehicles, showers, restrooms, locker rooms and latrines, degradation which military leaders opposed to no avail during Obama's first term and which, analysts predict, will impair unit cohesion and the military's core mission.[233]

From the Judeo-Christian Natural Law perspective of the America's 1776 charter and her Founding Fathers, in a nation which anchors human rights in an endowing, designing Creator, how can we prayerfully expect Heaven's help against Liberty's enemies if the standard-bearers of both major parties, if the pagan kings we would have reign over us, favor institutionalized sodomy, lesbianism and promiscuity in our armed forces?

During the 2012 campaign, Romney also has refused to respond to the Center for Military Readiness – Military Culture Coalition Presidential Survey, by which other GOP contenders ruled-out openly homosexual soldiers as well as the placement of females in front-line combat. Romney's pro-homosex outlook seems almost calculated to gall traditionalists overseas – not only our allies, but also our enemies who contend, with growing justification, that American culture has become hopelessly decadent. And now, it's increasingly clear that a Romney Presidency would further weave the GLBT agenda into U.S. national security and foreign policy.

---

[230] "The Employment Non-Discrimination Act (ENDA) is a proposed bill in the United States Congress that would prohibit discrimination in hiring and employment on the basis of sexual orientation or gender identity by civilian, nonreligious employers with at least 15 employees," (http://en.wikipedia.org/wiki/Employment_Non-Discrimination_Act#Transgender_protection). See "Testimony by Tony Perkins, President, Family Research Council in opposition to H.R. 3017, Employment Non-Discrimination Act, House Education and Labor Committee, September 29, 2009 (http://www.frc.org/testimony/testimony-in-opposition-to-hr-3017-employment-non-discrimination-act); "Free Markets, Not Just Freedom of Religion, Threatened by ENDA" (http://www.frc.org/get.cfm?i=PV08D07)

[231] http://thinkprogress.org/tag/employment-non-discrimination-act/page/2/

[232] "Romney Says He Will Continue Obama's Policy of Having Homosexuals in Military" (http://cnsnews.com/news/article/romney-says-he-will-continue-obamas-policy-having-homosexuals-military); http://freethoughtblogs.com/dispatches/2011/12/21/romney-v-romney-on dadt/;http://www.advocate.com/News/Daily_News/2011/12/12/Mitt_Romney_Now_Supports_Gays_in_the_Military/;http://freethoughtblogs.com/dispatches/2011/12/21/romney-v-romney-on-dadt/; http://www.renewamerica.com/columns/keyes/120426

[233] See, e.g., Mackubin Thomas Owens, "The Case Against Gays in the Military" *The Wall Street Journal*, (http://online.wsj.com/article/SB10001424052748703389004575033601528093416.html).

Romney Hires Out Gay Spokesman to Tackle Foreign Affairs and National Security Issues

MetroWeekly, Posted by Chris Geidner
April 19, 2012 10:00 PM

Mitt Romney's campaign tonight announced that it has hired Richard Grenell, an out gay former George W. Bush administration official, to serve as the presumptive Republican presidential nominee's "national security and foreign policy spokesman," according to a report from *The Washington Post* that did not mention Grenell's sexual orientation.

Grenell served through September 2008 in the Bush administration as a spokesman to the U.S. ambassador to the United Nations -- and told *The Advocate's* Kerry Eleveld as he Left the administration that it was his hope that New York would have marriage equality soon and that he would one day be able to marry his partner, Matt Lashey. The couple has been together 10 years. Log Cabin Republicans executive director R. Clarke Cooper, who also served in the Bush administration, tells Metro Weekly that Grenell will be "a tremendous asset" to the Romney campaign....

At the end of Grenell's service in the Bush administration, he took a notable whack at the administration, telling The Advocate's Kerry Eleveld of his effort to have his partner, Matt Lashey, listed in the United Nations' Blue Book, which is "a reference guide of contact information for different member states of the United Nations as well as diplomatic personnel and their spouses." Grenell had attempted to have Lashey's name added several times, to no avail. He told The Advocate back in 2008, "What put me over the edge was a friend and colleague who met her spouse after I was already with my partner -- they got married and subsequently were put into the Blue Book in a matter of days."

The State Department eventually told him that the Defense of Marriage Act prevented the listing. Although he protested the decision behind the scenes, Lashey's name was not ever added, which led to his coming forward to criticize the treatement publicly as he Left his post....Of his relationship with Lashey and the possibility of marriage, he told The Advocate in 2008, "It is not an option for us in New York, but hopefully someday soon it will be. In my mind, and in Matt's mind, this is it. We're married."[234]

Way back when there was no discernible right to gay marriage in the Massachusetts Constitution of 1780, Gen. George Washington classed homosexuality as a crime to be viewed with "abhorrence and detestation" as he ejected (but did not hang) a Lt. Enslin for making advances upon a fellow soldier.[235]

In June, 2012, however, the Pentagon celebrated Gay Pride Month in much the same manner that Romney seemed to suck-up to pederasty's recruiters, to sodomy's Sanduskys, by proclaiming "Gay Youth Pride Day."[236] In July, 2012, uniformed active-duty homo/bisexual U.S. soldiers marched for the first time, with Pentagon approval, at a gay pride parade.[237] All Tampa delegates who view that, and our cover photo, as healthy "progress" should vote for Mitt Romney on the First Ballot.

Mitt's Sexual Confusion

Weirdly, Romney's GLBT fawning – at first seeming to position him as a liberal vis-a-vis his sect's contemporary decrees on promiscuity and homosexuality, a bit like scofflaw Catholics such as Mario Cuomo or Joe Biden relative to Rome – actually aligns him *closer* to the polyamorous, homoerotic, screw-whatever-moves roots of Salt Lake City's sci-fi sex cult. This insight will undoubtedly escape Establishment types from the GOP's Mehlman-Grenell-Singer-Sandusky-GOProud-LogCabin wing, but let's think about it:

What's unfair about observing that Romney's pro-GLBT, pro-pedophile, pro-pederast, pro-gay soldiering, anti-Boy Scout policies effectively puts him into the camp of pervy Mormon Fundamentalists like Joseph Smith, Warren Jeffs, Brigham Young, Brigham Morris Young, John C. Bennett, Heber C. Kimball, Wilford Woodruff, Lorenzo Snow, Joseph Fielding Smith and Romney's own Nauvoo-born polygamist great grandfather, Miles Park Romney?

From the very start, Mormonism has been rife with homoeroticism, bisexuality, cross-dressing, nude same-sex Temple rituals, and incest.

---

[234] http://www.metroweekly.com/poliglot/2012/04/romney-hires-out-gay-spokesman-for-foreign-affairs.html
[235] http://www.thomasmore.org/press-releases/2012/06/george-washington-turning-over-his-grave-pentagon-celebrates-sodomy
[236] http://www.massresistance.org/docs/marriage/romney/GayYouthProclamation.pdf
[237] "Military marchers wear uniforms in gay pride parade," *USA Today* (http://www.usatoday.com/news/military/story/2012-07-22/military-gay-pride-parade/56419032/1?csp=34news

> [Former Brigham Young University history professor] D. Michael Quinn has suggested that early church leaders had a more tolerant view of homosexuality.... Valeen Avery suggested that Joseph Smith's son, David Hyrum Smith (1844–1904), may have had homosexual tendencies.... Quinn argues that several early church leaders—including Louise B. Felt, May Anderson, Evan Stephens, and Joseph Fielding Smith—may have either had homosexual tendencies or been involved in homosexual relationships....Quinn also claims that some active and prominent members of the church in Utah were not disciplined after publicizing that they were living in intimate relationships with their same-sex domestic partners, although there is no clear evidence these relationships involved sex. These included Evan Stephens, who had been director of the Mormon Tabernacle Choir until 1916 and is the author of numerous standard church hymns, who remained single but had intimate relationships and shared the same bed with a series of male domestic partners and traveling companions. Some of these relationships were described under a pseudonym in *The Children's Friend.* Also notable were Louise B. Felt and May Anderson, the church's first two general presidents of the Primary, who lived together in the same bedroom for decades....[238]

Prophet Joseph Smith awarded John C. Bennett, within months of his arrival at Nauvoo, the title of "Assistant President to the Church, placing him above either Smith's first counselor Rigdon or church patriarch, Hyrum Smith. Bennett also became chancellor of the University of Nauvoo, mayor of Nauvoo, and a general in the Nauvoo Legion." Yet, Bennett was a noted homosexual, bisexual and abortionist.[239] The same author, Connell O'Donovan, documents many homoerotic undercurrents in Mormonism and how

> ...Lesbian, Gay, and Bisexual Mormons have responded to their religion. In doing so, it became apparent to me that Mormon women found that the intensity of female homosociality available in Mormon structures created a vital space in which they could explore passionate, romantic relationships with each other. At the same time I have uncovered some of the problematics of male homosociality - its power to arbitrarily defend or exile men accused of entering into erotic relationships with other men. [240]

Mormon polygamy, writes O'Donovan, afforded opportunity for lesbianism among plural wives.

> Indeed at least one Mormon woman went so far as to request that her husband marry polygamously after she fell in love with another woman, so that the two women could openly live together. Sarah Louisa Bouton married Joseph Felt in 1866 as his first wife but according to a 1919 biography, around 1874, Louie (the masculinized nickname she used) met and "fell in love with" a young woman in her local LDS congregation named Alma Elizabeth (Lizzie) Mineer. After discovering her intense passion for Lizzie Mineer, a childless Louie encouraged Joseph to marry the young woman as a plural wife, explaining "that some day they would be privileged to share their happiness with some little ones." Joseph married Lizzie Mineer in 1876. But Lizzie's new responsibilities of bearing and raising children evidently proved too great a strain for her and Louie's relationship. Five years later Louie Felt fell in love with "another beautiful Latter-day Saint girl" named Lizzie Liddell, and again Joseph obligingly married her for Louie's sake. Thus Louie "opened her home and shared her love" with this second Lizzie. In 1883, 33 year old Louie Felt met 19 year-old May Anderson, and they also fell in love. This time, however, May did not marry Joseph Felt. In 1889 May moved in with Louie, and Joseph permanently moved out of the house Louie had built and bought on her own. Thus began one of the most intense, stable, and productive love relationships in turn-of-the-century Mormonism. These two women lived together for almost 40 years, and together presided over three of Mormonism's most significant institutions: the General Primary Association (for Mormon children), the Children's Friend (a magazine for young Mormons), and founding the Primary Children's Hospital. Louie and May were fairly open about the romantic and passionate aspects of their relationship, as reported in their biographies published in several early issues of the LDS *Children's Friend*.... [A recent] biography also calls the beginning of their relationship a "time of love feasting", and makes it clear that the two women shared the same bed. [241]

Could Mitt Romney have warmly had in mind LDS lesbian exemplars like these – or LDS scoutmaster pederasts[242] infesting LDS-sponsored Boy Scout Troops – when he brought about gay marriage in Massachusetts, pursuant to the legal petition of lead plaintiffs Julie and Hillary Goodridge (their wedded names for the two years their marriage lasted after Romney ordered state officials to begin solemnizing same-sex unions)?[243]

---

[238] http://en.wikipedia.org/wiki/Homosexuality_and_The_Church_of_Jesus_Christ_of_Latter-day_Saints#History_and_background

[239] Connell O'Donovan, *"The Abominable and Detestable Crime Against Nature": A Revised History of Homosexuality & Mormonism, 1840-1980*; 1994, 2004 (http://www.connellodonovan.com/abom.html; see also http://en.wikipedia.org/wiki/John_C._Bennett

[240] Connell O'Donovan, *"The Abominable and Detestable Crime Against Nature": A Revised History of Homosexuality & Mormonism, 1840-1980*; 1994, 2004 (http://www.connellodonovan.com/abom.html.

[241] Connell O'Donovan, *"The Abominable and Detestable Crime Against Nature": A Revised History of Homosexuality & Mormonism, 1840-1980*; 1994, 2004 (http://www.connellodonovan.com/abom.html.

[242] See, e.g., http://ldssexchildabuse.blogspot.com/; http://www.rickross.com/reference/mormon/mormon395.html; http://blogs.findlaw.com/decided/2010/04/first-verdict-in-molestation-case-returned-against-bsa.html; http://www.sltrib.com/lds/ci_13806832

[243] *"After 2 years, same-sex marriage icons split up" The Boston Globe,* (http://www.boston.com/news/local/articles/2006/07/21/after_2_years_same_sex_marriage_icons_split_up/)

No one is herein arguing against the niceness or human decency of any given homo/bisexual like Louie Felt, Hillary Goodridge, Ellen DeGeneres, Mary Cheney, Anderson Cooper or Barney Frank. Rather, we hold that a multiplicity of sex disorders and pathologies, frequently driven by fatherly abandonments and mainly-male sexual predators and pedophiles – evil rakes like Jerry Sandusky, Joseph Smith and Brigham Young – has tended to alienate America's young men and women from their inherent, Creator-endowed design.

While this is indeed a tragic feature of American infidelity to that Creator (and to one another in traditional marriage), it's no sound basis for the abandonment of hetero-monogamy in U.S. public policy, something Obama, Romney and GLBT activists have been pursuing with for many years. It's clear that Romney's pro-gay-everything stance in Rep. Frank's Massachusetts has been good politics for him so far. What's been fuzzy until now, however, is that Romney's warmth to every facet of the GLBT agenda is almost certainly rooted in homoerotic LDS subculture – and the likelihood that the reinstatement and nationalization of polygamy (and attendant pedophilia/pederasty) will logically follow the enshrinement of Massachusetts-style same-sex wedlock as a fundamental right under such a coming Supreme Court read of the U.S. Constitution.

If and when that happens, it's likely that Romney and many of his co-religionists will feel very much at home. O'Donovan writes that in 1923,

> [P]rominent Salt Lake Lesbian, Edith Mary Chapman opened her home just across the street from (and to the north of) Liberty Park as a boarding house for other Lesbians, most of whom were LDS or had a Mormon background.... [Her mother] Sarah Ann was married off polygamously at the age of 14 to the 42 year old George Handley. Sarah Ann was pregnant within a week of her marriage and at the age of 23 found herself the widowed mother of four small children. Embittered by her experiences in Mormonism (especially church-sanctioned pedogamy - adults marrying children), she left the church and joined the Anglican Communion.... [and] Sarah Ann's children were taken from her by Handley relatives to be raised Mormon under orders from LDS leaders....
>
> When Edith opened her home to other professional, Lesbian boarders in 1923, Grace Nickerson, an instructor at the LDS School of Music (in the McCune Mansion) was the first boarder in what I have nicknamed the Casa Lesbiana. A year later, Chapman met Mildred "Barry" Berryman, another Episcopalian Lesbian from Salt Lake (who had converted to Mormonism briefly in her youth, at least long enough to receive a Patriarchal Blessing, as documented by Michael Quinn). Mildred's first female lover had been Mae Anderson, a prominent violin teacher in Salt Lake (who would join the LDS School of Music faculty in 1924, where other prominent Mormon homo- and bisexuals taught). The relationship of Berryman and Anderson lasted until about 1922....when Edith met Mildred Berryman in 1924, she "fell desperately in love" and Barry Berryman moved into Edith's home. While their romantic relationship only lasted a short time, Barry continued living in the Lesbian boarding house until 1929.
>
> Berryman went on to complete her study of the homosexual community of Salt Lake (thoroughly addressed in Michael Quinn's history of homosexuality and Mormonism). After Grace Nickerson moved out of the house, Dorothy Graham replaced her. Dorothy was the Lesbian manager of the Coon Chicken Inn in Salt Lake (a well-known restaurant owned by her family, which featured male drag performers, such as Julian Eltinge, during the 1920s and 30s). Around this time, Carline Monson joined the women, as a live-in cook at the boarding house.[244]

O'Donovan notes that "This aunt of Apostle Thomas S. Monson" – incidentally, the current LDS President and Living Prophet to whom Mitt Romney and all Mormons are in religious submission[245] – "never married, although she referred to herself as "Mrs. Monson" on occasion. In the mid-1930s, Edith Chapman closed the boarding house, leaving the home to Carline Monson."[246]

As with Joseph Smith and his "buggery," bisexual Nauvoo Mayor John C. Bennett, similar prominence was granted to Joseph Fielding Smith, a descendant of the founder's brother, who was granted an LDS position which,

> had historically rivaled that of the church president himself. When Joseph Fielding Smith was ordained Patriarch to the Church on October 8, 1942, many Mormons were stunned because it was well known that the Drama professor at the University of Utah was a practicing homosexual, and it was even rumored in his own family that he had an arrest record for sexual vice. One of his favorite Drama pupils, Cynthia Blood, told me in a 1989 interview that "everybody on campus knew" that Prof. Smith was 'queer' and that he often "flitted amongst the boys".... However, should any of the Mormon faithful question whether a married, homosexual Drama teacher with a police record for having sex with his students was "called of God" to be Patriarch to the Church, Pres. David O. McKay affirmed earlier that week during October General Conference that, "Elder Smith's right to his office...is not only by [patriarchal] lineage but by direct

---

[244] Connell O'Donovan, *"The Abominable and Detestable Crime Against Nature": A Revised History of Homosexuality & Mormonism, 1840-1980*; 1994, 2004 (http://www.connellodonovan.com/abom.html.

[245] http://mormon.org/faq/present-day-prophet/

[246] Connell O'Donovan, *"The Abominable and Detestable Crime Against Nature": A Revised History of Homosexuality & Mormonism, 1840-1980*; 1994, 2004 (http://www.connellodonovan.com/abom.html.

inspiration to the President who holds the keys of the Priesthood". With this full assurance from a member of the First Presidency, the Mormon faithful are only Left with two options: either God in fact did not care that Joseph Fielding Smith was an adulterous homosexual, or the presiding prophet at that time, George Albert Smith, was in fact not receiving 'direct inspiration' from God in the governance of the Church, despite what McKay said.[247]

Pedophilia, homosexuality and extramarital sex are today formally disapproved as a matter of formal LDS doctrine, a feature of LDS Mormonism which causes some observers to wrongly infer that Mormonism is on common theological ground with traditional evangelicalism, Catholicism and Judaism. But, it may well be that the polytheist and theologically-polyamorous LDS has found it useful, from the beginning, to loudly protest deviation from American hetero-monogamy (as in the case of California Proposition 8), while secretly cultivating its destruction:

> The LDS Church supported a Salt Lake City ordinance protecting members of the LGBT community against discrimination in employment and housing while allowing religious institutions to consider lifestyles in actions such as hiring or providing university accommodations, while at the same time reaffirming that it remained "unequivocally committed to defending the bedrock foundation of marriage between a man and a woman." Gordon B. Hinckley, late president of the church officially welcomed gay people in the church, and affirmed them as good people in an interview "Now we have gays in the church. Good people. We take no action against such people – provided they don't become involved in transgression, sexual transgression. If they do, we do with them exactly what we'd do with heterosexuals who transgress"....The president of the LDS Church, Thomas S. Monson, has stated church members can disagree politically with the church's opposition to same-sex marriage, but if the disagreement turns into an apostasy situation, that would be inappropriate. The church also supports the Boy Scouts of America's ban on homosexual conduct. It is the largest sponsor of Boy Scout troops in the United States and has stated that it will end its nine-decade-long affiliation if homosexual conduct is permitted.[248]

Wethinks, however, that perhaps the LDS protesteth too much, loudly and formally forbidding what may often be winked at actual practice. As we have seen, Joseph Smith brazenly lied about his polygamy and pedophilia. Historian Quinn, a former BYU professor who today is openly gay, "has publicly argued that homosexual relationships, between both men and women, were quietly accepted by the Church of Jesus Christ of Latter-day Saints and its leadership up until the 1940s."[249] To escape federal anti-polygamy pressure and obtain statehood for Utah around the turn of the 20th Century, LDS officials shifted from the promotion of child brides and polyamory to threats of excommunication for those who continued to follow the teachings and examples of Smith and Brigham Young. LDS Prophet/Presidents Hinckley and Monson seem to have had homo/bisexuality within their own families.

Could ostensible LDS conventionality today – on everything from monogamy to Prop 8 – be institutional cover for a persisting Mormon subculture of polygamy, pedophilia and pederasty? While a monstrous thought, what better way for Mormon pedophiles to maintain predatory access to young men than to assure parents of LDS opposition to homo/bisex scoutmasters, while simply winking Romney-style, Penn-state style, at the horrific risks? The blog "LDS Mormon Child Sexual Abuse"[250] pleads:

> President Thomas S. Monson, ecclesiastical leaders and members of the Church of Jesus Christ of Latter-Day Saints: We will no longer remain silent about the sexual abuse of children in the church and organizations affiliated with the LDS Church like Boy Scouts of America ....we only see the tip of the iceberg, when various media report about cases of sexual childhood abuse among members of the LDS Church. We know that thousands of sexual childhood abuse cases never see the light of day, and that victims and their families suffer in quiet desperation.
>
> We know of hundreds of cases, w[h]ere local ecclesiastical leaders covered up and silenced victims and their families. We know of hundreds of cases were ecclesiastical leaders on all levels in the church hierarchy harbored sexual child predators and did nothing to prevent them from having access to children in positions of trust. We have letters from families pleading the First Presidency to intervene and stop the spiritual abuse of victims and families, when the perpetrators of the abuse were local ecclesiastical leaders like Bishops. Nothing happened! It has to stop now!

---

[247] O'Donovan adds:

> During the early part of the twentieth century, as Mormonism slowly but steadily grew, problematic issues surrounding isolationism versus universalism arose. Confrontation with homosexuality (which was itself becoming more and more publicized) and what to do with "out" homosexuals was inevitable. For example, in 1945, as reported by D. Michael Quinn, church leaders realized that there were quite a number of Mormon homosexuals who were meeting for sex at the Deseret Gym in downtown Salt Lake. ("Cruising for sex" had been going on there since at least 1930, as personally reported to me in the late 1980s by Spencer Kimball's Gay first cousin twice removed, Jack Pembroke [1913-2000], who began cruising there that year. Homosexual activities were constantly occuring in the showers and steam room at the Deseret Gymnasium in Salt Lake throughout the 1970s and 1980s, when I had a membership there. Several members of the Mormon Tabernacle Choir, one Tabernacle organist, and at least two General Authorities were participants in the sexual activies there, as personally witnessed by me or by a Gay employee I knew who worked there.)

[248] http://en.wikipedia.org/wiki/Homosexuality_and_The_Church_of_Jesus_Christ_of_Latter-day_Saints#History_and_background

[249] http://en.wikipedia.org/wiki/D._Michael_Quinn#cite_note-Interview_of_D._Michael_Quinn-1

[250] http://ldssexchildabuse.blogspot.com/; see also http://www.mormonabuse.com/

> We believe that protecting the image of the LDS Church is less important than preventing sexual child abuse.... The authority of these church leaders cannot be questioned and this blind faith is part of the problem. We have lost our patience and trust in Church leaders ability to handle and prevent sexual child abuse in the LDS Church. By starting this blog and documenting sexual childhood abuses we try to raise awareness to a problem you do not want to hear about. The church pays many millions of dollars every year to victims, that were betrayed by church leaders, who knowingly put "Worthy" priesthood holders and women in callings, where they have access to children, in spite of knowing that they have a history of sexually abusing children - sometimes for many decades.
>
> We are tired of the cover ups, the denial and even persecution of victims and their families, who do not obey the Church's order to keep silent. We even see members of the LDS Church defending the perpetrators and persecuting members of the press. You may think that paying millions of dollars to settle these cases outside worldly courtrooms, so they world will not hear about it, will make the problem go away. You are wrong!

The "tell," the "giveaway" underlying Romney's pro-GLBT record – as well as LDS-leftist support for the aforementioned Salt Lake City ordinance – is a common, pagan-ish premise that homo/bisexuals are morally entitled to non-discriminatory treatment – and to trample upon the property rights, association rights and religious liberties of objectors – because homo/bisexuality is, like race and gender, an inborn trait. (Pedophiles, marital cheats and violent spouse abusers sometimes argue similarly, contending that they're "just born that way.") As we'll soon see, however, science indicates otherwise.[251]

It seems evident, furthermore, that Mormonism's historic pedophilia/polygamy, secret homoerotic temple rituals and historic homosexual subculture have survived deep into Mitt Romney's lifetime inside and outside LDS Mormonism, perhaps in much the same way that founding Prophet Smith privately practiced that which he preached against. This has driven some truth-seeking ex-Mormons to the left (perhaps upset at the hypocritical way homosexuality is formally received within the LDS, even after its informal cultivation in rites described below) while driving others toward traditional Judeo-Christianity.

Naked Temple Rituals

Tricia Erickson, example of the latter and the daughter of an LDS Bishop, contends that at her own Mormon Temple wedding, she was required to disrobe against her will. "It was horrific....There I was standing naked. They brought this bowl of water, and started washing my body down and whispering prayers over my body. They stopped over the right and left breast, the navel and knees and prayed specific prayers."[252]

Tyson Dunn, similarly, writes of homoerotic Mormon temple rites on the website ex-mormon.org:[253]

> The first thing you go through when receiving your endowment for the first time is the washing and anointing. You strip naked and are given what is called a "shield" to wear. It's a big white oval of fabric, worn like a poncho, but open at the sides....The washing and anointing both consist of various parts of the body being touched by the fingertips of the temple worker performing the ordinance. They use a drop of water or oil on their fingertips, hence washing and anointing. They say a sort of prayer for the good health and function of each of the involved body parts. Unlike other priesthood ordinances, men wash and anoint men and women wash and anoint women.
>
> The parts of the body include the head, each ear, the eyes (I think it was across the brow), nose (bridge), lips, neck (nape), shoulders, back, breast (center of chest if I remember right), arms and hands (touch in one motion along length of each arm), vitals and bowels (point on the side, I think), loins, legs and feet (touch in one motion along length of each leg). The loins are supposed to be done by touching the side of the person parallel to their genitals, but more than one man has reported that perverted temple workers directly rubbed down the front of their penises. They seem to try to get away with it more with first-time missionaries who are young and don't know better.

To this, another ex-mormon responded:

> The thread on "naked touching" in the temple reminded me of something I had completely forgotten. Tyson Dunn's excellent explanation of the initiatory ordinance triggered my memory: While reading Dunn's post, I recalled an incident that occurred to one of the missionaries in the MTC in the Provo temple. One morning the guys in my room all went to the Provo temple to do temple work. At the last minute, we decided to do initiatories instead of doing an endowment session. Big mistake.

---

[251] See page 70 and forward.
[252] "Mormon Bishop's daughter spills Romney's 'Secrets'" (http://www.wnd.com/2011/10/354721/)
[253] http://www.exmormon.org/mormon/mormon366.htm

Instead of taking in an endowment session where we'd get to sit across the room from a bunch of veiled women, we spent two hours almost naked getting touched by old men. And it gets worse!

> It's weird enough going through the intiatory ordinance ONCE for your own endowment. But doing a two-hour initiatory session for the dead is borderline traumatic, especially for four young missionaries. I got through it without much touching, despite going around and around from little cubicle to little cubicle with my little poncho-think constantly flapping open.
>
> But when we completed the session, one of the Elders [a young Mormon man] with us came out of there completely white. He had this shocked look on his face as if something bad had happened to him. He refused to tell us what was wrong and stayed very quiet the rest of the day.
>
> A few days later he told me what happened. He said every time he went through the initiatory, one of the old men stroked his private parts with the oil. Strange, since this didn't happen to any of the rest of us, just him. He said he was so shocked and scared and he was in the temple, that he didn't know what to do. So he just let the old man keep doing it. Maybe he was making it up, but he sure looked shook up.

Below that entry, a female named "kc" added:

> Not only was I touched during my initiatory....
>
> but I KNOW I was not 'mistaken' or having a 'false memory' because my 2 friends and I used to actually go to the temple for hours and do initiatories for the dead! I went round and round in the little booths until I thought I would faint, being touched over and over until the oil was dripping down my body in certain spots.
>
> Yes, I had a sheet over me, open on the sides, and yes, a little old lady reached under the sheet with her COLD bony hands and touched my naked body. When she would bend and touch my legs her face was almost in my lap. When she anointed my breasts she touched above the breast area but when she anointed my vitals and bowels she often inadvertently brushed my breasts or nipples. IT WAS VERY UNCOMFORTABLE.
>
> So yeah. Naked touching.

Have Mitt and Ann Romney, as "Temple Mormons" experienced (or administered) this kind of rite themselves? In the age of Sandusky and pedophile LDS Scoutmasters, is Mitt Romney willing to call for the end of any and all such weird, secret rites? Other web respondents compared their youthful LDS temple experiences to the ritualized, cultic scenes in *Rosemary's Baby* and *The Wicker Man.*

Meanwhile, more conventional combinations of pedophilia and bathing have been reported at higher levels: In the 2010, the Utah House Majority leader, an LDS bishop, resigned over revelations that he had bathed nude in a hot tub with a 15-year-old girl (more or less following the moral example of Smith and other LDS leaders).[254]

And yet as we've seen, sexual predation has been central to Mormon culture from the beginning. LDS defenders will rightly note that Roman Catholics, Evangelicals, mainline Protestants, Jews and seculars, in the internet age, have had plenty of their own dirty linens exposed. That, however, only underscores one of the first premises of Jewish-Christian doctrine: Humanity is deeply sinful, and in deep need of help to keep sexual intimacy and marriage where the Edenic ideal seems to put it, between one consenting man and one woman divinely *designed* to "be fruitful and multiply."[255]

Although the Bible and all of human history duly records every conceivable deviation from the Edenic ideal – adultery, rape, incest, divorce, polygamy, promiscuity, homosexuality, pederasty, child sacrifice, spousal abuse, murder – these dark things have occurred among Jews and Christians (and all the rest of humanity) *in spite* of divine commands or ideals, not *because* G_d commanded them.

While any and all behaviors are compatible with a blind, materialist multiverse that randomly cast us upon the shores of the earth – and while many behaviors are compatible with polytheism and paganism –Judaism and Christianity are understood to exclude some of humanity's worst habits. The holy texts, prophets and power-brokers of Mitt Romney's Mormonism, on the other hand, have sanctioned from the very start things which average

[254] "Utah lawmaker quits over hot-tub revelation," *The Washington Post,* http://www.washingtonpost.com/wp-dyn/content/article/2010/03/13/AR2010031301999.html

[255] See Genesis 1:22 : ver 28; Ge 8:17; 9:1, 7, 19; 47:27; Leviticus 26:9; Ezekiel 36:11.

swing-state voters would find dark. For example, an informal "History of Sex in the Mormon Church" derived from D. Michael Quinn's book, *The Mormon Hierarchy: Extensions of Power,* reports:

> **19 Jar, 1851 - Utah legislature enacts law against "Sodomoy" by "any man or boy," but removes sodomoy from criminal code on 6 Mar. 1852, without explanation. As governor Brigham Young signs both laws. Due to absence of sodomy statue, Utah judge drops charges against soldier for raping LDS boy in 1864. Young claims Utah's legislators never criminalized sodomy and he declines to instruct them to do so for the next twelve years. Utah legislators criminalize sodomy in 1876 only because federally appointed governor asks them to adopt entire criminal code of California which has five-year imprisonment for sodomoy. For next twenty years LDS judges give 3-6 months of imprisonment to those convicted of homosexual rape, the same sentencing given to young males and females convicted of consensual fornication. Mormons of this era give no known explanations for any of these legislative and jurdicial actions/inactions.**[256]

More infamous than LDS pederasty, of course, was polygynous Mormon pedophilia:

> **Critics of polygamy in the early LDS Church claim that church leaders sometimes used polygamy to take advantage of young girls for immoral purposes. LDS historian George D. Smith studied 153 men who took plural wives in the early years of the Latter Day Saint movement, and found that two of the girls were thirteen years old, 13 girls were fourteen years old, 21 were fifteen years old, and 53 were sixteen years old. LDS historian Todd Compton documented that Joseph Smith married girls of age 13 or 14. Historian Stanly Hirshon documented cases of girls aged 10 and 11 being married to old men....**[257]

There were outbreaks of envy among Mormonism's sexual predators. Addressing outbound missionaries, LDS leader Heber C. Kimball said:

> **Brethren, I want you to understand that it is not to be as it has been heretofore. The brother missionaries have been in the habit of picking out the prettiest women for themselves before they get here, and bringing on the ugly ones for us; hereafter you have to bring them all here before taking any of them, and let us all have a fair shake.**
>
> On another occasion, he said "You are sent out as shepherds to gather sheep together; and remember that they are not your sheep ... do not make selections before they are brought home and put into the fold.". ... One third of the women of marriageable age and nearly all of the church leadership were involved in the practice.
>
> **Instances of coercion and deception related to plural marriage:** Critics of polygamy in the early LDS Church have documented several cases where deception and coercion were used to induce marriage, for example citing the case of Joseph Smith who warned some potential spouses of eternal damnation if they did not consent to be his wife. In 1893, married LDS Church member John D. Miles traveled to England and proposed to Caroline Owens, assuring her that he was not polygamous. She returned to Utah and participated in a wedding, only to find out after the ceremony that Miles was already married. She ran away, but Miles hunted her down and raped her. She eventually escaped, and filed a lawsuit against Miles that reached the Supreme Court and became a significant case in polygamy case law. Ann Eliza Young, nineteenth wife of Brigham Young, claimed that Young coerced her to marry him by threatening financial ruin of her brother.
>
> **Incestuous plural marriages:** Critics of polygamy in the early LDS Church claim that polygamy was used to justify marriage of close relatives that would otherwise be considered immoral. In 1843, Joseph Smith's diary records the marriage of John Bernhisel to his sister, Maria. In 1886, [LDS leader] Lorenzo Snow said that brothers and sisters should be able to get married. Former LDS Church member and prominent critic Fanny Stenhouse wrote in 1875:
>
>> **It would be quite impossible, with any regard to propriety, to relate all the horrible results of this disgraceful system.... Marriages have been contracted between the nearest of relatives; and old men tottering on the brink of the grave have been united to little girls scarcely in their teens; while unnatural alliances of every description, which in any other community would be regarded with disgust and abhorrence, are here entered into in the name of God.**[258]

The aforementioned "History of Sex in the Mormon Church" notes that incestuous relations seemed to have the blessing of the highest Mormon authorities:

> **8 Oct, 1854 - In what Apostle Wilford Woodruff describes as "the greatest sermon that ever was deliveed to the Latter Day Saints since they have been a people," Brigham Young announces from the pulpit: "I believe in Sisters marrying brothers, and brothers having their sisters for Wives. Why? because we cannot do otherwise.**

---

[256] http://www.exmormon.org/mormon/mormon036.htm
[257] http://en.wikipedia.org/wiki/Mormonism_and_polygamy#Criticism_of_plural_marriage
[258] http://en.wikipedia.org/wiki/Mormonism_and_polygamy#Criticism_of_plural_marriage

> **There are none others for me to and the opposite idea has resulted from the ignorant and foolish traditions of the nations of the earth." Young's secretary George D. Watt has already married his own half sister as a plural wife. Her letter to Young shows that he was initially "unfavorable" toward allowing them to marry, but this sermon reveals theological basis for Young's authorizing Watt's brother-sister marriage and the three children born of their union....**
>
> **15 July, 1886 - Apostle Lorenzo prophecises from the pulpit that in the future "brothers and sisters would marry each other in this church. All our horror at such a union was due entirely to prejudice, and the offspring of such unions would be as healthy and pure as any other. These were the decided views of President Young, when alive, for Bother Snow talked to him freely on this matter."** [259]

The hostility to hetero-monogamy and covered-up warmth for pedophilia and pederasty, woven-in to the DNA of Mormonism and Mitt Romney would seem, therefore, to make it a perfect intimate partner in the advancement of the GLBT Left's greatest anti-scientific myth, one that has captured the blind faith of our culture just as Joseph Smith's tall tales of golden plates, the Angel Moroni and the Book of Abraham suckered gullibles nearly two centuries ago: That some human beings are born gay.[260]

Romney's Top 10 Myths about Homosexuality

Mitt Romney, President Obama, Log Cabin Republicans, GOProud, Rand-wing atheists, *The New York Times*, most of News Corp (Fox News, *The Wall Street Journal,* etc.) and much of the rest of the media effectively function together as philosophically-materialist, pro-GLBT cheerleaders *against* the American Founders' monotheistic premises in The Declaration of Independence. And yet, if indeed our rights of Life and Liberty are Creator-endowed, then we necessarily are *designed creatures,* subject to "the Laws of Nature and of Nature's God."[261] We are necessarily non-random, non-accidental and *physically designed* beings who are, unavoidably and equally, accountable to our Creator for our conduct.

Such accountable conduct might well include things like sexual infidelity, abandonment, porn-fueled lust, child molestation and all forms of bodily abuse: Anorexia, gluttony, spousal abuse, clitorectomies, castration, substance addiction, STD proliferation, anal sex, fisting, pederasty, pedophilia and sadomasochism. If we are indeed "endowed by our Creator" with rights, breasts, wombs, vaginas, penises, hearts and *brains*… then *not quite everything can be fifty shades of gray.*

As with Mormonism's contest with monotheism and hetero-monogamy, Mitt Romney's warfare against the teleological and Natural Law premises of the American Founders rests upon entirely unproven, unscientific notions which are *almost* as groundless as the notion of lunar and solar inhabitants. Romney clings to a zealous faith – rooted in pagan-ish, polytheistic, polyamorous Mormon history – that homo/bisexuality is genetically determined, immutable and irresistible (just like race, gender and eye color).

As such, whether decreed by the finite pantheon of Mormonism or the blind, Darwinian gods of the multiverse, GLBT statists demand that those behaviors be enshrined, protected and promoted as a matter of civil rights and U.S. public policy, and they must be seen as compatible with good childrearing, and personal/public health.

Yet, there's absolutely no empirical proof that anyone is born gay [262] nor that GLBT behavior is healthy for individuals or society. We have already cited scientific evidence that homo/bisexuals are more likely to have serious mental health problems and engage in child sexual abuse. Jerry Sandusky's personal rejection of hetero-monogamy for homo/bisexuality was the logical and necessary condition of his pederasty.

For years, NBC's *Will and Grace,* by its very title, seemed to gleefully celebrate the willful abuse of humanity's heterosexual, hetero-monogamous design which, the Americans of 1776 believed, has so graciously been endowed to us by our Creator.

In terms of that divine endowment and design by which our human rights are anchored, men and women of all races and ethnicities are self-evidently moral equals (whether or not societies acknowledge that)… but procreative intercourse and anal sex are not. Nor, in terms of our design, can heterosexuality and lesbianism be regarded as

---

[259] http://www.exmormon.org/mormon/mormon036.htm

[260] See page 70 and forward.

[261] From *The Declaration of Independence.*

[262] See page 70 and forward.

equals. But to claim anything like that, Judaism and Christianity have historically argued, would be to deny, implicitly or explicitly, the existence of the One G_d of Abraham, Isaac, Jacob, Moses, Joshua, David, Solomon, Elijah, Isaiah, Jeremiah, Daniel, Peter, James, John and Jesus.

Traditional Judaism is unequivocal in its eschewal of homo/bisexuality. The popular Jewish website chabad.org says, "Jewish law unconditionally prohibits the homosexual act. Just as the heterosexual act is prohibited outside of marriage, regardless of personal desires, attractions or inclinations, so the homosexual act is forbidden."[263] That prohibition derives straight from the Books of Moses, as well as other Jewish Scriptures.[264]

Rabbi Yehuda Levin, leader of Union of Orthodox Rabbis of the United States and Canada and the Rabbinical Alliance of America (representing 1,200 rabbis and more than 2 million Orthodox and traditional Jews) calls Mitt Romney "a dangerous homosexualist" whose nomination must be averted: ""America is on the brink of collapse economically and morally. Capitalism alone cannot save it. No amount of financial tinkering can save a country which is morally bankrupt."[265]

Precious few Christian leaders have spoken so clearly. Yet a Jewish Pharisee, a rabbi who joined the Nazarene sect of Judaism later known as Christianity, wrote in the opening of his letter to the Romans:

> **The wrath of God is being revealed from heaven against all the godlessness and wickedness of people, who suppress the truth by their wickedness, since what may be known about God is plain to them, because God has made it plain to them. For since the creation of the world God's invisible qualities—his eternal power and divine nature—have been clearly seen, being understood from what has been made, so that people are without excuse.**
>
> **For although they knew God, they neither glorified him as God nor gave thanks to him, but their thinking became futile and their foolish hearts were darkened. Although they claimed to be wise, they became fools and exchanged the glory of the immortal God for images made to look like a mortal human being and birds and animals and reptiles. Therefore God gave them over in the sinful desires of their hearts to sexual impurity for the degrading of their bodies with one another.**
>
> **They exchanged the truth about God for a lie, and worshiped and served created things rather than the Creator—who is forever praised. Amen. Because of this, God gave them over to shameful lusts. Even their women exchanged natural sexual relations for unnatural ones. In the same way the men also abandoned natural relations with women and were inflamed with lust for one another. Men committed shameful acts with other men, and received in themselves the due penalty for their error.**

-- St. Paul, Letter to Romans, 1:18-26 (New International Version)

In the 1980's, when HIV-AIDS devastated gay populations (and heterosexual women and children who came into contact with HIV-AIDS infected body fluids), preachers who cited the preceding sentence were scolded by GLBT activists and media allies for their judgmentalism.

Yet were they with us today, Paul, Moses, Jesus and other Biblical figures[266] might just as well have been referencing CDC and public health reports about the objective health hazards of homosexuality. SSS (Same-Sex as Sandusky, i.e., anal intercourse) is vastly more dangerous than vaginal sex; it poses very serious risks not only to gay men, but to abused/manipulated women, assaulted children and experimenting teenagers.[267] The practice physically misuses a part of the anatomy that is comprised of delicate, easily-torn, fluid-absorbing mucous membranes which affords opportunity for infection, and contains toxic microorganisms, such as *E. coli,* exposed nowhere else on the body.

Penetration can be painful and result in rectal prolapse, incontinence, hemorrhoids and ulcers. Anal sex is associated with human papilloma virus (HPV),[268] HIV/AIDS, bacterial infection hepatitis A; hepatitis B; hepatitis C;

---

[263] http://www.chabad.org/library/article_cdo/aid/663504/jewish/Do-Homosexuals-Fit-into-the-Jewish-Community.htm
[264] See, e.g., Leviticus 18:22 and 20:13.
[265] http://www.rabbilevin.com/2012/01/850-orthodox-jewish-clergymen-call.html
[266] See, e.g., Matthew 10:14-15; I Corinthians 1 6:9-10; Timothy 1 1:9-10; Jude 1:7
[267] In some teenage subcultures, e.g., within various mainstream Mormon communities, there is today an affinity for an imagined "technical virginity" which permits anal sex in lieu of vaginal intercourse. Among Mormon adolescents, this may be some kind of swirled ethic that combines Bill Clinton's technical distinctions pertaining to the definition. See, for example, the terms "Mormon Tresspass," "Mormon Glory," "Mormon Virgin" and "Mormon F-----g" at urbandictionary.com
[268] Wherever the location, HPV is dangerous. The Centers for Disease Control reports (www.cdc.gov/hpv/WhatIsHPV.html) that genital human papillomavirus (HPV) "is the most common sexually transmitted infection (STI). There are more than 40 HPV types that can infect the genital areas of males and females," manifesting as genital warts, cancers, or both. This cheery CDC website, run by the Obama Administration, continues:

herpes simplex; Kaposi's sarcoma-associated herpesvirus (HHV-8); lymphogranuloma venereum; Mycoplasma hominis; Mycoplasma genitalium; salmonellosis; shigella; syphilis; tuberculosis; Ureaplasma urealyticum.typhus, amoebiasis; chlamydia; cryptosporidiosis; giardiasis; gonorrhea and syphilis.

Most anal cancer cases are linked to HPV, according to the American Cancer Society and NIH-funded studies by the Fred Hutchinson Cancer Research Center ("Changing Trends in Sexual Behavior May Explain Rising Incidence of Anal Cancer Among American Men and Women," 2004) with the practice of receptive anal sex yielding a sevenfold increase in incidence. [269] Writing for *Slate*, William Saletan reports that

> [A]nal sex is far more dangerous than oral sex. According to data released earlier this year by the Centers for Disease Control, the probability of HIV acquisition by the receptive partner in unprotected oral sex with an HIV carrier is one per 10,000 acts. In vaginal sex, it's 10 per 10,000 acts. In anal sex, it's 50 per 10,000 acts. Do the math….A CDC fact sheet explains the risks of anal sex. First, 'the lining of the rectum is thin and may allow the [HIV] virus to enter the body.' Second, 'condoms are more likely to break during anal sex than during vaginal sex.'
>
> These risks don't just apply to HIV. According to the new survey report, the risk of transmission of other sexually transmitted diseases is likewise 'higher for anal than for oral sex,' and the risk 'from oral sex is also believed to be lower than for vaginal intercourse.'" Yet for much of the media "anal sex is too icky to mention in print. But not too icky to have been tried by 35 percent of young women and 40 to 44 percent of young men—or to have killed some of them. Not that there's anything wrong with it, as Jerry Seinfeld might say.[270]

Unless, of course, it's wrong to defy one's biological engineering specifications, wrong to deny our G_d-given design? We seem to widely recognize that when it comes to pathological stuff like binge drinking, anorexia, obesity, inhaling tobacco smoke or doing crystal meth; we seem willfully blind, however, to the enormous hazards of abusing the human alimentary canal.

> HPV is passed on through genital contact, most often during vaginal and anal sex. HPV may also be passed on during oral sex and genital-to-genital contact. HPV can be passed on between straight and same-sex partners—even when the infected partner has no signs or symptoms. A person can have HPV even if years have passed since he or she had sexual contact with an infected person. Most infected persons do not realize they are infected or that they are passing the virus on to a sex partner. It is also possible to get more than one type of HPV. Rarely, a pregnant woman with genital HPV can pass HPV to her baby during delivery…. Approximately 20 million Americans are currently infected with HPV. Another 6 million people become newly infected each year. HPV is so common that at least 50% of sexually active men and women get it at some point in their lives….Each year, about 12,000 women get cervical cancer in the U.S. Almost all of these cancers are HPV-associated. 1,500 women who get HPV-associated vulvar cancer; 500 women who get HPV-associated vaginal cancer 400 men who get HPV-associated penile cancer; 2,700 women and 1,500 men who get HPV-associated anal cancer; 1,500 women and 5,600 men who get HPV-associated oropharyngeal cancers (cancers of the back of throat including base of tongue and tonsils)…. Certain populations are at higher risk for some HPV-related health problems. This includes gay and bisexual men, and people with weak immune systems (including those who have HIV/AIDS)….It is estimated that less than 2,000 children get juvenile-onset RRP every year in the U.S…. Vaccines can protect males and females against some of the most common types of HPV that can lead to disease and cancer….condoms may not fully protect against HPV. People can also lower their chances of getting HPV by being in a faithful relationship with one partner; limiting their number of sex partners; and choosing a partner who has had no or few prior sex partners. But even people with only one lifetime sex partner can get HPV [if the other is infected]. And it may not be possible to determine if a partner who has been sexually active in the past is currently infected. That's why the only sure way to prevent HPV is to avoid all sexual activity.

Bottom line: President Obama's CDC could help refill the ranks of Catholic celibates (thinned in many cases by HPV's deadlier STD cousin, HIV), write speeches for puritanical U.S. Rep. Michele Bachmann (on the benefits of extramarital abstinence) or for Gov. Rick Perry (on why, perhaps, he shouldn't have called it a mistake to make HPV immunization normative for adolescent girls in Texas). About 475,000 cases of cervical cancer and 250,000 deaths – virtually all HPV-related – occur worldwide. About 5,000 of those occur annually in the USA: That's around half again the death toll from 9/11, or from all combat-related deaths in Afghanistan and Iraq since 9/11.

[269] According to the American Cancer Society web page on anal cancer (www.cancer.org/Cancer/AnalCancer/.../anal-cancer-risk-factors):

> For men, the 2 main factors influencing the risk of genital HPV infection are circumcision and the number of sexual partners. Men who are circumcised (have had the foreskin of the penis removed) have a lower chance of becoming and staying infected with HPV. The risk of being infected with HPV is also strongly linked to having many sexual partners (over a man's lifetime).
>
> For women, certain factors have been linked to an increased risk of genital HPV infection, such as:
> Starting to have sex at an early age, Having many sexual partners, Having sex with a partner who has had many other partners, Having sex with uncircumcised males. In a study that looked at risk factors for anal HPV infection in women, risk was increased in younger women and in those who had more than 5 sexual partners in their lifetime. Ever having anal sex also increased risk.
>
> Circumcision and HPV: Men who have not been circumcised are more likely to be infected with HPV and pass it on to their partners. The reasons for this are unclear. It may be that the skin on the glans of the penis goes through changes that make it more resistant to HPV infection. Another theory is that the surface of the foreskin (which is removed by circumcision) is more easily infected by HPV. Still, circumcision does not completely protect against HPV infection -- men who are circumcised can still get HPV and pass it on to their partners.
>
> Condoms and HPV: Condoms can provide some protection against HPV, but they do not completely prevent infection. One study found that when condoms are used correctly they can lower the genital HPV infection rate in women by about 70% - but they need to be used every time sex occurs. This study did not look at the effect of condom use on anal HPV infection. In another study, men who used condoms less than half of the time had a higher risk of HPV infection. Condoms cannot protect completely because they don't cover every possible HPV-infected area of the body, such as skin of the genital or anal area. Still, condoms provide some protection against HPV, and they also protect against HIV and some other sexually transmitted diseases. Condoms (when used by the male partner) also seem to help genital HPV infections clear (go away) faster in both women and men.
>
> Other cancers: Ever having cancer of the cervix, vagina, or vulva is linked to an increased risk of anal cancer. This is likely because these cancers are also caused by infection with HPV. Although it is likely that having penile cancer, which is also linked to HPV infection, would increase the risk of anal cancer, this link has not been shown in studies.
>
> HIV infection: People infected with the human immunodeficiency virus (HIV), the virus that causes AIDS, are much more likely to get anal cancer than those not infected with this virus. Effective drug treatment for HIV has lowered the risk for many AIDS related diseases, but it hasn't lowered the anal cancer rate.
>
> Sexual activity: Having multiple sex partners increases the risk of infection with HIV and HPV. It also increases the risk of anal cancer. Receptive anal intercourse also increases the risk of anal cancer in both men and women, particularly in those younger than the age of 30….

[270] William Saletan, "Ass Backwards: The media's rampant silence about anal sex," *Slate* (http://www.slate.com/articles/health_and_science/human_nature/2005/09/ass_backwards.html)

Same Sex as Sandusky

Three millennia ago, Moses called it an "abomination"[271] – the same pejorative used by Joseph Smith[272], authoritative holy prophet of the Romney family, for all religions apart from his historic sex cult. This, of course, is the same polytheistic-polyamorous Mormonism at war with American monotheism and hetero-monogamy from its very start (and whose misled adherents have frequently honored latter-day LDS proscriptions on polygamy, pedophilia and sodomy in the breach).

Two millennia ago, as we've seen, St. Paul contended that homo/bisexuality entailed exchanging "the truth about God for a lie," the worship and service of "created things rather than the Creator.... Because of this, God gave them over to shameful lusts.... men also abandoned natural relations with women and were inflamed with lust for one another. Men committed shameful acts with other men, and received in themselves the due penalty for their error."[273]

In Judaism and Christianity, worshiping created things rather than the Creator – idolatry – is the "abomination which causes desolation"[274] and yields the kind of horrors which devastate individuals and whole societies (drought, plague, national conquest, etc.) In their moves to solemnize sodomy and facilitate promiscuity, Barack Obama, Mitt Romney and their GLBT allies have been making war on traditional Judeo-Christian hetero-monogamy and monotheism, core to traditions regarded by latter-day prophet Joseph Smith as "abominations".

Just as Moses and Paul did in a pre-scientific age, Sprigg in his *The Top 10 Myths about Homosexuality* challenges an essentially pagan sort of wishful thinking that "Homosexual conduct is not harmful to one's physical health." Reiterating some of the empirical findings above, he asserts that,

> Both because of high-risk behavior patterns, such as sexual promiscuity, and because of the harm to the body from specific sexual acts, homosexuals are at greater risk than heterosexuals for sexually transmitted diseases and other forms of illness and injury. The most obvious and dramatic example of the negative consequences of homosexual conduct among men is the AIDS epidemic. In 2009, a gay newspaper reported, "Gay and bisexual men account for half of new HIV infections in the U.S. and have AIDS at a rate more than 50 times greater than other groups, according to Centers for Disease Control & Prevention data . . . ."[46]
>
> Through 2007, 274,184 American men had died of AIDS whose only risk factor was sex with other men. When men who had sex with men and engaged in injection drug use are added to that total, we find that more than two thirds of the total male AIDS deaths in America (68%) have been among homosexual men.[47]
>
> HIV/AIDS is not the only sexually transmitted disease for which homosexual men are at risk. The CDC warns, "Men who have sex with men (MSM) are at elevated risk for certain sexually transmitted diseases (STDs), including Hepatitis A, Hepatitis B, HIV/AIDS, syphilis, gonorrhea, and chlamydia."[48] As early as 1976—even before the onset of the AIDS epidemic—doctors had identified a "clinical pattern of anorectal and colon diseases encountered with unusual frequency in . . . [male] homosexual patients," resulting from the practice of anal intercourse, which they dubbed "the gay bowel syndrome."
>
> An analysis of 260 medical records reported in the Annals of Clinical and Laboratory Science found: The clinical diagnoses in decreasing order of frequency include condyloma acuminata, hemorrhoids, nonspecific proctitis, anal fistula, perirectal abscess, anal fissure, amebiasis, benign polyps, viral hepatitis, gonorrhea, syphilis, anorectal trauma and foreign bodies, shigellosis, rectal ulcers and lymphogranuloma venereum. . . . In evaluating proctologic problems in the gay male, all of the known sexually transmitted diseases should be considered. . . . Concurrent infections with 2 or more pathogens should be anticipated.[49]
>
> Although not as dramatic, similar problems are also found among lesbians. In 2007, a medical journal reported, "Women who identified as lesbians have a 2.5-fold increased likelihood of BV [bacterial vaginosis] compared with

---

[271] Leviticus 18:22 and 20:13.

[272] Joseph Smith, the founder of Romney's Mormonism, aka, The Church of Jesus Christ of Latter-day Saints, claims that God commanded him: "...I must join none of them [other denominations], for they were all wrong...that all their creeds were an abomination in His sight" (Joseph Smith History 1:19); "The Roman Catholic, Greek, and Protestant church, is the great corrupt, ecclesiastical power, represented by great Babylon...." (Orson Pratt, *Writings of an Apostle,* "Divine Authenticity," no.6, p.84); "There is no salvation outside The Church of Jesus Christ of Latter-day Saints..." (Bruce McConkie, *Mormon Doctrine,* p. 670); "The Christian world, so called, are heathens as to their knowledge of the salvation of God." (Brigham Young, *Journal of Discourses* 8:171); all as quoted in McCann, "How Does the Mormon Church Really View other Churches?" (http://www.spotlightministries.org.uk/morm&churches.htm). Also: "Does Mormonism Attack Other Religions?" (http://carm.org/does-mormonism-attack-other-religions).

[273] As if to mercifully mitigate the impact of such error is the Abrahamic, Mosaic, Jewish and Judeo-Christian custom of circumcision – a practice which, especially to males, seems at first to defy common sense. As a matter of empirical science, however, what the pagan world and anti-Semites have from ancient times seen as senseless mutilation actually helps protect against the spread of HPV, HIV and other sexually-transmitted diseases associated with homosexuality in particular and sexual promiscuity in general. See http://www.cdc.gov/hiv/resources/factsheets/circumcision.htm

[274] See, e.g., Daniel 9:27; 11:31; 12:11. Also: Matthew 24:15; Mark 13:14.

heterosexual women."[50] As with mental health problems (see Myth No.5), the Gay and Lesbian Medical Association has neatly summarized the elevated risks to physical health experienced by homosexuals:

- "That men who have sex with men are at an increased risk of HIV infection is well known . . . . However, the last few years have seen the return of many unsafe sex practices."
- "Men who have sex with men are at an increased risk of sexually transmitted infection with the viruses that cause the serious condition of the liver known as hepatitis. These infections can be potentially fatal, and can lead to very serious long-term issues such as cirrhosis and liver cancer."
- "Sexually transmitted diseases (STDs) occur in sexually active gay men at a high rate. This includes STD infections for which effective treatment is available (syphilis, gonorrhea, chlamydia, pubic lice, and others), and for which no cure is available (HIV, Hepatitis A, B, or C virus, Human Papilloma Virus, etc.)."
- "Of all the sexually transmitted infections gay men are at risk for, human papilloma virus —which cause anal and genital warts — is often thought to be little more than an unsightly inconvenience. However, these infections may play a role in the increased rates of anal cancers in gay men. . . . [R]ecurrences of the warts are very common, and the rate at which the infection can be spread between partners is very high."[51]

Lesbians also face significant risks, according to the GLMA:

- "Lesbians have the richest concentration of risk factors for breast cancer than [sic] any subset of women in the world."
- "Smoking and obesity are the most prevalent risk factors for heart disease among lesbians . . ."
- "Lesbians have higher risks for many of the gynecologic cancers."[275]

Men and women obviously are not *designed* for homo/bisexuality – and *especially* not little boys, girls or teens who tend to be the targets of predatory males like Jerry Sandusky, Joseph Smith and Brigham Young.

Human Rights and Homosexuality

Yet, if the purposeful, endowing Creator honored in America's 1776 Declaration has no real existence but was merely a mirage to America's monotheistic Founders – if we are but mindless, accidental byproducts of a random multiverse or some chance-driven, pagan-ish reality with no absolute, designing G_d... then it's obviously absurd to speak of human design *or human rights*.

Why? Because if we are *not* in fact biologically designed, if we and our children are *not* products of a benevolent intelligence, then in what sense can human beings be "endowed by their Creator with certain unalienable rights" to "Life, Liberty and the Pursuit of Happiness"?

All of that must have been a fanciful figment of the colonial imagination – a mere, rhetorical fig leaf to cover what is, and always is, the naked exercise of force by one or another group of accidental animals over others of their own species (*homo sapiens*) and others (the rest of the biosphere which we consume for our survival).

And if that's so, then the "American Experiment" and "American Exceptionalism" would, in fact, be no more exceptional, in a moral or ethical sense, than any other form of government – Monarchism, Communism, Nazism, Sharia Islam, etc. How can an entirely accidental, undesigned humanity be measurable by any objective moral or ethical standard? Fidelity and infidelity, kindness and cruelty, persuasion and coercion, liberty and tyranny, humanitarianism and genocide: In an ultimately random, mindless cosmos, none can be of greater real value than any other.

---

[275] Peter Sprigg, *The Top 10 Myths about Homosexuality,* (Family Research Council, http://downloads.frc.org/EF/EF10F01.pdf), at 26-29. Here are cited sources for "Myth 6":

46 Dyana Bagby, "Gay, bi men 50 times more likely to have HIV: CDC reports hard data at National HIV Prevention Conference," Washington Blade, August 28, 2009.

47 Centers for Disease Control and Prevention. HIV/AIDS Surveillance Report, 2007. Vol. 19. Atlanta: U.S. Department of Health and Human Services, Centers for Disease Control and Prevention; 2009; p. 19. http://www.cdc.gov/hiv/topics/surveillance/resources/reports/

48 Centers for Disease Control and Prevention, "Viral Hepatitis And Men Who Have Sex With Men," online at: http://www.cdc.gov/hepatitis/Populations/msm.htm (accessed February 5, 2010).

49 H. L. Kazal, N. Sohn, J. I. Carrasco, J. G. Robilotti, and W. E. Delaney, "The gay bowel syndrome: clinico-pathologic correlation in 260 cases," Annals of Clinical and Laboratory Science 1976, Vol 6, Issue 2, 184-192; abstract online at: http://www.annclinlabsci.org/cgi/content/abstract/6/2/184

50 Amy L. Evans, Andrew J. Scally, Sarah J. Wellard, Janet D. Wilson, "Prevalence of bacterial vaginosis in lesbians and heterosexual women in a community setting," Sexually Transmitted Infections 2007; 83:470-475; abstract; online at: http://sti.bmj.com/content/83/6/470.abstract

51 Victor M. B. Silenzio, "Top 10 Things Gay Men Should Discuss with their Healthcare Provider" (San Francisco: Gay & Lesbian Medical Association); accessed April 1, 2010; online at: http://www.glma.org/_data/n_0001/resources/live/Top%20Ten%20Gay%20Men.pdf

52 Katherine A. O'Hanlan, "Top 10 Things Lesbians Should Discuss with their Healthcare Provider" (San Francisco: Gay & Lesbian Medical Association); accessed April 1, 2010; online at: http://www.glma.org/_data/n_0001/resources/live/Top%20Ten%20Lesbians.pdf

To speak of human rights, women's rights, children's rights, negro rights, religious rights, speech rights, privacy rights, gay rights, animal rights and any other kind of right as a transcending, deontological "ought" – rather than merely wished-for policies conferred (or not) by ephemeral tyrants or governing majorities – would seem rather absurd in a multiverse or universe that is ultimately blind, material and without intelligent design, no?

Incorporating just such a faith in 1903, philosopher Bertrand Russell wrote this soaring catechism for the likes of Bill Maher, Richard Dawkins and others of the metaphysical Left:

> **That man is the product of causes which had no prevision of the end they were achieving; that his origin, his growth, his hopes and fears, his loves and his beliefs, are but the outcome of accidental collocations of atoms; that no fire, no heroism, no intensity of thought and feeling can preserve an individual life beyond the grave; that all the labors of the ages, all the devotion, all the inspirations, all the noonday brightness of human genius, are destined to extinction in the vast death of the solar system, and that the temple of Man's achievement must inevitably be buried beneath the debris of the universe in ruins – all these things, if not beyond dispute, are yet so nearly certain, that no philosophy which rejects them can hope to stand. Only within the scaffolding of these truths, only on the firm foundation of unyielding despair can the soul's habitation henceforth be safely built.**[276]

And indeed, it is this deeply religious catechism which many on the materialist Right more or less recite to themselves, as if mumbling their way through an atheistic rosary in order to fit in with their more secular, more fashionable social peers (Fox News anchors, Beltway activists, members of Congress, Wall Street Journal editors?).

Embarrassed by their heritage, perhaps desperate to fit in, they seem to abandon the "the Supreme Judge of the world" honored in the Declaration by Judeo-Christian monotheists who risked everything to sign it. They seem to go all wobbly at the thought of upholding the benevolent, designing, rights-endowing Creator honored in their nation's founding charter. Yet Russell, a 20th Century high priest of secularism and materialism, was every bit the huckster and charlatan Joseph Smith was. Summing up his "Free Man's Worship" above, Russell writes that "Such, in outline, but even more purposeless, more void of meaning, is the world which Science presents for our belief."

That Russell's atheistic faith is manifestly unscientific, that it is not at all logically necessary, should be obvious to any critical thinker: How, for example, does the learned skeptic know that humanity is "but the outcome of accidental collocations of atoms"? How does Russell know that nothing "can preserve an individual life beyond the grave"? How the heck does he know that everything is "destined to extinction in the vast death of the solar system"? How could he, a disciple of (capital "S") Science, know that these things are "so nearly certain, that no philosophy which rejects them can hope to stand."?

Empirical observation, the application of the scientific method *per se*, by its very nature can demonstrate *nothing* about the non-existence of a Creator who may not be subject to ordinary sensory perception – or who may purposefully hide himself, awaiting discovery by each created soul, behind the teleological design of a humanity made in the *Imago Dei* and in the background – cosmic microwave radiation or dark matter – of our habitation.

Yet, the U.S. Supreme Court essentially embraced Russell's faith when it ruled over the course of 1962-63 that government must be neutral toward atheism. Or at least, with regard to American public life and public policy, the Court rejected the crucial premise of the American Founders, and their Declaration, in their recognition of an endowing, designing Creator. In Engel v. Vitale (1962), a 6-1 majority ruled this government-approved school prayer unconstitutional:

> Almighty God, we acknowledge our dependence upon Thee, and we beg Thy blessings upon us, our parents, our teachers and our Country.

Writing with good intentions for the majority, Justice Hugo Black said that, in large part to escape "systematic religious persecution,"

> the Founders brought into being our Nation, our Constitution, and our Bill of Rights, with its prohibition against any governmental establishment of religion.... It has been argued that to apply the Constitution in such a way as to prohibit state laws respecting an establishment of religious services in public schools is to indicate a hostility toward religion or toward prayer. Nothing, of course, could be more wrong.... men of... faith in the power of prayer ... led the fight for

[276] Bertrand Russell, "A Free Man's Worship," (http://www.philosophicalsociety.com/Archives/A%20Free%20Man's%20Worship.htm)

> adoption of our Constitution and also for our Bill of Rights with the very guarantees of religious freedom that forbid the sort of governmental activity which New York has attempted here. These men knew that the First Amendment, which tried to put an end to governmental control of religion and of prayer, was not written to destroy either. They knew, rather, that it was written to quiet well justified fears which nearly all of them felt arising out of an awareness that governments of the past had shackled men's tongues to make them speak only the religious thoughts that government wanted them to speak and to pray only to the God that government wanted them to pray to. It is neither sacrilegious nor anti-religious to say that each separate government in this country should stay out of the business of writing or sanctioning official prayers and leave that purely religious function to the people themselves and to those the people choose to look to for religious guidance.
>
> It is true that New York's establishment of its Regents' prayer as an officially approved religious doctrine of that State does not amount to a total establishment of one particular religious sect to the exclusion of all others -- that, indeed, the governmental endorsement of that prayer seems relatively insignificant when compared to the governmental encroachments upon religion which were commonplace 200 years ago. To those who may subscribe to the view that, because the Regents' official prayer is so brief and general there can be no danger to religious freedom in its governmental establishment, however, it may be appropriate to say in the words of James Madison, the author of the First Amendment:
>
> > [I]t is proper to take alarm at the first experiment on our liberties. . . . Who does not see that the same authority which can establish Christianity, in exclusion of all other Religions, may establish with the same ease any particular sect of Christians, in exclusion of all other Sects? That the same authority which can force a citizen to contribute three pence only of his property for the support of any one establishment may force him to conform to any other establishment in all cases whatsoever?

And yet, while the First Amendment forbade any governmental establishment of religion (while protecting the free exercise thereof), it did *not* negate the benevolent monotheism of the nation's 1776 Declaration, as expressed by the same founding generation. That, however, was the overreaching effect of *Abingdon School District v. Schempp.*[277] In that 1963 ruling, an 8-1 majority articulated a First Amendment "neutrality test":

> The test may be stated as follows: what are the purpose and the primary effect of the enactment? If either is the advancement or inhibition of religion, then the enactment exceeds the scope of legislative power as circumscribed by the Constitution. That is to say that, to withstand the strictures of the Establishment Clause, there must be a secular legislative purpose and a primary effect that neither advances nor inhibits religion.

In a lonely dissent cheered by religious conservatives, Justice Stewart wrote,

> If religious exercises are held to be an impermissible activity in schools, religion is placed in an artificial and state-created disadvantage.... And a refusal to permit religious exercises thus is seen, not as the realization of state neutrality, but rather as the establishment of a religion of secularism, or at least, as governmental support of the beliefs of those who think that religious exercises should be conducted only in private

With 20/20 hindsight, however, many conservatives and libertarians of the Right may by now recognize that having any government-run school (or other government entity, such as the military) dictate sectarian prayers, devotional readings, etc. imposes unacceptable risks to the liberties of all. Once familiar with the doctrines of Mormonism, for example, could responsible Jewish or Christian parents living in Provo *ever* be warm to the thought of their own children being subjected to public school devotionals from the weird sci-fi writings of Joseph Smith?

The fatal conceit of the *Abingdon* majority, however, may be the notion that American government – today consuming an enormous share of U.S. GDP – could somehow maintain neutrality with regard to the benevolent, endowing, designing Creator upon whom the Founders predicated the entire American experiment. As we've all pretty much learned since 1963, American public life, public schools – and public institutions like the military, Medicare, Medicaid, RomneyCare, ObamaCare, the Centers for Disease Control, and all of U.S. public policy – depend upon a worldview about humanity, upon one version or another of human anthropology.

If we are but "accidental collocations of atoms" descended from a common biological ancestor along with fish, fungi and *E.coli* bacteria in an ultimately mindless, materialist multiverse, that's certainly one religious viewpoint. If we are, as Mitt Romney and all Mormon Bishops must believe, the embodied "spirit babies" of our finite, fleshly "Heavenly Father and Heavenly Mother" who themselves are descended from an infinite regression of finite gods (and whom each of us can join in an in an infinite progression as gods ourselves)... well, that's certainly another religious viewpoint.

---

[277] http://www.law.cornell.edu/supct/html/historics/USSC_CR_0374_0203_ZO.html

The Founders' View

But *neither* view of humanity, neither that of Prophet Bertrand Russell nor the racist polytheism of Prophet Joseph Smith, is very compatible with the formal creed of the Founders as articulated in the American Declaration. And, if any honest reading of the First Amendment must be consistent with a straight take on the Declaration (each written by the same founding generation), then nothing at odds with that from the judiciary (e.g., Russell's view) can work for U.S. policy.

Is the Constitution is rightly read through the monotheistic lens of the Declaration (as Lincoln and the abolitionists read it in their fight to free the slaves)? Can our government honor the Being who created us equal, the "Supreme Judge of the world" upon whom our unalienable rights to "Life, Liberty and the Pursuit of Happiness" depend? If the Declaration has bearing and rightly binds us today – anchoring human rights outside of government and in humanity's Creator – then how can it possibly be an unconstitutional "advancement of religion" for U.S. public policy to uphold monotheism, Creator-endowed design and for that matter, Creator endowed hetero-monogamy?

The Warren Court in *Engel* and *Abingdon* fancied, perhaps with the noblest of motives, that government could somehow avoid taking any side at all. Yet of course, our nation's 1776 charter, the Declaration of Independence, *does* indeed take sides: Not for one Christian denomination over another, nor for Christianity over Judaism; the Establishment Clause clearly forbids that.

However, the founding Americans who framed the First Amendment (to protect the free exercise of religion, freedom of the press, free speech, etc.) had previously risked *everything* on the monotheistic claims of the Declaration. In Philadelphia, as they mutually pledged "to each other our lives, our fortunes and our sacred honor," they bet absolutely everything – personally and on behalf of their nation – on their purposeful, benevolent and endowing Creator, on the "protection of divine providence."

In other words, the American Founders who framed the Declaration and the First Amendment tilted *decisively* in favor of a personal, monotheistic and designing G_d – for an assertion about reality entirely consistent with Judaism and Christianity, *yet enormously inconsistent* with: Atheism, materialism (e.g., Russell's "scientific materialism"), Objectivism (Ayn Rand's atheistic individualism), hard agnosticism ("no one can ever know..."), soft agnosticism ("someone may know, but I don't yet know..."), empiricism or scientism ("nothing which cannot be perceived via the senses or sensory aid is real"), Epicureanism (a materialist cosmos in which maximizing pleasure and minimizing pain is the ultimate objective), pantheism, emperor worship, Occultism, Scientology, Satanism, polytheism, paganism, Mormonism, etc.

The Declaration's metaphysic is also inconsistent with deism, at least to the extent any American Founder at one time or another in life leaned toward a version that envisions a remote, uncaring, and uninvolved deity who wound-up the cosmos like a clock... and then spirited himself away from terrestrial and human affairs. That then-fashionable, Enlightenment view from the salons of Paris was figuratively shouted-down in Philadelphia; it is rejected by the words of a Declaration of *dependence* upon a Creator who is proclaimed to be the endowing, providing and just Judge who made all humans equal.

To any extent the Muslim deity may rightly be regarded as deistically remote – or, as some scholars hold, a tyrannical "greatest deity" in a polytheistic pantheon, a bellicose Arabian moon god of war supremacized by Muhammad and demanding dark things like jihad, child sacrifice and the destruction of Jews and Christians (who comprised America's 1776 generation, yet who are held unequal to those in submission to the Q'ranic Allah) – it also would seem that the Declaration, the USA's charter, carved out little space for Sharia-style Islam.

If the First Amendment's Establishment Clause forbids the government-enforced supremacy of one Judeo-Christian denomination over others – and no one debates that – then it *certainly* rules-out the supremacy of supremacist Islam (or supremacist Communism, Nazism, Mormonism, etc., pragmatically intolerant views which, in any case, had zero subscribers in the Founding generation).

On the premise that the Declaration's endowing, designing Creator made us moral equals – and had rather miraculously enabled the American Republic to free itself from Britain about four-score years prior – Lincoln fought to preserve the Union and free the slaves. Similarly, on the inference that the "Supreme Judge of the world" designed us for heterosexuality and procreation, then maybe a public policy which– for the sake of personal health, social health and adherence to the "Laws of Nature and of Nature's God" – aims to confine penetration to vaginal intercourse, and that to traditional monogamy... might indeed be a *good* one?

No one is arguing herein for the prosecution or persecution of (non-pedophile) homo/bisexuals. No one's arguing for the punishment of anyone who fails to recognize that the Declaration's Creator, the benevolent endower of our rights, must also have endowed and designed us for heterosexuality and reproduction. No one is herein arguing against GLBT freedom of association, freedom of contract. Nor are we in any way arguing herein for the criminal punishment of citizens who succumb to adulterous or homo/bisexual desires.

L'chaim, Barney Frank!

Our hope, rather, is for Tampa's GOP delegates, the Republican Party and American society to recognize – by first recognizing or presupposing the Declaration's benevolent and endowing Creator – that which can so reasonably be inferred from the biological design of men and women.

The Democratic Party is set to go all the way with Obama – to go all the way with homo/bisexuality, abortion and reproductive nihilism – by embracing SSS/SSM (Same-Sex Marriage, Same-Sex as Sandusky[278]) at their Raleigh convention. By contrast, our hope is that, by not even trying to out-gay Obama, by nobly abstaining from a RINO frontrunner who has been so blind to all of these things,[279] we may begin to correct a national course which has veered way off track from the Founder's vision.

In other words, if the benevolent, endowing Creator cited by the Declaration's monotheistic signatories purposefully *made us this way,* if indeed we're *designed for heterosexuality,* then maybe a public policy that aims to confine sex to marriage, and marriage and childrearing to a man and a woman, and unborn babies to the class of legally-protected persons… might be a vastly *better one* than the current, pro-death, pro-GLBT and effectively pro-pedophile agenda which both Obama and Romney have been pushing?

A possible added benefit: Maybe the hypothesis of a designing Creator can help explain why so many empirical (yet media-ignored) social science studies have emerged to gut the following GLBT whoppers:

- "Children raised by homosexuals are no different from children raised by heterosexuals, nor do they suffer harm."
- "Homosexuals are no more likely to molest children than heterosexuals." (Discussed above).
- "Homosexuals do not experience a higher level of psychological disorders than heterosexuals." (Discussed above).
- "Homosexual relationships are just the same as heterosexual ones, except for the gender of the partners."
- "Sexual orientation can never change."
- "Efforts to change someone's sexual orientation from homosexual to heterosexual are harmful and unethical."

Each of these mainstays of GLBT mythology is undermined or undone by science cited in *The Top 10 Myths about Homosexuality*. So too is the notion that GLBT numbers have any great electoral significance. Sprigg writes that,

> of the small number of people who have ever experienced homosexuality on any of the three measures of sexual orientation (attractions, behavior, and self-identification), the number who have been exclusively homosexual on all three measures throughout their lives is vanishingly small—only 0.6% of men and 0.2% of women. Even if we go by the measure of self-identification alone, the percentage of the population who identify as homosexual or bisexual is quite small. Convincing evidence of these has come from an unlikely source—a consortium of 31 of the leading homosexual rights groups in America. In a friend-of-the-court brief they filed in the Supreme Court's *Lawrence v. Texas* sodomy case in 2003" –

---

[278] Anal intercourse which, coerced or uncoerced, is toxic to human health – a practice for which human beings are not designed – yet central to the broad GLBT/pedophila-pederast movement (see page 56 forward). In this appalling sense, it is the Republican frontrunner who has led from behind: Whether adult-youth, youth-youth, or adult -adult interaction, Romney has been joined to them at the figurative hips for years: Romney's chiding of the Boy Scouts (http://massresistance.org/romney/videos/index.html), for example, could have been scripted by NAMBLA (the North American Man-Boy Love Association), despite well-known cases of LDS pedophiles within the Boy Scouts. Likewise with Romney's infamously obsequious, brown-nosing letter to the Log Cabin Republicans. (http://www.boston.com/news/daily/11/romneyletterbaywindows.pdf).

[279] Logically, one can view homo/bisexuality as an understandable reaction to predatory males, as a psychological disorder, as a willful human deviation from divine design, as a pathology, or even as a public health and disease threat, without any implication of hatred or venom toward those who have been engaged in GLBT conduct – and without necessarily impinging upon freedom of association, contract rights, property rights, free speech rights, etc. of gays and lesbians. Logically, American society and public policy could generally discourage homo/bisexuality, pedophilia, transgenderism and other disorders and deviations from hetero-monogamy while allowing some social space for said (as has been the historic case with prostitution, pornography, etc.) By contrast, "Marriage Equality" – redefining legal marriage to include homo/bisexuality, bigamy, polygamy, pedogamy, etc. – obviously represents governmental endorsement of those practices.

[NOTE: the ruling in which Scalia's dissent signaled to Gov. Romney, less than a year before he brought about the USA's first gay marriages in Massachusetts, that institutionalized homosexuality is the key to reinstating legal American polygamy]

> -- they admitted the following:
>
> The most widely accepted study of sexual practices in the United States is the National Health and Social Life Survey (NHSLS). The NHSLS found that 2.8% of the male, and 1.4% of the female, population identify themselves as gay, lesbian, or bisexual.[280]

Most of that population, overwhelmingly loyal to the Democratic Party and the Democratic incumbent who came out this summer for homosexual wedlock, is very unlikely to cast its votes for a Republican who, albeit the author of gay marriage in the USA, opportunistically and transparently tacked right with an ambitious eye to his 2008 and 2012 GOP Presidential campaigns.

L'chaim, Barney Frank! Mazel tov!: If science demonstrates that gay people are born that way just as some are born with black skin, blue eyes, or ovaries – if it's just the way some of us are inherently made or literally designed – shouldn't we all be joyously celebrating the respective summer nuptials of Barney Frank and Mary Cheney as a good thing? Shouldn't we all be helping the GLBT movement to add the faces of Mitt Romney – the man who brought SSM/SSS to the USA – and Barack Obama, the first US President to endorse it, to Mount Rushmore?

Gays, lesbians, progressives – not to mention freethinkers on the Right – who would deny the Founders' Creator, the being who beneficently endows all humans "with certain unalienable rights," might have a hard time coherently invoking the idea of a transcendent, unalienable right to anal intercourse, fisting, polygamy, pedophilia or the abortion of unborn babies; in a materialist multiverse or universe, any "right" to those things – *or to anything* – must necessarily be merely political, a matter of arbitrary claim or man-made positive law.

Yet, there undeniably are many within the GLBT movement and among their supporters on the right and left who do not formally deny the Declaration's Creator, nor the more specified G_d of Judaism and Christianity. What about *their* "unalienable rights"?

Suppose that, despite arguments from Natural Law and Design, it were scientifically established that up to three percent of humanity is *born gay.* What if – despite Genesis (from Eden to Sodom and Gomorrah), despite Moses

---

[280] *Lawrence v. Texas,* Docket No. 02-102 (U.S. SupremeCourt), brief of amici curiae Human Rights Campaign et al., 16 January 2003, p. 16 (footnote 42), as discussed and cited in Sprigg, *The Top 10 Myths about Homosexuality,* (Family Research Council, http://downloads.frc.org/EF/EF10F01.pdf), at 21.

and the balance of the Tanakh, despite Jesus and St. Paul – we could confirm that homo/bisexuals, pedophiles or marital cheaters are just "made that way," that their sexual behaviors are inborn, immutable and irresistible?

In that case, wouldn't President Obama's summer endorsement of gay marriage seem a good thing? Wouldn't it seem only fair? Wouldn't Mitt Romney's covert creation of U.S. gay marriage – and Romney's overt support for GLBT adoption, childrearing, curricula, soldiering, hiring, non-discrimination, etc. – just seem like good, common sense? Wouldn't we all be morally obliged to join with friends and family of Mary Cheney and Barney Frank in joyfully celebrating their recent same-sex nuptials?

After all, gays, lesbians, bisexuals and transgenders have no more responsibility for their sexuality than do African-Americans for their skin tone, women for their ovaries, or a Tay-Sachs infant for her disability, *right?*

Anderson Cooper was Born Gay?

CNN anchor Anderson Cooper dog-piled onto President Obama's summer decision to come out of the closet for gay marriage ... by coming out himself: "The fact is," he said, "I'm gay, always have been, always will be."

But, is that good journalism? Is it really so?

As a fellow human being and bearer of the *Imago Dei,* we wish Mr. Cooper good health, long life, happiness and Heaven's very best. We pray that he survives, along with Neil Patrick Harris, Ellen DeGeneres (and other homo/bisexually-inclined souls whom we know and love in our families and among our friends) on the happiest side of the GLBT bell curve – or better, in accord with his G_d-given heterosexual design.

As we've seen, the science indicates homo/bisexuality is generally and deeply harmful to mental and physical health. And, just as with other dangerous-living celebs, those who survive remain on our radar, while those who don't – e.g., Freddie Mercury, Perry Ellis, Rock Hudson, Anthony Perkins, Brad Davis, Alvin Ailey, Terry Dolan, etc. – kind of just seem to disappear.

In any case, the empirical evidence indicates Mr. Cooper is almost certainly in error if he contends that he was *born homosexual,* that his "gayness" is genetically determined like a person's race, gender or eye color. In *The Top 10 Myths about Homosexuality,* Sprigg writes that the GLBT agenda

> has involved an effort to define the benefits homosexuals seek as a matter of "civil rights," comparable to that which African Americans fought for in the 1960's; and to define disapproval of homosexual conduct as a form of "bigotry," comparable to a racist ideology of white supremacy. However, these themes only make sense if, in fact, a homosexual "orientation" is a characteristic that is comparable to race.
>
> But racial discrimination is not wrong merely because a group of people complained loudly and long that it is wrong. Racial discrimination is irrational and invidious because of what I call the five "I's"—the fact that, as a personal characteristic, race is inborn, involuntary, immutable, innocuous and [protected] in the Constitution. Homosexual activists would have us believe that the same is true of their homosexuality.

Sprigg writes that, although some attractions may be involuntary (but not immutable), science indicates that the decision to engage in homo/bisexuality is voluntary – just as voluntary, we might add, as the decisions of John Edwards and Mark Sanford to cheat on their wives. Yet, per Sprigg, it's clear that GLBT activists have duped a chunk of the U.S. population and its policymakers into believing that

> homosexual "orientation" is something they are born with, cannot choose whether to accept or reject, and cannot change; and that it does no harm (to themselves or to society).... However, these are empirical questions, subject to being verified or refuted based on the evidence. And the evidence produced by research has simply not been kind to this theoretical underpinning of the homosexual movement. It has become more and more clear that none of the "five-I" criteria apply to the choice to engage in homosexual conduct.

If homo/bisexuality is inherent, then discriminatory attitudes or policies toward practitioners – by Biblical authorities, religious leaders, or civil society – would seem to be unfair, maybe just plain wrong. Even if the science shows, as we have seen, that homo/bisexuality is associated with physical and mental illness, and with abuse of the sort Jerry Sandusky inflicted on his young victims, perhaps Sandusky and every member of the broad, recruitment-inclined "GLBT community" are only doing what their genes programmed them to do.

Except, the science doesn't support that. Sprigg writes that, following three studies hyped in the early 1990's to suggest that homosexuality is biologically determined,[281]

> **[M]ore rigorous studies of identical twin pairs have essentially made it impossible to argue for the genetic determination of homosexuality. Since identical ("monozygotic," in the scientific literature) twins have identical genes, if homosexuality were genetically fixed at birth, we should expect that whenever one twin is homosexual, the other twin would be homosexual (a "concordance rate" of 100%).** [282]
>
> **.... Researchers Peter Bearman and Hannah Brückner, from Columbia and Yale respectively, studied data from the National Longitudinal Study of Adolescent Health, and found .... concordance rates of only 6.7% for male and 5.3% for female identical twins. In fact, their study neatly refuted several of the biological theories for the origin of homosexuality, finding social experiences in childhood to be far more significant:**
>
>> **[T]he pattern of concordance (similarity across pairs) of same-sex preference for sibling pairs does not suggest genetic influence independent of social context. Our data falsify the hormone transfer hypothesis by isolating a single condition that eliminates the opposite-sex twin effect we observe—the presence of an older same-sex sibling. We also consider and reject a speculative evolutionary theory that rests on observing birth-order effects on same-sex orientation. In contrast, our results support the hypothesis that less gendered socialization in early childhood and preadolescence shapes subsequent same-sex romantic preferences.** [283]

In the early 1990's – when Mitt Romney was telling gay activists that President Clinton's efforts to integrate homo/bisexuality into the U.S. military needed to go farther – junk science hinted that maybe homosexuality is inherent. Today, however, the science make it quite clear:

Homosexuality and lesbianism are *not* genetically determined; no one is "born gay."

Nor has careful science found homosexual attractions, conduct and self-identification – some or all of which are included in the strategically-vague term "sexual orientation" – to be immutable.[284] At least "two studies have found that a large percentage (46% in one survey, and more than half in another) of all men who have ever engaged in homosexual conduct did so only before age 15 and never since." [285] Although leftist, RINO and media mythology denies it, "personal testimonies, survey data and clinical research all make clear that change from a predominantly homosexual to a predominantly heterosexual orientation is possible."[286]

So, why would a self-proclaimed "data-driven" person like Romney cling so hard to a GLBT agenda? Why cling to an invalid analogy which likens non-inherent, mutable and resistible homo/bisexual behavior to inherent traits like race and gender? For that matter, why would a "data-driven" Romney embrace junk science on anthropogenic global warming, why would he buy the shaky claim that climate change is a man-made phenomenon which justifies

---

[281] Sprigg details that,

> The widespread, popular belief that science has proven a biological or genetic origin to homosexuality can be traced to the publicity which surrounded three studies published in the early 1990's. In August of 1991, researcher Simon LeVay published a study based on post-mortem examinations of the brains of cadavers. He concluded that differences in a particular brain structure suggested "that sexual orientation has a biological substrate." In December of 1991, researchers J. Michael Bailey and Richard C. Pillard published a study of identical and fraternal twins and adoptive brothers, and found that "the pattern of rates of homosexuality . . . was generally consistent with substantial genetic influence." Finally, in 1993, researcher Dean Hamer claimed to have found a specific "chromosomal region" containing "a gene that contributes to homosexual orientation in males." These studies suffered from serious methodological weaknesses, such as small sample sizes, non-random samples and even possible mis-classification of their subjects. Other scientists have been unable to replicate these dramatic findings. These problems led two psychiatrists to conclude, "Critical review shows the evidence favoring a biologic theory to be lacking. . . . In fact, the current trend may be to underrate the explanatory power of extant psychosocial models." (William Byne and Bruce Parsons, "Human Sexual Orientation: The Biologic Theories Reappraised," *Archives of General Psychiatry,* 50 (March 1993): 228, 236, cited in Sprigg, *The Top 10 Myths about Homosexuality,* (Family Research Council, http://downloads.frc.org/EF/EF10F01.pdf), at 6.

[282] Sprigg adds:

> Even Michael Bailey himself, co-author of the landmark 1991 twins study (which supposedly found a concordance rate of about 50%), conducted a subsequent study on a larger sample of Australian twins. As summarized by other researchers, "They found twenty-seven identical male twin pairs where at least one of the twin brothers was gay, but in only three of the pairs was the second twin brother gay as well"6 (a "concordance rate" of only eleven percent). (Stanton L. Jones and Mark A Yarhouse, *Ex-gays? A Longitudinal Study of Religiously Mediated Change in Sexual Orientation*, Downers Grove, Ill.: IVP Academic, 2007, p. 124; summarizing findings of: J. Michael Bailey, Michael P. Dunne, and Nicholas G. Martin, "Genetic and environmental influences on sexual orientation and its correlates in an Australian twin sample," *Journal of Personality and Social Psychology,* Vol. 78(3), March 2000, 524-536.

[283] Peter S. Bearman and Hannah Brückner, "Opposite-Sex Twins and Adolescent Same-Sex Attraction," American Journal of Sociology Vol. 107, No. 5, (March 2002), 1179-1205, as cited in Sprigg, *The Top 10 Myths about Homosexuality,* (Family Research Council, http://downloads.frc.org/EF/EF10F01.pdf), at 7.

[284] Calculated from Tables 2 and 3 in Robert E. Fay, Charles F. Turner, Albert D. Klassen, John H. Gagnon, "Prevalence and Patterns of Same-Gender Sexual Contact among Men, *Science,* New Series, Vol. 243, Issue 4889 (20 January 1989): 341-42, as cited by Sprigg, note 22; John H. Gagnon and William Simon, *Sexual conduct: The social sources of human sexuality* (Chicago: Aldine, 1993), pp. 131-32; cited in Laumann et al., p. 289, footnote 8.

[285] See, e.g., Robert L. Spitzer, M.D., "Can Some Gay Men and Lesbians Change Their Sexual Orientation? 200 Participants Reporting a Change from Homosexual to Heterosexual Orientation," Archives of Sexual Behavior 32, no. 5 (October 2003): 413.

[286] Sprigg, note 22, at 13, summarizing citations including James E. Phelan, Neil Whitehead, Philip M. Sutton, "What Research Shows: NARTH's Response to the APA Claims on Homosexuality," *Journal of Human Sexuality* Vol. 1 (National Association for Research and Therapy of Homosexuality, 2009), p. 32; J. Nicolosi, A. D. Byrd, and R. W. Potts, "Retrospective self-reports of changes in homosexual orientation: A consumer survey of conversion therapy clients," *Psychological Reports* 86, pp. 689-702. Cited in: Phelan et al., p. 12; Stanton L. Jones and Mark A Yarhouse, *Ex-gays? A Longitudinal Study of Religiously Mediated Change in Sexual Orientation* (Downers Grove, Ill.: IVP Academic, 2007), p. 369.

government regulation and taxation of carbon dioxide (just as uninsured human illness justifies government takeover of health care?)

Maybe this: Mormonism has required of Romney and his forebears such a stunning level of credulity, such a child-like gullibility, such mindless submission to authority… that his B.S. detector is broken: Heck, if someone honors pedophile prophets who preach solar residents and racism, who can really be surprised that he'd fall for the junk science of global warming and "gay genes"?[287] What else would we expect from the USA's first Sci-Fi President?

Mitt Romney grew up during a century in which the LDS was trying to downplay such history, to conform and advance within a larger U.S. society which had, up into the 1960's, largely embraced hetero-monogamy, marital and sexual fidelity between one man and one woman for life. As extramarital sex, serial adultery, open marriage, easy divorce, abortion, homosexuality, pedophilia and child porn became increasingly vogue, however, Romney discovered that wider American society was toying with sexual practices which had been dark undercurrents of his Mormonism from the start.

When Romney ran in liberal Massachusetts on a pro-abortion, pro-gay-everything RINO platform against Ted Kennedy for the U.S. Senate in 1994, he was a long way from the conformism of contemporary Salt Lake City… but very close to the sexual relativism of his Mormon forebears: By the hook-up standards of 1990s New England, hard-loving LDS polyamorists of the 1890's were friggin' progressives! A decade later, when the moment arrived for him to deliver on his brown-nosing to his Log Cabin friends, Romney pioneered the USA's first gay marriage regime and laid the groundwork for Mormon payback on polygamy.

Today, Republicans stand on the brink of nominating the Manchurian Candidate from GOProud and Provo, our LDS - Log Cabin advocate of sexual confusion, our own weird version of Gov. Jim McGreevey.[288] While feigning his support for traditional hetero-monogamy – as did his Presidency-seeking Prophet Joseph Smith in the 1840's – Mitt Romney has been working longer and harder to gut one-man, one-woman marriage in American public policy than has President Obama. For Paul Singer, Peter Thiel and every pro-GLBT billionaire who wants to see the Republican ticket and RNC platform "go gay" that's undoubtedly a good thing.

The GLBT endgame, however, is not simply male-male or female-female "Marriage Equality" on the groundless notion that people are born gay.[289] Nor is it the wide-open style polyamory (homoerotic, pedophile, polygynous, etc.) of Utah Territory and Romney's forebears. Rather, the logical end to which both Romney and Obama have been aiming, consciously or unconsciously, is the effective extinguishment of Jewish-Christian monotheism in America – lights out for the Faith of our Fathers.

If Tampa's delegates effectively reject the monotheism of the Declaration to make a polytheist their nominee, we believe that, one way or another, historians will mark 2012 as a crucial turning point. By ensuring President Obama's re-election (or an unlikely yet possible Romney Presidency), Tampa's unbound delegates would, we fear, become deeply responsible for the end of the American Republic.

Our Manhattan Project

To any and all confused souls like Gov. McGreevey, Gov. Romney, Ric Grenell and Anderson Cooper, each tempted in one way or another to regard human hetero-monogamy as a negotiable element of Natural Law and Divine Design; to each of you as bearers of the *Imago Dei,* we wish to respectfully repeat these words of *The Manhattan Declaration*:

> We acknowledge that there are those who are disposed towards homosexual and polyamorous conduct and relationships, just as there are those who are disposed towards other forms of immoral conduct… We, no less than they, are sinners who have fallen short of God's intention for our lives….Some who enter into same-sex and polyamorous relationships no doubt regard their unions as truly marital. They fail to understand, however, that marriage

---

[287] Each kind of junk science requires statist socio-economic intervention by government that might make good sense from the vantage point of authoritarian Salt Lake City: "Gay genes" not only help rationalize the homoeroticism so long a part of Mormon subculture; they morally demand gay marriage which, on similar constitutional logic, requires the reinstatement of legal polygamy. Meanwhile, CO2 regulation to impede global warming helps ensure better skiing at Park City and Sundance. For credulous authoritarians, any story rationalizes the exercise of coercive power.

[288] McGreevey was the 52nd Governor of New Jersey, a Democrate who, after fathering children in two marriages that admittedly included bisexual threesomes and at least one extramarital homosexual affair, resigned his office, declared that he was gay, divorced his wife, and began pursuing a new career as an Episcopalian priest. "McGreevey was the first and, to date, the only openly gay state governor in United States history." (http://en.wikipedia.org/wiki/Jim_McGreevey).

[289] See page 70 and forward.

> is made possible by the sexual complementarity of man and woman, and that the comprehensive, multi-level sharing of life that marriage is includes bodily unity of the sort that unites husband and wife biologically as a reproductive unit....
>
> The human person is a dynamic unity of body, mind, and spirit. Marriage is what one man and one woman establish when, forsaking all others and pledging lifelong commitment, they found a sharing of life at every level of being—the biological, the emotional, the dispositional, the rational, the spiritual— on a commitment that is sealed, completed and actualized by loving sexual intercourse in which the spouses become one flesh, not in some merely metaphorical sense, but by fulfilling together the behavioral conditions of procreation. That is why in the Christian tradition, and historically in Western law, consummated marriages are not dissoluble or annullable on the ground of infertility, even though the nature of the marital relationship is shaped and structured by its intrinsic orientation to the great good of procreation....

To Mitt Romney, the author of gay marriage in America, we must particularly reiterate these words from *The Manhattan Declaration*:

> [T]he assumption that the legal status of one set of marriage relationships affects no other would not only argue for same sex partnerships; it could be asserted with equal validity for *polyamorous partnerships, polygamous households, even adult brothers, sisters, or brothers and sisters living in incestuous relationships.* Should these, as a matter of equality or civil rights, be recognized as lawful marriages, and would they have no effects on other relationships? No. The truth is that marriage is not something abstract or neutral that the law may legitimately define and re-define to please those who are powerful and influential. No one has a civil right to have a non-marital relationship treated as a marriage. [Emphasis added].

As we've reviewed herein, it is well-established that the prophets of LDS Mormonism have engaged in all of the italicized practices above and promoted them as normative. We and most of swing-state America, however, believe that:

> Marriage is an objective reality—a covenantal union of husband and wife—that it is the duty of the law to recognize and support for the sake of justice and the common good. If it fails to do so, genuine social harms follow. First, the religious liberty of those for whom this is a matter of conscience is jeopardized. Second, the rights of parents are abused as family life and sex education programs in schools are used to teach children that an enlightened understanding recognizes as "marriages" sexual partnerships that many parents believe are intrinsically non-marital and immoral. Third, the common good of civil society is damaged when the law itself, in its critical pedagogical function, becomes a tool for eroding a sound understanding of marriage on which the flourishing of the marriage culture in any society vitally depends. Sadly, we are today far from having a thriving marriage culture. But if we are to begin the critically important process of reforming our laws and mores to rebuild such a culture, the last thing we can afford to do is to re-define marriage in such a way as to embody in our laws a false proclamation about what marriage is....

Gov. Romney: Jewish-Christian religious liberties have been under assault, from your time in Massachusetts through President Obama's tenure in Washington:

> in the effort to weaken or eliminate conscience clauses, and therefore to compel pro-life institutions (including religiously affiliated hospitals and clinics), and pro-life physicians, surgeons, nurses, and other health care professionals, to refer for abortions and, in certain cases, even to perform or participate in abortions. We see it in the use of anti- discrimination statutes to force religious institutions, businesses, and service providers of various sorts to comply with activities they judge to be deeply immoral or go out of business. After the judicial imposition of "same-sex marriage" in Massachusetts, for example

[*Your* doing, Governor!]

> Catholic Charities chose with great reluctance to end its century-long work of helping to place orphaned children in good homes rather than comply with a legal mandate that it place children in same-sex households in violation of Catholic moral teaching. In New Jersey, after the establishment of a quasi-marital "civil unions" scheme, a Methodist institution was stripped of its tax exempt status when it declined, as a matter of religious conscience, to permit a facility it owned and operated to be used for ceremonies blessing homosexual unions. In Canada and some European nations, Christian clergy have been prosecuted for preaching Biblical norms against the practice of homosexuality. New hate-crime laws in America raise the specter of the same practice here.
>
> In recent decades a growing body of case law has paralleled the decline in respect for religious values in the media, the academy and political leadership, resulting in restrictions on the free exercise of religion. We view this as an ominous development, not only because of its threat to the individual liberty guaranteed to every person, regardless of his or her faith, but because the trend also threatens the common welfare and the culture of freedom on which our system of republican government is founded. Restrictions on the freedom of conscience or the ability to hire people of one's own faith or conscientious moral convictions for religious institutions, for example, undermines the viability of the intermediate structures of society, the essential buffer against the overweening authority of the state, resulting in the soft despotism Tocqueville so prophetically warned of. Disintegration of civil society is a prelude to tyranny.

On all three foci of *The Manhattan Declaration* – Life, Marriage/Sexuality and Religious Liberty – and corresponding Presidential pledges (*The Marriage Vow, The Pro-Life Presidential Leadership Pledge*, *The Personhood Pledge* and *The Repeal ObamaCare Pledge*) unsigned by Romney, the GOP frontrunner's current, impenitence is plainly unacceptable:

Romney has made absolutely no apologies for the coercive, anti-life, anti-liberty *substance* of RomneyCare (the model for ObamaCare), nor has he backed off in any manner from his formal support for an essentially pagan GLBT agenda which Greco-Roman polytheists of old could easily have embraced. One might reasonably suspect that any *Manhattan Declaration* signatory who would knowingly contend otherwise, or who may wish to maintain a shameful silence on these things, is either a Romney money recipient or, perhaps, is angling for access to an imaginary Romney Administration.[290]

Yet, the hard truth is: If Tampa's delegates don't dump the USA's squishy Founding Father of Gay Marriage[291] for a genuine conservative, they will squander an enormous potential GOP advantage over President Obama in the Presidential and overlapping U.S. Senate swing states: Obama came out for gay marriage this summer because Axelrod knows Romney is so badly compromised on the issue, he can be gutted on it in the swing states if he tries to leverage it – a bit like the Bob Dole ticket, with a personal history of adultery, being unable to leverage the "character issue" against Bill Clinton in 1996.

POTUS SWING STATE	ELECTORAL COLLEGE VOTES	SENATE SWING STATE?	PRO HETERO-MONOGAMY? GAY MARRIAGE REJECTED?	STOP ROMinee MESSAGING YET?	STOP ROMinee MESSAGING PENDING?
FL	29	YES	Y- By Voters -2008		YES
PA	20	DEM HARD	Y-By Legislature	YES	YES
OH	18	YES	Y- By Voters - 2004	YES	YES
MI	16	YES	Y- By Voters - 2004	YES	YES
NC	15		Y-By Legislature	YES	YES
VA	13	YES	Y- By Voters -2006		YES
IN	11	YES	Y-By Legislature		YES
AZ	11	YES	Y- By Voters - 2008	YES	YES
WI	10	YES	Y- By Voters -2006	YES	YES
MO	10	YES	Y- By Voters - 200X	YES	YES
CO	9		Y- By Voters - 2006	YES	YES
IA	6	SUPREME RET	3 Justices Ousted - 2010	YES	YES
NV	6	YES	Y- By Voters -2008		YES
NM	5	YES			YES
MT	3	YES	Y- By Voters -2004		YES
15 States	182	13 States	14 States	9 States	15 States

NOTES: Most Presidential swing states are also U.S. Senate swing states, either "toss-ups" or soft "light blue" or "light red" leaners as tracked by Real Clear Politics.[292] In Iowa, where voters ousted three state supreme court justices in 2010 retention elections for imposing gay marriage on the citizenry, there is no Senate contest, but another of the pro-GLBT justices is up. Columns on the right indicate actual and pending states for messaging that makes clear Romney's role as the Founding Father of U.S. Gay Marriage.[293]

[290] Tangibly green and legal "goodwill bribes" from the Romney camp are one thing, but for all Judeo-Christian *Manhattan Declaration* signatories who would trade their credibility or their souls for the latter, we say: *Joseph Smith's visions and polytheistic claims may be more likely than a Romney Presidency.*

[291] Open letter critiques of Romney's Leftist statism on sexuality and other issues list a former Massachusetts assistant U.S. attorney, law professors, a state judge and lawmaker, clerics, independent scholars, lawyers, physicians, activists and media professionals among Romney's detractors. have dogged him for years, public policy scandals which none of Romney's recent underfunded opponenta have effectively exploited (but which will not pose a resource problem for undermining him in the swing states this fall if he is nominated in Tampa): "An Open Letter to Mitt Romney," (http://theinteramerican.org/blogs/law-and-government/324-letter-to-governor-romney-by-john-haskins.html), ""An Open Letter to Rush Limbaugh"(http://www.rushtellthetruth.blogspot.com/);"A Warning to the 'Conservative Elites' about Mitt Romney" (http://theinteramerican.org/commentary/322-a-stern-warning-to-the-qconservative-elitesq-about-mitt-romney.html)

[292] See http://www.realclearpolitics.com/epolls/2012/president/2012_elections_electoral_college_map_no_toss_ups.html; ; http://www.realclearpolitics.com/epolls/2012/president/2012_elections_electoral_college_map.html; http://www.realclearpolitics.com/epolls/2012/senate/2012_elections_senate_map.html

[293] See page 70 and forward.

By nominating a true pro-family conservative at Tampa, however, everything changes. Not only is it politically necessary to reject Romney for **A BETTER NOMINEE AT TAMPA** (as a reasonable response to the man's racist religion alone); the table above also underscores why a pro-growth, pro-defense GOP nominee *who happens to eschew gay marriage and the GLBT agenda as a function of compassion, conviction and good science* should be able beat an incumbent who expressly supports SSM/SSS.

As such, crucial swing voters – including those in traditional Bible Belt areas – will choose between a devil they know and a beguiling GOP nominee who now *says* he's against gay marriage, yet who clearly brought it about, and most of the GLBT Agenda, in the state he governed.

Armed with the truth, therefore, we aim to encourage all Tampa delegates to **ABSTAIN ON THE FIRST BALLOT IN FAVOR OF A NEW NAME** whom *they* choose on Second-Ballot or later consideration in an Open Republican National Convention. By such lawful and rules-based means, genuinely *republican* RNC delegates can select a courageous and principled pro-Liberty champion, a seasoned and battle-tested David, who will have at least a shot at felling the giant statist who now occupies the White House.

If all our "DUMP ROMNEY" pleas to Tampa's delegates go ignored, however, the appalling facts on Romney's record, current statist stands and *his racist, anti-Jewish, anti-Christian sci-fi religion* will inevitably become clear to POTUS and Senate swing-state voters – and President Obama will almost certainly re-elected.[294]

Can we really Dump Romney?

There will be 2,286 Republican delegates at Tampa.

If he is to do what his Prophet Joseph Smith was unable to do in his Presidential campaign of 1844 – become the USA's first polytheist President – then Mitt Romney will need at least 1,144 delegates to submit to him with their votes on the first ballot.

However, anti-Romney voting this year for Ron Paul, Rick Santorum and Newt Gingrich, along with delegates unlinked to Romney, makes it quite possible that their combined numbers (between 750 and 1,800, depending on the counting methodology) can ally with a modest number of emancipated Romney "Harem Delegates" (who realize they are entirely unbound, that they are free by Republican Party Rules to prudently and conscientiously abstain from corrupting themselves as one of Romney's 1,144) so as to deny Romney a first-ballot win.

Meanwhile, every Tampa delegate who is RINO, pro-GLBT, pro-abortion, pro-CO2 regulation, pro-RomneyCare, pro-ObamaCare, from Massachusetts, from Utah, a Mormon or some other kind of "Rombot" will be working furiously to deny Second-Ballot consideration of all other Presidential possibilities besides Mitt Romney. Should Tampa's first ballot go by without Romney's nomination, support for Romney will evaporate like a puddle of water in the Utah desert on a hot August day.

Rightly fearful of that, these "Harem Delegates" and others within the Romney-bought GOP Establishment can be expected to desperately fib, lie, threaten, extort, cheat, bully and bribe – like LDS Mormon leaders of yore – to induce other delegates to surrender their minds, and their small-r *republican duty* to exercise conscientious judgment rather than robotically do what they're commanded at Tampa.

Everyone knows that were solid Republicans who did not feel they had the financial firepower to compete with Mitt Romney's millions in the 2012 GOP Presidential Primaries. Vastly better leaders like Mitch Daniels, Bobby Jindal, Tom Coburn, Mike Huckabee, Jim DeMint, Chris Christie, Allen West, Peter Pace, Jerry Boykin, Duncan Hunter, John Boehner, Bob McDonnell, John Kasich, Scott Walker, Paul Ryan, Marco Rubio, Josh Mandel, Jim Inhofe, Jeff Sessions, Pat Roberts, Sarah Palin, Rob Portman, Todd Akin and dozens more demurred… while others like Ron Paul, Tim Pawlenty, Michele Bachmann, Rick Santorum, Rick Perry, Newt Gingrich and Herman Cain gave it their best.

---

[294] Of course, some swing-state voters will acquiesce to a Romney-led GOP ticket just as some did in the losing Bush '92, Dole '96 and McCain '08 campaigns. The GOP tickets of '92, '96 and '08 carried enough heavy public policy baggage (e.g., broken tax pledges, RINO spending, half-hearted social conservatism, etc.) and personal character baggage (e.g., infidelity, hot tempers, etc.) to flatten-out all GOP electoral fervor and sufficiently explain the Democrat margins of victory. The GOP's putative Massachusetts Messiah, however, *is much further* left of Bush I, Dole and McCain on public policy; his character infidelities (to constitutionalism, to hetero-monogamy, to the sanctity of human life, to basic political and religious liberties) are legion. On policy grounds alone, and without reference to the eccentricities of Mormonism, we would urge thinking RNC delegates to abstain from Romney on the First Ballot and thereby throw open the convention to another, saner 2012 nominee. .

But, Romney is not entitled to the GOP nomination because he is worth millions, because he spent millions, or because prominent pro-GLBT activists like Paul Singer[295] have spent millions on him. Because 100% of Tampa's delegates are in fact totally unbound by Republican National Committee Rules to any delegate and vote their consciences on the First Ballot, it remains fully possible, and indeed our moral imperative:

TO DRAFT A PRESIDENTIAL TICKET LEADER OF TRUE COURAGE, SACRIFICE AND PRINCIPLE – A PRO-GROWTH, PRO-LIBERTY, PRO-FAMILY, LIMITED-GOV CONSTITUTIONALIST – TO BE THE 2012 REPUBLICAN PRESIDENTIAL NOMINEE.

HE (OR SHE) WOULD IDEALLY BE A RELUCTANT CINCINATTUS, ONE WHO UNDERSTANDS OUR ENEMIES, HAS DEFENDED AMERICAN LIVES AND WORN THE UNIFORM OF THE UNITED STATES MILITARY; ONE WHO KNOWS DIRECTLY THE HORRORS OF WAR, WHO NEED PROVE NOTHING ABOUT HIS OWN MANHOOD THROUGH WARMONGERING, WHO WILL TREAT ALL U.S. TROOPS AS IF HIS OWN SONS AND WHO WILL NOT COMMIT THEM WITHOUT CONSTITUTIONAL JUSTIFICATION.

HE SHOULD BE ONE WHO, ONLY WITH THE BACKING OF CONGRESS, WANTS TO HELP RID THE WORLD OF MONSTERS LIKE KONY, QADDAFI AND BIN LADEN (AS EVEN PRESIDENT OBAMA HAS BEEN WILLING TO DO) WHILE STANDING STEADFAST BY OUR FRIENDS SUCH AS ISRAEL AND HER DEFENDERS OF JUDEA AND SAMARIA (AS OBAMA HAS MADE CLEAR HE IS UNWILLING TO DO). HE SHOULD BE READY ON DAY ONE – LIKE A GEORGE WASHINGTON, ANDREW JACKSON, ULYSESS GRANT OR DWIGHT EISENHOWER – TO PROTECT ALL OF AMERICA'S CITIZENS AND INTERESTS ON THIS DANGEROUS GLOBE.

Any U.S. leader mentioned above, especially those who competed in the 2012 arena, could be considered for the GOP ticket. But, we believe it rightly should be *led* by a man who has stood in harm's way for Life and Liberty, who would be ready on day one to assume the job of Commander-in-Chief.

> **Mr. Romney doesn't meet that test, nor – as a tragically-duped disciple of Joseph Smith, Brigham Young and their sci-fi polytheism – does he even meet the three most basic tests Tampa delegates could apply for a potential U.S. Presidential nominee: Mental competency, swing-state winnability and a core belief in the absolute, endowing, designing Creator honored in The Declaration of Independence, the Founders' infinite, personal and monotheistic "Supreme Judge of the world."**

As we have seen, Romney believes in many finite gods and, as any LDS Mormon must, he believes – on the testimony of a charlatan named Joseph Smith – that he and his wife can become gods. But Americans do not want or need a finite god, an authoritarian Caesar, to rule over us. One such hubris-filled aspirant – Barack Obama – is enough. Rather, we need a humble man, a willing and liberty-loving servant who, with the Founders, acknowledges "the Laws of Nature and of Nature's God."

Here's why it's not too late for the Republican Party to nominate such a person:

- **RNC delegates are NOT bound by a suicide pact.** This will make it clear: If facts emerged on August 15 showing Romney (or any potential nominee) to be a wife-beater, shoplifter, cross-dresser, inside trader, exhibitionist, pornographer, suicidal, terminally ill, a pedophile or a kooky cult member… it obviously wouldn't matter how many so-called "bound" delegates he has accrued so far; wise and responsible Republican National Convention delegates, out of principle and political pragmatism, *would inevitably choose to nominate someone better.* Thus, if Romney has no real lock on the nomination lock for such sensational circumstances, he has no real lock on the nomination at all.

- **Romney *is* a member of a kooky cult – a Missionary, Priest, President and Bishop** in an historic sex cult rife with pedophilia, racism, anti-Semitism, adultery, polygamy, homoeroticism and sci-fi weirdness from the very start. Would Tampa's delegates ever, in their wildest dreams, anoint an authoritarian cult leader like Joseph Smith, Brigham Young, Jim Jones, David Koresh, Charles Manson or L. Ron Hubbard to be their nominee for the Presidency?

---

[295] Romney supporter Paul E. Singer, the billionaire head of Elliot Management, has a homosexual son who was married in Massachusetts pursuant to Romney's inauguration of gay marriage in Massachusetts. Frank Bruni, "The GOP's Gay Trajectory", *The New York Times,* June 6, 2012 (http://www.nytimes.com/2012/06/10/opinion/sunday/the-gops-gay-trajectory.html?pagewanted=all).

If not, then how can they nominate the duped disciple of such a man? How can they nominate a gullible, duplicitous and brainwashed *clerical leader* of such a cult? As we have seen, Romney is indeed the disciple of manipulative, polytheistic charlatans. No Tampa delegate needs to become an expert in Mormonism, nor take a position on every one of its exotic dogmas, in order to see one thing clearly:

> When the pro-Obama media enlightens swing-state voters on Mormonism this fall, Romney – if we foolishly nominate him at the end of August – would epitomize our collective abandonment of Judeo-Christian monotheism were he to win, yet is all but certain for defeat: Even now, before everything hits the fan, Romney is *already* losing the Electoral College in a rout which threatens GOP Senate prospects in the overlapping swing states.[296]

- **RNC Rules allow 100% of Tampa's delegates to "Conscientiously Abstain" on the crucial First Ballot.** Any and all mindlessly-loyal "Rombots" or "Harem Delegates" will want to skip this section; it requires some analytical capacity and thought. For the vast majority of the GOP's 2012 Tampa delegates, however, what follows will offers decisive guidance on their **Delegate's Right to Abstain** on the First Ballot.

> On November 25, we co-authored a ***Politico* commentary** called "A rogue convention? How GOP party rules may surprise in 2012" that struck a chord with many readers. Those highlighting or responding to our piece include the **Washington Post's The Fix** (calling it a "must read"), **Andrew Sullivan's The Dish** in "The Daily Beast", the influential conservative website **Hot Air**, **Election Law blog**, **Ballot Access News**, and political analyst **Michael Barone**. You can read a torrent of comments about the piece at some of these links. We also have had reactions directly from representatives and members of the RNC.
>
> Our piece focuses on the Republican National Committee rules governing how delegates are chosen for the Republican national convention next August and what those delegates are bound to do – and not do -- at the convention....While not predicting a "brokered convention," we explain the legal and political arguments for why it might happen. The combination of Rule 38, widespread use of winner-take-all primaries, and a Republican electorate that to date is not thrilled with its announced presidential candidates may invite a convention challenge.
>
> Some critics, like Barone, have claimed that we misread Rule 38's prohibition against what's called "the unit rule," but in fact they misunderstand our point. Barone say we have it wrong that the unit rule ban doesn't allow state parties to use winner-take-all primaries in which the plurality winner of a state earns all that state's delegates. But we aren't claiming that the rule prevents winner-take-all primaries (at least after April 1st, as the party in 2010 did vote to prohibit winner-take-all primaries before April 1st except in the four states given special rights: Iowa, Nevada, New Hampshire and, the one state using a winner-take-all primary, South Carolina).
>
> **Rather, we explain that the RNC rules' provision on the unit rule make it clear that delegates aren't bound to vote according to how most delegates from their state are voting. In fact, delegates can vote according to their own judgment and conscience,** and that this is most likely to take place in a state where a state party's winner-take-all rule has allowed a candidate to win all delegates primarily due to a split in the majority vote, or due to votes cast by non-Republican voters participating in the contest.
>
> To explain our case, we look to the language of Rule 38, which was adopted in its current form in 1964. The rule states: "no delegate shall be bound by any attempt of any state or Congressional district to impose the unit rule." The unit rule does not prohibit a state from using a winner-take-all primary in the same way that Rule 15(b) prohibits most states from using a winner-take-all primary when holding a contest earlier than April 1st. **However, the unit rule does prohibit binding delegates to vote according to how a majority of delegates from their state vote – again, a scenario most likely to occur in a state using the winner-take-all rule.**
>
> As set out in the **Rules of the Republican Party**, delegates have the ability to vote according to the delegates' preference, even if that is contrary to the outcome of each state's primary. According to **one source, the legal counsel for the Republican National Convention in 2008 stated: "[The] RNC does not recognize a state's binding of national delegates, but considers each delegate a free agent who can vote for whoever they choose." Thus, if a delegate were to challenge his or her ability to vote as a free agent, he or she would have grounds under Rule 38.**

---

[296] Seehttp://www.realclearpolitics.com/epolls/2012/president/2012_elections_electoral_college_map_no_toss_ups.html; http://www.realclearpolitics.com/epolls/2012/president/2012_elections_electoral_college_map.html; http://www.realclearpolitics.com/epolls/2012/senate/2012_elections_senate_map.html; Nate Silver's forecast/now-cast at http://fivethirtyeight.blogs.nytimes.com/.

For further clarification on the meaning of Rule 38, it is instructive to look to the debate in 1964 when the RNC debated whether to strike the Rule 38 language from a proposed amendment that was adopted that year. The debate begins on page 64 of **this source. The RNC voted 59 to 41 to keep the rule in the amendment, noting that it helped to clarify a longstanding practice that a delegate was free to take exception to the roll call, and was free to vote his or her preference. Those who sought to strike the rule feared that its inclusion in the rules would give delegates freedom from both a non-existent legal obligation and a moral obligation to vote according to instructions from their state. However, even these opponents of the rule admitted that there never has been any legal obligation for a delegate to do so.**

The contrast between the actual Republican Party rules governing its convention and most people's understanding of the role of the primaries underscores the way that the party system has changed rapidly in today's modern era. Many of the RNC rules come from a time when conventions chose nominees and the party was a meaningful institution, representing an association of individuals coming together, articulating platform positions, and choosing candidates to stand for those positions.

With that understanding, the rules governing a party are those of a private group, not a government entity. A private group should have the right to nominate candidates however it wants, which is a fact that some analysts like Barone seem to have difficulty grasping, Last March, for example, Barone went so far as to criticize current nomination grounds under the bizarre pretext that the U.S. Constitution doesn't spell out what parties should do. He wrote, "The weakest part of our political system is the presidential-nomination process. And it's not coincidental that it's the part of the federal system that finds least guidance in the Constitution." Not only does the Constitution leave electoral rules quite vague - with nothing on how U.S House Members should be chosen beyond the fact of being elected, for example, and nothing whatsoever on how states must pick electors to the Electoral College -- but it would be strange indeed for the Constitution to mandate how private associations should pick their leaders.

Even though it certainly matters today whether a presidential candidate is a Republican or Democrat, parties are less meaningful as associations and much more important as "brands" in an electoral politics driven by consultants, big money, and, the one upside, more voters. **To many in the major parties, party conventions now are essentially showcases for candidates determined before the convention**.

In this atmosphere, selection of candidates can take place in a winner-take-all manner because candidates and their backers do not care if elected delegates accurately reflect the differences of opinion among Republican voters. When conventions don't really matter, state parties can blithely dismiss the impact of RNC penalties like losing half their delegates due to advancing the date of their primary, as is the case for several states .... [However,] **We believe that this difference between the letter of the rules and the way they have come to be interpreted could lead to some surprises in 2012.**[297]

- **Republican Delegates' Right of Conscience,** their conscientious-objector Right to Abstain from voting for Mitt Romney on the First Ballot, is further underscored by this responsive legal commentary:

To buttress your points, please note the following:

1. Rule 29 (a) clearly states that "Each delegate to the convention shall be entitled to one (1) vote ..." This provision, which may seem self-evident, establishes from a practical point of view, that NOTHING, not even a state rule supposedly binding the delegate, can prevent the delegate from voting his or her conscience, since he or she is clearly "entitled", ie. has a RIGHT, under Rule 29(a) to his or her vote, otherwise that right is meaningless.

2. Rule 37(b) provides that in the balloting by state delegations, the chairman of each state delegation announces the delegation's vote counts for each candidate, BUT that if any delegate takes exception to the correctness of the delegate count, "the chairman of the convention shall direct the roll of members of such delegation to be called, and the result shall be recorded in accordance with the vote of the several delegates in such delegation". In otherwords, EVERY delegate has a vote, and no one can speak for or cast that vote for him at the national convention.[298]

- **Even on the plainly false notion that Tampa delegates would be otherwise "bound" to vote for Romney on the First Ballot,** the preceding legal commentator notes that:

Rule 11(a) provides that "The Republican National Committee shall not, without the prior written and filed approval of all members of the Republican National Committee from the state involved,

---

[297] Rob Richie, Elise Helgesen, "Response to "A Rogue Convention?" (http://www.fairvote.org/response-to-a-rogue-convention-how-gop-party-rules-may-surprise-in-201).
[298] Responsive legal commentary to Rob Richie, Elise Helgesen, "Response to "A Rogue Convention?" (http://www.fairvote.org/response-to-a-rogue-convention-how-gop-party-rules-may-surprise-in-201), just below the main article.

contribute money or in-kind aid to any candidate ... except the nominee of the Republican Party or a candidate who is unopposed the the Republican primary after thefiling deadline for that office." Rule 11(b) provides that "No person nominated by the Republican National Committee in violation of this rule shall be recognized by the Republican National Committee as the nominee of the Republican Party from that state." Amazingly, the Romney Campaign has been advertising online a "joint fundraising committee with the Republican National Committee", namely Romney Victory, Inc., which includes Romney for President, Inc., the RNC and several state and national Republican committees. Clearly the RNC has authorized and/or at permitted the online, nationwide disseminaton of this advertising, which clear supports and endorses Romney. This advertising and endorsement, supported and paid for in part by the RNC, constitutes "in-kind aid" as defined by FEC rules, that is prohibited by Rule 11.

Since Romney's nomination should not recognized in those states in which Rule 11 has been violated by the RNC (and of course, also by his committees), possible a majority of states, and since delegates, even if otherwise bound by state rules, should not be required and in fact should be prohibited from voting for a nominee who is ineligible under the rules, each delegate is now armed with further justification and right to vote for a candidate other than Romney. Ron Paul and other delegates, even including Romney delegates, should avoid voting for an ineligible candidate and clearly one whose candidacy has received an unfair boost from the RNC. Delegates also have solid ground to contest the validity of ANY state delegation that received Romney aid in violation of Rule 11.[299]

- **Entirely apart from RNC Rules and state claims, Federal law seems to protect the right of every Tampa delegate to abstain from Romney on the First Ballot.**

  In more recent discoveries, they have found that 42 USC § 1971 - Voting Rights[300] supports the claim that voters cannot be forced by anyone to vote for any candidate he or she does not favor.

  > **"No person, whether acting under color of law or otherwise, shall intimidate, threaten, coerce, or attempt to intimidate, threaten, or coerce any other person for the purpose of interfering with the right of such other person to vote or to vote as he may choose, or of causing such other person to vote for, or not to vote for, any candidate for the office of President, Vice President, presidential elector, Member of the Senate, or Member of the House of Representatives, Delegates or Commissioners from the Territories or possessions, at any general, special, or primary election held solely or in part for the purpose of selecting or electing any such candidate."** - 42 USC § 1971 - Voting Rights.

  The response from the rest of the Republican Party was that this does not account for conventions or nominations. However, this latest finding will trump that claim. 11 CFR 100.2 - Election (2 U.S.C. 431(1))[301] clearly states that:

  > **"Caucus or Convention. A caucus or convention of a political party is an election if the caucus or convention has the authority to select a nominee for federal office on behalf of that party."** - 11 CFR 100.2 - Election (2 U.S.C. 431(1)).

  Federal law has the ability to trump all state laws as well as party rules.... For a video interpretation, click on this link: http://www.youtube.com/watch?v=GiEbNncoSG0&feature=plcp

- **Even on the error that RNC delegates are "bound" against abstaining on the First Ballot, RNC delegates *can* vote to suspend the rules.** Just as Romney's lawless forces demand that RNC rules be set aside to give him winner-take-all numbers from Florida and Arizona, so responsible RNC delegates can vote to set aside any rule which might *seem* to require collective GOP suicide in the Presidential and Senate swing states.

- **Even on the falsehood that some Tampa delegates are "bound" against abstaining on First Ballot,** former Santorum strategist John Yob wrote on April 5:

  > There are a couple of fundamental flaws with the delegate counts that the media keeps that reveals that this race is much closer than they report: .... Florida, Arizona, and quite possibly Puerto Rico will be proportional rather than Winner Take All. They broke RNC rules by going winner take all before the window and therefore RNC Members

[299] Responsive legal commentary to Rob Richie, Elise Helgesen, "Response to "A Rogue Convention?" (http://www.fairvote.org/response-to-a-rogue-convention-how-gop-party-rules-may-surprise-in-201), just below the main article.
[300] http://www.law.cornell.edu/uscode/text/42/1971
[301] http://cfr.vlex.com/vid/100-2-election-431-1-19624312

and/or the convention [could] enforce the rules and make the delegations proportional. This will reduce Romney's delegate total substantially and increase the other three candidates' respective delegate totals.... Unbound delegates – The media continues to put unbound delegates in their counts in the territories and other states. These folks can change their mind, or have yet to make up their mind, and should not be counted as if they are bound.

RNC action to enforce its own rules for Florida and Arizona, in other words, would reduce Romney's inflated count of "leaner" delegates who are, in fact, unbound on the first ballot. Strictly speaking, 100% of all Tampa delegates are unbound. An RNC National Committeeman explains here, furthermore, why Romney can have no certainty even about his unbound Florida and Arizona "leaners."[302]

- **RNC delegates have asserted themselves in previous Open Conventions:** For example, "During the 1920 Republican Convention in Chicago, Maj. Gen. Leonard Wood won a plurality of the vote on the first ballot, while Sen. Warren Harding came in a distant sixth place. Over the course of the next 10 ballots, Wood's support rose and then fell, while Harding methodically accumulated a larger and larger percentage of the vote until he finally achieved a majority to become the GOP nominee and, ultimately, the 29th president of the United States." [303]

- **The very definition of a "small-r republican"** requires that Republican National Convention delegates exercise their own sober judgment on behalf of fellow citizens who have sent them as their elected representatives to Tampa. As adverse facts on Romney *are freshly recognized* by GOP delegates, *each delegate has an ethical duty* to soberly exercise his individual, *republican* judgment concerning said facts and how they are likely to adversely impact November, their party, and their nation. Living up to their party's proud name, for example, most Republican Congressmen and Senators *do not and should not* robotically mime ill-conceived or mobocratic demands of their constituencies on Capitol Hill – and neither should elected RNC delegates do so at Tampa.

- **The Party of Lincoln should not reward Romney's RINO lawlessness and thuggery.** As America's Founding Father of Gay Marriage, as a function of documented cheating by his "Mormon Mafia" and GOP Establishment forces on GOP delegate selection, and in his religiously-based, ends-justify-means lying, Mitt Romney is toxic to the Republican Party's brand; for those reasons alone, he should not be rewarded with the 2012 Republican nomination.

- **An Open Republican Convention at Tampa – in which patriotic delegates boldly reject the foregone conclusion by the Associated Press and the rest of the media that Romney is the inevitable GOP Nominee – would be reviving for the Republican Party and our Nation.** From *The American Spectator*, "if no candidate enters a convention with majority support [it would be] a contested, open convention. This would be a good thing for the party. First, the drama would be riveting. The convention would actually mean something rather than being a mere propaganda vehicle....The public would see 'ordinary Americans' making the momentous decision about who should be the nominee seeking the post powerful position in the world. The resulting impression would be a very good one for the party and the eventual nominee. ... The nominee who emerges from a contested convention could thus do so with a huge surge of momentum to take the fight to Barack Obama in the fall." [304]

Conclusion: American Monotheism, Monogamy and Survival

We believe that American monotheism – the Judeo-Christian Natural Law faith of our Founders in a benevolent, endowing and designing Creator as expressed in The Declaration of Independence – is essential to the survival of this great Republic. It is the bedrock beneath the First Amendment, the metaphysical premise upon which all our liberties stand.

We believe that hetero-monogamy – the American Institution of Marriage between one man and one woman for the good of children and unborn American generations – should be U.S. public policy, to the exclusion of same-sex, polygamous, pedogamous, zoogamous or other imagined forms of wedlock. Its formal abandonment, as President Obama seeks and as Mitt Romney has so obsequiously facilitated, would constitute a bright-line demarcation of our nation's leap into multiverse materialism, polytheistic paganism, or both.

---

[302] http://www.redstate.com/morton_c_blackwell/2012/03/19/delegates/

[303] http://www.realclearpolitics.com/articles/2012/03/15/how_gingrichs_candidacy_could_help_santorum__113488-2.html. Ironically, Romney's vacuity is much like that of Harding, regarded as one of our worst US presidents; we are arguing herein for dutiful GOP delegates to displace him, ideally with AN ENTIRELY NEW NAME OF STATURE tied to military service and sacrifice, as was that of forsaken Maj. Gen. Wood.

[304] http://spectator.org/archives/2012/04/02/this-race-is-far-from-over/1

We believe that Romney – hostile to American monotheism and hetero-monogamy either as a matter of his public record or his lifetime clerical role a priest, missionary, stake president and Bishop of an intolerant, authoritarian and polytheistic sex cult – would be disastrous for the nation, the Republican Party and its brand were he somehow to win... but that the writing's already on the wall, and indelibly etched into the swing states and the Electoral College, that he will lose.

We believe fear and ignorance are the *only* reasons that any faithful Jew, Christian or Republican delegate is even *considering* supporting Romney on the first Tampa ballot: Fear that there's no courageous "David" within the GOP with the stones to take on the (pro-Palestinian) Philistine who occupies the West Wing of the White House;[305] fear that House and Senate Republicans are too wimpy to play hardball with Obama if he wins another term; ignorance of the fact that no GOP delegate is bound to back Romney; and ignorance that each and every "small-r" *republican* representing the GOP in Tampa has **A REPUBLICAN RIGHT TO EXERCISE PERSONAL JUDGMENT, TO VOTE HIS OR HER CONSCIENCE AND TO CONSCIENTIOUSLY ABSTAIN FROM BACKING ROMNEY ON THE CRUCIAL FIRST BALLOT.**

Finally, because a Romney nomination would defy so many *Manhattan Declaration* principles and so certainly assure Republican defeat this November, it is our united, ecumenical intent to detail, in a National Press Club news conference prior to October: Our Coalitional Plan, already under execution on a seven-figure budget (which we seek to grow into 8-9 figures for more visible TV-radio purposes), to direct millions of fact-based robo-calls, emails, texts and other forms of messaging – including earned media via our Speakers Bureau Invitees – so as to thoroughly expose Romney's record, integrity issues, character issues, his polytheism and his hostility to hetero-monogamy.[306]

To help prevent Jewish and Christian flocks from being misled by bad shepherding (as a function of the religious or Republican credentialing of false guides), allied forces are pushing a rich array of Bible studies and small group teaching materials on Mormon polytheism.[307]

Also, another truth-telling document and movement has recently emerged, "For the Sake of the Gospel":[308] Launched by evangelical theologians and apologists such as Norman Geisler, R.C. Sproul, John Ankerberg, Kerby Anderson and ex-Mormons, their purpose, in line with ours, is to implore the USA's Christian leadership to explain to their masses that Romney's Mormonism is indeed a racist, anti-Semite and anti-Christian cult. They plead with evangelical shepherds down to local pastors, to

> **[Be] "clearly and unequivocally distancing yourself and Biblical Christianity from [Romney's] Mormon beliefs.... the general population should not be left with any uncertainty whether the theological cult of which Mitt Romney is a faithful member, namely The Church of Jesus Christ of Latter-day Saints (Mormons), and historic evangelical Christianity are one and the same faith. This we adamantly deny!.... Since its inception in the 19th century, The Church of Jesus Christ of Latter Day Saints has deceptively labeled itself a "Christian" church. Its leaders used the historical accounts and key figures found in the Bible, but they ignore or contradict the Bible's central theology.... Mormonism is not only "unbiblical," regarding most of the essential truths that make up the Gospel of Jesus Christ, but, as stated previously, it is profoundly "anti-Christian."**

In solidarity with the courageous souls of that movement, behind *The Manhattan Declaration,* and behind the aforementioned Presidential pledge documents, the Jews and Christians Together coalition to **"DUMP ROMNEY"** intends to communicate with the pastors, priests and rabbis of every Jewish, Catholic, Orthodox, Protestant and Evangelical Christian congregation in the nation, especially those in the 15 POTUS and Senate swing states listed above.

---

[305] For inspiration, any such potential GOP champion might wish to read I Samuel 17, especially verse 26: *"Who is this uncircumcised Philistine that he should defy the armies of the living God?"*

[306] For any GOP delegates who imagine Romney's Tampa coronation to be an inevitable and good thing, all of our coalitional "DUMP ROMNEY" efforts could be considered usefully inoculatory in Presidential and Senate swing states: Since the media will find clever ways to enlighten the toss-up states on Romney's record and eccentric religious beliefs, it's arguably much better that it all come out sooner rather than later. Our central aim, however, is even more emphatically constructive: To DUMP ROMNEY in an open Tampa convention which, instead, nominates a genuine *republican* standard bearer for more likely victory in the POTUS and Senate swing states.

[307] Examples: Exposé of Mormonism - Blue Letter Bible - Study Tools (www.blueletterbible.org/study/cults/exposem/);Mormon Bible Studies - Life After Ministries for LDS Church (www.lifeafter.org/studies.asp); Tips for Witnessing to Mormons (www.contenderministries.org/mormonism/witnesstips.php); Ask Catholics What We Believe: Mormonism vs. Catholicism (catholicseries.blogspot.com/2009/05/this-is-open-blog_10.html);Mormonism,Latter Day Saints, and the Bible - The Gospel Way (www.gospelway.com/religiousgroups/mormonism.php);Mormonism - Bible Study Tools (www.biblestudytools.com/commentaries/.../related.../mormonism.html); Is Mormonism considered a "false teaching"? | Bible.org - Worlds ...(bible.org/question/mormonism-considered-"false-teaching"); Mormonism - Bible Study Lesson - THE GOSPEL OF CHRIST (www.thegospelofchrist.com/transcripts/.../add_04_mormonism.html); Mormon View of the Bible | Why Mormonism (whymormonism.org/31/bible);Mormonism, LDS, Church of Jesus Christ of Latter-day saints ... (carm.org/Mormonism); A Biblical Response to Mormons|The Bible and Mormonism ...(carm.org/biblical-response-to-mormons);Mormonism - Bible-Study-Lessons.com (www.bible-study-lessons.com/Mormonism.html); The Mormon Cult: Yes, Mormons Are a Cult, By Definition - Just Like ...(mormoncult.org/);The Plain Truth about the Mormons (www.biblebelievers.com/jmelton/Mormons.html); The truth about the LDS Mormon Cult (www.angelfire.com/az2/arizonadry/davidwhitmer.html)

[308] See "Mitt Romney, Mormonism and the Christian Vote: A Biblical Call to Christian Ministers and Leaders," (http://forthesakeofthegospel.com/document/)

Furthermore and to every extent budget allows, we intend to deploy participating **Speakers Bureau Invitees**[309] (see the Appendix which follows) to speak before media and live audiences in said swing states. This is an expanding list of prominent figures who know full well – or by now ought to know – what Romney is all about, and why the Republican Party's 100% unbound delegates have a *solemn duty* to abstain from supporting him on the First Ballot.

Finally – and in keeping with a fashionable, essentially pagan Obama/Romney sexual confusion which refuses to discriminate between innate Creator-endowed traits like race versus resistible disorders and behaviors like homosexuality, pedophila and polyamory – we hereby refuse to discriminate between pro-monotheist support from the Right (e.g., Judeo-Christian conservatives, Natural Law libertarians, industrial interests, etc.) and funds from elsewhere which also may be offered to help expose Romney's Mormon racism, anti-Semitism and authoritarian, sci-fi polytheism before it's too late: To fulfill the mission we've defined herein, we intend to accept support from any domestic source, anonymous or disclosed.

All gifts (whether identified contributions, anonymous wires or unidentifiable cashier's checks) will be treated in the same way – agnostically – with regard to our efforts to help "DUMP ROMNEY."

BANK WIRING/DEPOSIT INSTRUCTIONS:

- **By wire:** **Jews and Christians Together -- "DUMP ROMNEY"**
  ABA Routing Number: 026009593
  Account Number: 0758570749

  Bank of America – CAO1380101
  330 S. Santa Fe Avenue
  Vista, California 92084

  Phone: 760-643-2152

- **By mail:** **Jews and Christians Together -- "DUMP ROMNEY"**
  PO Box 1115
  Vista, CA 92085

To President Obama and Gov. Romney: As Christian signatories to *The Manhattan Declaration*, as Jewish affirmers of that within it which is consistent with Judaism, or as American monotheists who stand in solidarity with its core pro-Life, pro-Marriage and pro-First Amendment Religious Liberty aims,

> [W]e take seriously the Biblical admonition to respect and obey those in authority. We believe in law and in the rule of law. We recognize the duty to comply with laws whether we happen to like them or not, unless the laws are gravely unjust or require those subject to them to do something unjust or otherwise immoral. The biblical purpose of law is to preserve order and serve justice and the common good; yet laws that are unjust—and especially laws that purport to compel citizens to do what is unjust—undermine the common good, rather than serve it.
>
> Going back to the earliest days of the church, Christians have refused to compromise their proclamation of the gospel. In Acts 4, Peter and John were ordered to stop preaching. Their answer was, "Judge for yourselves whether it is right in God's sight to obey you rather than God. For we cannot help speaking about what we have seen and heard." Through the centuries, Christianity has taught that civil disobedience is not only permitted, but sometimes required. There is no more eloquent defense of the rights and duties of religious conscience than the one offered by Martin Luther King, Jr., in his Letter from a Birmingham Jail. Writing from an explicitly Christian perspective, and citing Christian writers such as Augustine and Aquinas, King taught that just laws elevate and ennoble human beings because they are rooted in the moral law whose ultimate source is God Himself. Unjust laws degrade human beings. Inasmuch as they can claim no authority beyond sheer human will, they lack any power to bind in conscience. King's willingness to go to jail, rather than comply with legal injustice, was exemplary and inspiring.
>
> Because we honor justice and the common good, we will not comply with any edict that purports to compel our institutions to participate in abortions, embryo-destructive research, assisted suicide and euthanasia, or any other anti-

[309] See Appendix.

> life act; nor will we bend to any rule purporting to force us to bless immoral sexual partnerships, treat them as marriages or the equivalent, or refrain from proclaiming the truth, as we know it, about morality and immorality and marriage and the family. We will fully and ungrudgingly render to Caesar what is Caesar's. But under no circumstances will we render to Caesar what is God's.[310]

Yet, as if to fulfill Mormonism's weird White Horse Prophecy,[311] Tampa's entirely-unbound GOP delegates stand on the verge of nominating a man who believes, as did the Caesars, that he is on the way to his own exaltation and godhood.

That kind of silliness may play in Gov. Moonbeam's California, or in Barney Frank's Massachusetts, or even in GOP Utah.But, it won't play in the swing states.

And so, by now it should be clear:

Tampa's delegates have a solemn responsibility to conscientiously abstain from Romney on the crucial First Ballot, to dump him in Tampa.

And – for the sake of our Republic and all we cherish – to nominate a David.

[310] http://www.manhattandeclaration.org/the-movement/movement.aspx

[311] Diane Tanner, "Joseph Smith's 'White Horse' Prophecy,"(http://www.utlm.org/onlineresources/whitehorseprophecy.htm); Sally Denton, "Romney and the White Horse Prophecy" (http://www.salon.com/2012/01/29/mitt_and_the_white_horse_prophecy/).

DUMP ROMNEY

Why Tampa's Republican Delegates must Dump Romney to Defeat Obama

Swing-State Speakers Bureau Invitees

Any consenting invitee among the religious, intellectual, activist, delegate or Republican leaders listed below (as well as interested additions possibly to be included) may be booked by our public relations professionals for TV, radio or other speaking venues impacting GOP delegates or the 2012 Swing States.[312] Communications objectives can include any topic discussed in the text above, including:

Distancing the GOP from the racially-toxic and anti-Semitic texts to which Romney is tied and has yet to repudiate; explaining that LDS Mormonism holds all other religious faiths to be "abominations"; distancing the monotheistic faiths of Judaism, Christianity and the American Founding Fathers from Mitt Romney's polytheism (as pled for at www.forthesakeofthegospel.com); illuminating Romney's record as America's Founding Father of Gay Marriage and the connectivity to Mormonism's historic hostility to hetero-monogamy; revealing the shocking additional content of The Romney Files; conveying how Mormon Bishop Romney himself *is* 2012's Jeremiah Wright; and helping our fellow GOP delegates and swing state voters grasp that Romney is already losing the Electoral College in a rout. Most importantly, invitees who volunteer must be willing and prepared (via the information herein) to help make the case for why **TAMPA'S 100% UNBOUND REPUBLICAN DELEGATES SHOULD ABSTAIN FROM VOTING FOR MITT ROMNEY ON THE FIRST BALLOT** to help ensure the nomination of a viable candidate (another 2012 contender or **AN ENTIRELY NEW NAME**) for the defeat of President Obama in the swing states.[313]

To accept said, to decline, to revise data or to request an addition in connection with the listing below, please write to Sara Bethel (sarabethel586@hotmail.com) or David Bethel (davidbethel70ce@yahoo.com).[314] In an effort to avoid confusion in connection with said listing, it is intended that any invitee who gives notice regarding his/her preference for Romney to receive the 2012 GOP Presidential nomination (rather than for *someone else* to receive it in Tampa)[315] will, as a courtesy, be noted at http://www.JewsandChristiansTogether.org; we emphatically *do not*

---

[312] Although it is assumed for practical purposes that each invitee likely concurs with our core **DUMP ROMNEY** premise – that Tampa's GOP delegates should exercise all their rights and authority to pick a better nominee – no representation whatsoever is herein made that every invitee concurs with every word, phrase, thought or sentiment of this document, nor is any representation herein made concerning anyone's opposition to Mr. Romney (or support for him) in the tragic, completely avoidable event of his Presidential nomination at Tampa. Furthermore, no representation is herein made that any particular listee opposes Romney at this point (summer, 2012) for the GOP nomination. Affiliations are indicated for ID purposes only and no representations are herein made or implied with regard to institutions or organizations; all media bookings will be for individuals in their personal capacities as concerned U.S. citizens, rather than in their institutional or affiliational capacities, pursuant to appropriate consent from each such party to to Sara (sarabethel586@hotmail.com) or David (davidbethel70ce@yahoo.com).

[313] For the very real potential event that Presidential primaries may yield a presumptive nominee discovered to have a fatal political problem – e.g., a history of mental illness, suicide attempts, pedophilia, incest, spousal abuse, bisexuality, Satanism, embezzlement, emailing lewd photographs of himself, involvement in a kooky cult, etc.. – RNC Rules ultimately empower delegates to ABSTAIN or vote their consciences, in entirely unbound fashion, on every ballot – *including, necessarily,* the First Ballot (after which no one contends any delegate is bound). In this manner, the Republican Party sensibly protects both the nation and its brand by upholding "small-r" republicanism; by empowering elected delegates to dutifully exercise their good judgment and wisdom, rather than binding them to "small d" democratic or "mobocratic" election results which can be unduly influenced by money, mass hysteria, misleading advertising, bad journalism, foreign interests, extortion, etc. See www.thereal2012delegatecount.com; "Response to "A Rogue Convention?" (http://www.fairvote.org/response-to-a-rogue-convention-how-gop-party-rules-may-surprise-in-201); "A Rogue Convention? How GOP party rules may surprise in 2012"(http://www.politico.com/news/stories/1111/69048_Page2.html); Reality Check: Republican Delegates "Unbound"? (http://www.youtube.com/watch?v=anWsU93fFsk&feature=relmfu); http://www.examiner.com/article/rnc-delegates-not-bound-to-any-candidate-on-first-ballot. Entirely apart from existing RNC Rules which uphold the right of all Tampa delegates to abstain -- and apart from the fact that any adverse RNC rule can in any case be set aside or revised by the convention itself! -- Federal law also seems to protect the voting rights of Tampa delegates to abstain on the crucial First Ballot: "Federal Law: All Delegates are Unbound" (http://www.examiner.com/article/federal-law-all-delegates-are-unbound); "Federal law proves that all delegates are unbound: All delegates must see this" (http://www.dailypaul.com/237770/federal-law-proves-all-delegates-are-unbound-all-delegates-must-see-this). See page 70 and forward. In any case, it is indisputable that the Republican National Convention has the legal authority to dump Romney at Tampa and choose a more viable nominee.

[314] The editors, whose personal roots extend into California, Massachusetts, Rhode Island, Indiana, Illinois, Arizona and New Jersey, wish to thank each of our contributors. We also wish to thank GOP delegates from those and all 50 states whose patriotism and courage may yet save the USA. It has been our honor to work with all of you. G_d save the America.

[315] Or, who otherwise wishes to decline the invitation herein.

wish to convey that anyone who actually *prefers* Mitt Romney for the GOP nomination and Presidency stands among other faithful American patriots, Jews and Christians together, listed below. Furthermore, no representation of any kind is made herein with regard to the person or persons preferred ahead of Mr. Romney (if any), by anyone listed below, for the Tampa nomination.

- Steve Baldwin, fmr executive director, Council on National Policy (DC); former California State Assemblyman.
- Dr. Gary Cass, president, DefendChristians.org (CA)
- Brian Camenker, president, MassResistance (MA)
- Amy Contrada, author, *Mitt Romney's Deception: His Stealth Promotion of "Gay Rights" and "Gay Marriage" in Massachusetts*
- Tricia Erickson, author, *Can Mitt Romney Serve Two Masters?*
- Rabbi Yehuda Levin, spokesman, Rabbinical Alliance of America (NY); former spokesman,The Union of Orthodox Rabbis of the U.S. and Canada
- Dr. James Dobson, founder, Family Talk Radio and Focus on the Family (CO)
- Dr. Norman Geisler, Theologian
- John Haskins, Parents' Rights Coalition
- Peter LaBarbera, president, Americans for Truth (IL)
- Rev. O'Neill Dozier, pastor, Worldwide Christian Center (FL)
- Dr. Peter Jones, Theologian
- Jason Jones, Iamwholelife.com
- Kerby Anderson, Probe Ministries
- Rabbi Daniel Lapin, founder, Toward Tradition
- Joseph Morris, president, Lincoln Legal Foundation (IL)
- Phyllis Schlafly, president, Eagle Forum (IL-MO)
- Bob Vander Plaats, president, The Family Leader (IA)
- Bishop Harry Jackson (MD)
- Tom Trento, president, The United West (FL)
- Keith Mason, Personhood USA
- Rabbi Joshua Leiman
- Dr. John Ankerberg, host, *The John Ankerberg Show*
- Dr. R.C. Sproul, Jr., Theologian
- Rabbi Isaac Levy, Jews for Morality
- Robert George, Professor, McCormick Professor of Jurisprudence, Princeton University (NJ)
- Troy Newman, president, Operation Rescue and Pro Life Nation (KS)
- Bill Wichterman, former chief of staff, U.S. Sen. Bill Frist (TN)
- Rabbi Nossan Leiter, New York Torah Hotline
- Dr. Allen Unruh, South Dakota Tea Party
- Timothy George, Professor, Beeson Divinity School, Samford University
- Phyllis Schlafly, president, Eagle Forum
- Penny Nance, president, Concerned Women for America
- Beverly LaHaye, chairman, Concerned Women for America
- Sandy Rios, Family PAC Federal
- Paul Caprio, president, Family PAC
- Gary Kreep, Esq., president, United States Justice Foundation
- Robert Knight, a draftsman of the federal Defense of Marriage Act
- Foster Friess, Jackson, WY
- Linda Harvey, Mission America
- Rev. Ted Pike, National Prayer Network
- Randy Thomasson, Campaign for Children and Families
- Dr. Chuck Baldwin, radio host, columnist
- Paul Likoudis, The Wanderer
- Rev. Stephen Bennett, Stephen Bennett Ministries
- Phil Lawler, Catholic World News
- Rev. Scott Lively, Esq., Defend the Family
- Dr. William Greene, RightMarch.com
- Michael Heath, Christian Civic League of Maine
- David E. Smith, Illinois Family Institute
- Gary Glenn, American Family Association of Michigan
- Diane Gramley, American Family Association of Pennsylvania
- Micah Clark, American Family Association of Indiana
- Kevin McCoy, West Virginia Family Foundation
- Stephen Cable, Vermont Center for American Cultural Renewal
- Joe Glover, Family Policy Network (National)
- Terry Moffitt, Family Policy Network of North Carolina
- Marnie Deaton, Family Policy Network of Virginia
- Danny Eason, Family Policy Network of Texas
- Matt Chancey, Family Policy Network of Alabama
- Ron Shank, Family Policy Network of Tennessee
- John R. Diggs, Jr., M.D., leading expert on the medical risks of homosexuality
- Sonja Dalton, Real Civil Rights Illinois
- Allyson Smith, Americans for Truth/California
- Bunny S. Galladora, Woman's Christian Temperance Union
- Dr. Paul Cameron, Family Research Institute
- James Hartline, The Hartline Report
- Jan Markell, Olive Tree Ministries & Radio
- Bill Cotter, Operation Rescue Boston
- Rabbi Mordechai W. Weberman, Rabbinical Advisory Board, Torah Loyal Jews
- Rabbi David Eidensohn, Generalcentral.com
- R. T. Neary, ProLife Massachusetts
- Mike O'Neil, CPF/The Fatherhood Coalition, Massachusetts
- John F. Russo, Marriage & Family, Massachusetts
- Stacy Harp, Active Christian Media, host, The Right View
- Rena Havens, Mothers Against Pedophilia
- Rev. Michael Carl, Constitution Party of Massachusetts
- Leslee Unruh, Abstinence Clearinghouse
- Carl Parnell, author, From Schoolhouse to Courthouse
- Pastor Che Ahn, Harvest Rock Church (Pasadena, CA)
- Dr. Robert C. Cannada, Jr., Chancellor and CEO of Reformed Theological Seminary (Orlando, FL)
- Michael J. Walsh, J.D.
- Galen Carey, Director of Government Affairs, National Association of Evangelicals (Washington, DC)
- Dr. Bryan Chapell, President, Covenant Theological Seminary (St. Louis, MO)
- Most Rev. Charles J. Chaput, Archbishop, Roman Catholic Archdiocese of Denver, CO
- Timothy A. Chichester, President, Catholic Family Association of America
- Most Rev. A. Dale Climie, Archbishop of the Western Province and Asia, Conservative Anglican Church of North America
-
- Timothy Clinton
- President, American Association of Christian Counselors (Forest, VA)
-
- Most Rev. Paul S. Coakley
- Bishop, Roman Catholic Diocese of Salina, KS
-
- Terry Colafrancesco
- President of Caritas of Birmingham
-
- Most Rev. George W. Coleman
- Bishop, Roman Catholic Diocese of Fall River, MA
-
- Dr. Kenneth J. Collins
- Professor of Historical Theology and Wesley Studies, Asbury Theological Seminary (Wilmore, KY)
-
- Chuck Colson
- Founder, the Chuck Colson Center for Christian Worldview (Lansdowne, VA)
-
- Dr. Mark Coppenger
- Managing Editor, Kairos Journal
-
- Most Rev. Salvatore Joseph Cordileone
- Bishop, Roman Catholic Diocese of Oakland, CA
-
- Dr. Barry H. Corey
- President, Biola University (La Mirada, CA)
-
- Dr. Gary Culpepper
- Associate Professor, Providence College (Providence, RI)
-
- Jim Daly
- President and CEO, Focus on the Family (Colorado Springs, CO)
-
- Marjorie Dannenfelser
- President, Susan B. Anthony List (Arlington, VA)
-
- Rev. Deacon Thomas J. Davis

- Associate Director, The Pope John Paul II Bioethics Center at Holy Apostles College and Seminary
- Rev. Daniel Delgado
- Board of Directors, National Hispanic Christian Leadership Conference & Pastor, Third Day Missions Church (Staten Island, NY)
- Patrick Deneen
- Tasakopoulos-Kounalakis, Associate Professor, Director, Tocqueville Forum on the Roots of American Democracy, Georgetown University (Washington D.C.)
- Most Rev. Frank J. Dewane
- Bishop, Roman Catholic Diocese of Venice, FL
- Most Rev. Nicholas DiMarzio
- Bishop, Roman Catholic Diocese of Brooklyn, NY
- Dr. James Dobson
- Founder, Family Talk (Colorado Springs, CO)
- Dr. David Dockery
- President, Union University (Jackson, TN)
- Most Rev. Timothy Dolan
- Archbishop, Roman Catholic Archdiocese of New York, NY
- Dr. William Donohue
- President, Catholic League (New York, NY)
- Dr. James T. Draper, Jr.
- President Emeritus, LifeWay (Nashville, TN)
- Dinesh D'Souza
- Writer & Speaker (Rancho Santa Fe, CA)
- Dr. J. Ligon Duncan
- Senior Minister, First Presbyterian Church, & President, Alliance of Confessing Evangelicals
- Most Rev. Robert Wm. Duncan
- Archbishop and Primate, Anglican Church in North America (Ambridge, PA)
- Dr. Michael Easley
- President Emeritus, Moody Bible Institute (Chicago, IL)
- Dr. William Edgar
- Professor, Westminster Theological Seminary (Philadelphia, PA)
- Brett Elder
- Executive Director, Stewardship Council (Grand Rapids, MI)
- Rev. Joel Elowsky
- Drew University (Madison, NJ)
- His Grace, The Right Reverend Bishop Basil Essey
- The Right Reverend Bishop of the Antiochian Orthodox Christian Diocese of Wichita and Mid-America (Wichita, KS)
- Rev. Jonathan Falwell
- Senior Pastor, Thomas Road Baptist Church (Lynchburg, VA)
- Most Rev. Kevin J. Farrell
- Bishop, Roman Catholic Diocese of Dallas, TX
- Most Rev. John C. Favalora
- Archbishop, Roman Catholic Archdiocese of Miami, FL
- William J. Federer
- President, Amerisearch, Inc. (St. Louis, MO)
- Most Rev. David E. Fellhauer
- Bishop, Roman Catholic Diocese of Victoria, TX
- Fr. Joseph D. Fessio
- Founder and Editor, Ignatius Press (San Francisco, CA)
- Most Reverend Robert W. Finn
- Bishop, Roman Catholic Diocese of Kansas City-St. Joseph, MO
- His Eminence John Cardinal Foley
- Grand Master, Equestrian Order of the Holy Sepulchre of Jerusalem, Rome (Italy)
- Carmen Fowler
- President & Executive Editor, Presbyterian Lay Committee (Lenoir, NC)
- Robert Gagnon
- Associate Professor of New Testament, Pittsburgh Theological Seminary (Pittsburgh, PA)
- Rabbi Abraham Stolzenberg, Young Israel
- Rabbi Joseph Rosenbluh, Young Israel
- Dr. Daniel Akin, President, Southeastern Baptist Theological Seminary (Wake Forest, NC)
- Randy Alcorn, Founder and Director, Eternal Perspective Ministries (EPM) (Sandy, OR)
- Rt. Rev. David Anderson, President and CEO, American Anglican Council (Atlanta, GA)
- Morton Blackwell, The Leadership Institute
- Rev. Dr. Gordon L. Anderson, President, North Central University, Minneapolis, MN
- Leith Anderson, President of National Association of Evangelicals (Washington, DC)
- Rabbi Yoseph Freedman, Bais Yisrael Torah Center, Morality Commission
- Most Rev. Samuel J. Aquila, Bishop, Roman Catholic Diocese of Fargo, ND
- Joseph Farah, WND.com (VA)
- Carole K. Ardizzone, TV Show Host and Speaker, INSP Television (Charlotte, NC)
- Kay Arthur, CEO and Co-founder, Precept Ministries International (Chattanooga, TN)
- Dr. Mark L. Bailey, President, Dallas Theological Seminary (Dallas, TX)
- Rev. Rick Warren, Saddleback Church (CA)
- Franklin Graham, Samaritan's Purse (NC)
- Steven Baer, former president, United Republican Fund of Illinois
- Most Rev. Robert J. Baker, S.T.D., Bishop, Roman Catholic Diocese of Birmingham, AL
- Most Rev. Craig W. Bates, Archbishop,International Communion of the Charismatic Episcopal Church (Malverne, NY)
- Gary Bauer, President, American Values; Chairman, Campaign for Working Families (Washington D.C.)
- Joel Belz, Founder, World Magazine (Asheville, NC)
- Rev. Michael L. Beresford, (Charlotte, NC)
- Rev. Thomas V. Berg, President, Westchester Institute for Ethics and the Human Person (New York)
- Ken Boa, President, Reflections Ministries (Atlanta, GA)
- Most Rev. Paul G. Bootkoski, Bishop, Roman Catholic Diocese of Metuchen, NJ
- Dorinda C. Bordlee, Esq., Executive Director and Senior Counsel, Bioethics Defense Fund (New Orleans, LA)
- Joseph Bottum, Editor, First Things (New York, NY)
- Pastor Randy & Sarah Brannon, Senior Pastor, Grace Community Church (Madera, CA)
- Most Rev. Robert H. Brom, Bishop, Roman Catholic Diocese of San Diego, CA
- Steve Brown, National radio broadcaster, Key Life (Maitland, FL)
- Most Rev. Robert A. Brucato, Retired Auxiliary Bishop, Roman Catholic Archdiocese of New York, NY
- Most Rev. Daniel M. Buechlein, O.S.B, Archbishop, Roman Catholic Archdiocese of Indianapolis, IN
- Most Rev. Michael F. Burbidge, Bishop, Roman Catholic Diocese of Raleigh, NC
- Archbishop Cyril Salim Bustros, Eparch, Melkite Greek-Catholic Eparchy of Newton, MA (Melkites in the United States)
- Brian Burch, president, CatholicVote.com
- Most Rev. William Patrick Callahan, Auxiliary Bishop, Roman Catholic Diocese of Milwaukee, WI
- Dr. Carlos Campo, President, Regent University (Virginia Beach, VA)
- Commissioner Israel L. Gaither
- National Commander, The Salvation Army
- Most Rev. Victor Galeone
- Bishop, Roman Catholic Diocese of St. Augustine, FL
- Maggie Gallagher
- President, National Organization for Marriage (Manassas, VA)

- Most Rev. James H. Garland
- Bishop Emeritus, Roman Catholic Diocese of Marquette, MI
- Dr. Jim Garlow
- Senior Pastor, Skyline Church (La Mesa, CA)
- Steven Garofalo
- Founder, National Apologetics Training Center (Charlotte, NC)
- Dr. Robert P. George
- McCormick Professor of Jurisprudence, Princeton University (Princeton, NJ)
- Dr. Timothy George
- Dean and Professor of Divinity, Beeson Divinity School at Samford University (Birmingham, AL)
- Most Rev. Joseph J. Gerry, O.S.B., Ph.D.
- Bishop Emeritus, Roman Catholic Diocese of Portland, ME
- Thomas Gilson
- Director of Strategic Processes, Campus Crusade for Christ International (Norfolk, VA)
- Most Rev. Irl A. Gladfelter
- Metropolitan Archbishop, The Anglo-Lutheran Catholic Church
- Dr. Jack Graham
- Pastor, Prestonwood Baptist Church (Plano, TX)
- Dr. Wayne Grudem
- Research Professor of Theological and Biblical Studies, Phoenix Seminary (Phoenix, AZ)
- Dr. Cornell "Corkie" Haan
- National Facilitator of Spiritual Unity, The Mission America Coalition (Palm Desert, CA)
- Most Rev. Joseph Hart
- Bishop Emeritus, Roman Catholic Diocese of Cheyenne, WY
- Fr. Chad Hatfield
- Chancellor, CEO. And Archpriest, St Vladimir's Orthodox Theological Seminary (Yonkers, NY)
- Most Rev. Edward L Haynes
- Metropolitan Archbishop,Nicene Orthodox Church (Chattanooga, TN)
- Alec Hill
- President, InterVarsity Christian Fellowship/USA
- Dr. Dennis Hollinger
- President and Professor of Christian Ethics, Gordon-Conwell Theological Seminary (South Hamilton, MA)
- Dr. Jeanette Hsieh
- Executive VP and Provost, Trinity International University (Deerfield, IL)
- Dr. John A. Huffman, Jr.
- Senior Pastor, St. Andrews Presbyterian Church (Newport Beach, CA) and Chairman of the Board,Christianity Today International (Carol Stream, IL)
- Dr. Edith M. Humphrey
- William F. Orr Professor of New Testament, Pittsburgh Theological Seminary
- Rev. Ken Hutcherson
- Pastor, Antioch Bible Church (Kirkland, WA)
- Bishop Harry R. Jackson, Jr.
- Senior Pastor, Hope Christian Church (Beltsville, MD)
- Fr. Johannes L. Jacobse
- President, American Orthodox Institute and Editor, OrthodoxyToday.org (Naples, FL)
- Most Rev. Michael Jarrell
- Bishop, Roman Catholic Diocese of Lafayette, LA
- Most Rev. Daniel R. Jenky
- Bishop, Roman Catholic Diocese of Peoria, IL
- Jerry Jenkins
- Author (Black Forest, CO)
- Most Rev. Peter J. Jugis
- Bishop, Roman Catholic Diocese of Charlotte, NC
- Camille Kampouris
- Editorial Board, Kairos Journal
- Emmanuel A. Kampouris
- Publisher, Kairos Journal
- Rev. Tim Keller
- Senior Pastor, Redeemer Presbyterian Church (New York, NY)
- Most Rev. Donald J. Kettler
- Bishop, Roman Catholic Diocese of Fairbanks, AK
- Dr. Alveda King
- Director of African American Outreach, Priests for Life
- Most Reverend John F. Kinney
- Bishop, Roman Catholic Diocese of Saint Cloud, MN
- Most Rev. Edward U. Kmiec
- Bishop, Roman Catholic Diocese of Buffalo, NY
- Most Rev. Emmanuel Musaba Kolini
- Primate, Anglican Church of Rwanda (Kigali, Rwanda)
- Dr. Peter Kreeft
- Professor of Philosophy, Boston College (MA) and at The Kings College (NY)
- Most Rev. Joseph E. Kurtz
- Archbishop, Roman Catholic Archdiocese of Louisville, KY
- Jim Kushiner
- Editor, Touchstone (Chicago, IL)
- Dr. Richard Land
- President, The Ethics & Religious Liberty Commission of the SBC (Washington, DC)
- Jim Law
- Senior Associate Pastor, First Baptist Church (Woodstock, GA)
- Dr. Matthew Levering
- Associate Professor of Theology, Ave Maria University (Naples, FL)
- Dr. Peter Lillback
- President, The Providence Forum (West Conshohocken, PA)
- Dr. Duane Litfin
- President, Wheaton College (Wheaton, IL)
- Rev. Edward M. Lohse, J.C.L.
- Chancellor and Vocation Director, Roman Catholic Diocese of Erie, PA
- V. Rev. Rodney H. Longmire, Jr.
- Canon Missioner of the Diocese of the Central States, The Reformed Episcopal Church
- Most Rev. Paul S. Loverde
- Bishop, Roman Catholic Diocese of Arlington, VA
- Rev. Herb Lusk
- Pastor, Greater Exodus Baptist Church (Philadelphia, PA)
- Dr. Erwin W. Lutzer
- Pastor, The Moody Church (Chicago, IL)
- His Eminence Adam Cardinal Maida
- Archbishop Emeritus, Roman Catholic Diocese of Detroit, MI

-
- Most Rev. Richard J. Malone
- Bishop, Roman Catholic Diocese of Portland, ME
-
- Gregory John Mansour
- Bishop of Saint Maron of Brooklyn (Maronite), New York
-
- Rev. Francis Martin
- Professor of New Testament, Dominican House of Studies, Washington D.C.
-
- Dr. Joseph Mattera
- Bishop & Senior Pastor, Resurrection Church (Brooklyn, NY)
-
- Phil Maxwell
- Pastor, Gateway Church (Bridgewater, NJ)
-
- Rt. Rev. Mark Maymon
- Bishop of Toledo and the Midwest, Antiochian Orthodox Christian Archdiocese of North America
-
- Josh McDowell
- Founder, Josh McDowell Ministry (Plano, TX)
-
- Zachary Wyatt
- Woody Burton
- Wm. C "Bill" McGee
- Winslow, Daniel
- Windol Weaver
- Willie Talton
- Tim Ackert
- Thomas Wyse
- Thomas Willmott
- Thomas 'Tommy' E. Pope
- Thomas 'Tom' R. Young, Jr.
- Thomas 'Tom' H. Wagoner
- Thomas 'Tom' F. Trail
- Thomas 'Tom' F. Loertscher
- Thomas 'Tom' F. Koch
- Thomas 'Tom' E. Lubnau II
- Thomas 'Tom' D. Corbin
- Ed McBroom
- Ed Hooper
- Ed Henry
- Ed Goedhart
- Ed Garner
- Ed Charbonneau
- Ed Buttrey
- Earle McCormick
- Earl Poleski
- Earl Ehrhart
- E.S. (Buck) Newton
- E Forrest Hamilton
- Dwight Wrangham
- Dwight Scharnhorst
- Dwight Cook
- Dwight A. Loftis
- Dwayne Umbarger
- Dwayne Bohac
- Dwayne Alons
- Duwayne Bridges
- Dustin Hightower
- Dustin A. Degree
- Durant, Peter
- Duncan Frey Kilmartin
- Duncan Baird
- Duane Milne
- Duane DeKrey
- Drew Darby
- Drew A. Perkins
- Doyle Heffley
- Douglas Vaughn Broxson
- Thomas 'Tom' A. Lockhart
- Thomas Saviello
- Thomas Sands
- Thomas Quigley
- Thomas Niehaus
- Thomas Nelson
- Thomas Murt
- Thomas Martin
- Thomas Long
- Thomas Lee Johnson
- Thomas Knollman
- Thomas Killion
- Thomas F. Hansen
- Thomas E. Saunders
- Thomas Dermody
- Thomas Dempsey
- Thomas Davis Rust
- thomas Carmody
- Thomas C. Wright, Jr.
- Thomas C. Alexander
- Fr. Joseph Marquis
- Sacred Heart Byzantine Catholic Church
-
- Dr. Thomas Marshall
- Head of Christ the Cornerstone Academy & Adjunct Professor, Liberty University (Lynchburg, VA)
-
- Roy Masters
- Foundation of Human Understanding
-
- Rev. James A. Matteson
- Immutable Word Ministries
-
- Pastor Kim D. May
- Liberty Christian Fellowship Organization
-
- Rev. James K. McCaslin, Jr.
- Assistant to the Bishop, Gulf Atlantic Diocese of the Anglican Church in North America
-
- Bruce McCoy
- Canaan Baptist Church, St. Louis, MO, and President of the Missouri Baptist Convention
-
- Patti McTee
- Grand Prairie Prayer Net
-
- Amy Mildenberg
- Bethel Presbyterian Church
-
- Daniel Millward
- Redeemer Presbyterian Church
-
- Stephen D. Minnis
- President, Benedictine College
-
- Tom Monaghan
- Chancellor, Ave Maria University
-
- Rev. Paul A. Monahan
- Holy Family Roman Catholic Church (Council Bluffs, IA)
-
- Fidel "Butch" Montoya
- H. S. Power & Light - Latino Faith Initiative Organization
-
- Dr. Dale Morgan
- Pastor, Dorcas Baptist Church (Jack, AL)
-
- Allen Morris
- Co-Founder and President, Concerned Methodists, Inc.
-
- Feda Morton
- Conservative candidate for Congress in VA-05
-
- Dan and Sharon Nejedlo
- SS. Peter and Paul Catholic Church (Hortonville, WI)
-
- Carl H. Nelson
- President, Greater Minnesota Association of Evangelicals
-
- Ed Neuenschwander
- President, Corporate Spiritual Consulting and Pastor of aCross Marin Christian Fellowship (Marin County, CA)
-
- Tom Newell
- Heartland Family Church
-
- John Newton
- Rector, Messiah Episcopal Church (St Paul, MN)
-

- Dr. George Ohlschlager
- Chairman, Law and Ethics Committee, American Association of Christian Counselors
-
- Pam Olsen
- Florida Prayer Network and the International House of Prayer
-
- LJ O'Neill
- Skippack Church of the Brethren
-
- Hector L. Padron
-
- Executive Vice President, Coral Ridge Ministries
-
- Hank Parker
- Pastor, Grace Alive Outreach Church
-
- Dr. Doug Partin
- Pastor, The Christian Church, Los Alamos, NM
-
- Rick Patterson
- First Southern Baptist Church (Hemet, CA)
-
- David Payne
- Pastor, Lifesong Church, Millbury, MA
-
- Rev. Michael Penikis
- Hope Lutheran Church, Shawnee, KS
-
- Pastor Charles Perkins
- Good Shepherd Church of the Nazarene
-
- Michael Philliber
- Providence Presbyterian Church (PCA) and President of the Midland Ministerial Alliance, Midland, TX
-
- Rev. Pat Pierce
- Pastor, Deep Water Lutheran Church, Mosinee, WI
-
- VADM John M. Poindexter, USN (Ret)
- Former National Security advisor to President Ronald Reagan
-
- Ray Popham
- Pastor, Oasis Church International Overseer, Called To All Nations Ministries, Inc.
-
- Pastor Rick Porter
- Victorious Living Chapel (Columbus, OH)
- Thomas Brunner
- Thomas Beadle
- Thomas B. Hooker
- Thomas A. Greason
- Thom Tillis
- Thom Goolsby
- Themis Klarides
- William Wadsworth
- William Tracy Arnold
- William Shirley
- William Sharer
- William Rogers
- William R. Romine
- William R. "Bobby" Outten
- William Payne
- William L Proctor
- William Kretschmar
- William 'Jeb' Steward
- William J. Howell
- WILLIAM J. FRANK
- William D Snyder
- William C. Friend
- William C Denny
- William Brawley
- William Brady Jr.
- William 'Billy' H. O'Dell
- William 'Bill' T. Doyle
- William 'Bill' R. Whitmire
- William 'Bill' R. Landen
- William 'Bill' P. Avery
- William 'Bill' M. Hixon
- William 'Bill' M. Chumley
- William 'Bill' G. Herbkersman
- William 'Bill' F. Canfield
- William 'Bill' E. Sandifer III
- William 'Bill' E. Crosby
- William Batchelder
- William Aman
- William Adolph
- William A Current Sr
- Will W Weatherford
- Will Tallman
- Will Longwitz
- Will Kraus
- Will Ford Hartnett
- Whit Betts
- Wesley Richardson
- Wesley Meredith
- Wesley Belter
- Wes Westmoreland
- Wes Long
- Wes Keller
- Wes Culver
- Wendy McNamara
- Wendy K. Nanney
- Wendell Willard
- WENDELL R. BEITZEL
- Webster, Daniel
- Wayne Wallingford
- Wayne Trottier
- Wayne Smith
- Wayne Parry
- Wayne Niederhauser
- Wayne Krieger
- Wayne Johnson
- Wayne Harper
- Wayne H. Johnson
- Wayne Christian
- Wayne A. Schmidt
- Warren Limmer
- Warren Kampf
- WARREN E. MILLER
- Warren Daniel
- Warren Chisum
- Ward Franz
- Wanda Taylor Jennings
- Wanda Brown
- Walter E. Duke
- Walt Rogers
- Wally Hicks
- W. Greg Ryberg
- W. Brian White
- W Keith Perry
- W Gregory Steube
- W Briggs Hopson III
- Vonnie Pietsch
- Vito Barbieri
- Vincent 'Vince' Illuzzi
- Vincent Candelora
- Vincent Buys
- Vince Dean
- Vieira, David
- Videt Carmichael
- Victor Gaston
- Vicky Steiner
- Vicki Truitt
- Vicki Strong
- Vicki Schneider
- Vicki Schmidt
- Vicki Berger
- Vic Williams
- Vic Williams
- Vic Gilliam
- Vernon Asbill
- Vernie McGaha
- Verdell Jackson
- Vaneta Becker
- Vance Dennis
- Van Wanggaard
- Van Taylor
- Valerie Clark
- Valarie Hodges
- Val Stevens
- Val Rausch

- Val Peterson
- V. Stephen 'Steve' Moss
- Tyson Rope Larson
- Tyler Clark
- Ty Masterson
- Tryon D. Lewis
- Trudi Walend
- Trudi K Williams
- Troy Balderson
- Troy Andes
- Trip Pittman
- Travis Holdman
- Tracy R. Edge
- TR Rowe
- Tory Rocca
- Tonya Schuitmaker
- Tony Smith
- Tony Shipley
- Tony Ross
- Tony O. Wilt
- TONY McCONKEY
- Tony McBrayer
- Tony Hwang
- Tony Grindberg
- Tony Fulton
- Tony Dugger
- Toni Boucher
- Tona Rozum
- Tommy Woods
- Tommy Tucker
- Tommy Taylor
- Tommy Smith
- Tommy M. Stringer
- Tommy Gollott
- Tommy Benton
- Tom Winson
- Tom Whatley
- Tom Weldon
- Tom Weathersby
- Tom Taylor
- Tom Shaw
- Tom Rice
- Tom Reeder, Jr.
- Tom Patton
- Tom Murry
- Tom McMillin
- Tom McCall
- Tom Loehner
- Tom Kirby
- Tom Jensen
- Tom Harman
- Tom Hansen
- Tom Grady
- Tom Goodson
- Tom Forese
- Tom Forese
- Tom Flanigan
- Tom Dickson
- Tom Davis
- Tom Creighton
- Tom Craddick
- Tom Casperson
- Tom Carlson
- Tom Burditt
- Tom Buford
- Tom Bivins
- Tom Azinger
- Tom Apodaca
- Todd Weiler
- Todd Stephens
- Todd Smith
- Todd Schlekeway
- Todd Rock
- Todd Richardson
- Todd Porter
- Todd Kiser
- Todd K. Atwater
- Todd Greeson
- Todd Ames Hunter
- Toby Barker
- Tina Pickett
- Timothy LeGeyt
- Timothy Krieger
- Timothy Jones
- Timothy Derickson
- Timothy D. Hugo
- Timothy Burns
- Timothy Begalka
- Timmy Ladner
- Timm Ormsby
- Tim Wirgau
- Tim Wesco
- Tim Summers
- Tim Stubson
- Tim Schaffer
- Tim Rave
- Tim Owens
- Tim Neese
- Tim Moore
- Tim L. Corder, Sr.
- Tim Kleinschmidt
- Tim Kapucian
- Tim Hennessey
- Tim Freeman
- Tim Flakoll
- Tim D Moffitt
- Tim Brown
- Tim Armstead
- Thad T. Viers
- Thad Altman
- Terry Wanzek
- Terry Rogers
- Terry Rice
- Terry R. Nealey
- Terry Murphy
- Terry Moulton
- Terry Johnson
- Terry G. Kilgore
- Terry England
- Terry Burton
- Terry Bruce
- Terry Brown
- Terry Boose
- Terry Blair
- Terrie Wood
- Terrie Huntington
- Terri Proud
- Terri Proud
- Terri Lynn Weaver
- Terri Collins
- Ted Vogt
- Ted Vogt
- Ted Lillie
- Ted Ferrioli
- Ted Daley
- Taylor F Barras
- Taylor Brown
- Tarr, Bruce
- Tarah Toohil
- Tanya Cook
- Tan Parker
- Tammie Wilson
- Tad Perry
- T.J. Berry
- T. Scott Garrett
- Sylvia Allen
- Suzi Schmidt
- Suzanne Crouch
- Susan Wagle
- SUSAN W. KREBS
- Susan Morissette
- SUSAN L. M. AUMANN
- Susan King
- SUSAN K. McCOMAS
- Susan Holmes
- Susan Helm
- Susan Glick
- Susan Fagan
- Sue Wilson Beffort
- Sue Wallis
- Sue Rezin
- Sue Entlicher

- Sue Ellspermann
- Sue Allen
- Stuart Reid
- Stuart Ingle
- Stuart Bishop
- Stuart Adams
- Stewart J Greenleaf
- Stewart Iverson
- Stewart Barlow
- Steven Tilley
- Steven 'Steve' P. Thayn
- Steven 'Steve' J. Vick
- STEVEN R. SCHUH
- Steven Olson
- Steven Neville
- Steve Yarbrough
- Steve Wood
- Steve Urie
- Steve Urie
- Steve Thompson
- Steve Southerland
- Steve Smith
- Steve Russell
- Steve Pylant
- Steve Pierce
- Steve Oelrich
- Steve McMillan
- Steve McManus
- Steve McDaniel
- Steve Massengill
- Steve Litzow
- Steve Lathrop
- Steve Kettering
- Steve Hurst
- Steve Horne
- Steve Hickey
- Steve Harshman
- Steve Harshman
- Steve Hall
- Steve Eliason
- Steve Davisson
- Steve Davis
- Steve Crisafulli
- Steve Court
- Steve Court
- Steve Cookson
- Steve Clouse
- Steve B. Montenegro
- Steve B. Montenegro
- Steve Abrams
- Steve A. Parker
- Stephen Wise
- Stephen Urquhart
- STEPHEN S. HERSHEY, JR.
- Stephen Pugh
- Stephen Morris
- Stephen L Precourt
- Stephen Hartgen
- Stephen Handy
- Stephen Carter
- Stephen Bloom
- Stephen Barrar
- Stephen Allison
- Stephen A. Meeks
- Stephen A. LaRoque
- Stephanie Malone
- Stefani Carter
- Stanley Lyson
- Stanley Cox
- Stanford Adelstein
- Stan Saylor
- Stan Cooper
- Stan Bingham
- Stacey Guerin
- Stacey Fitts
- Stacey Dahl
- Stacey Campfield
- Stace Nelson
- Spencer Berry
- Speaker Beth Harwell
- Smola, Todd
- Slade Blackwell
- Simone Champagne
- Sid Miller
- Shirley J. McKague
- Shirley B Randleman
- Sheryl L. Nuxoll
- Sheryl Delozier
- Sherrie Sprenger
- Sherri Smith Buffington
- Sherman Mack
- Shelly Short
- Shelley Keeney
- Shelley Hughes
- Sheila Solon
- Sheila Harsdorf
- Sheila Butt
- Shawn Lindsay
- Shawn Harrison
- Shawn Hamerlinck
- Shawn A. Keough
- Sharon Tyler
- Sharon L. Block
- Sharon Cooper
- Shantel Krebs
- Shannon S. Erickson
- Shannon Jones
- Shannon C. McMillan
- Shane Schoeller
- Shane R. Martin
- Shane Cultra
- Shadrack McGill
- Seth McKeel
- Seth Grove
- Senator Michael Baumgartner
- Selim Noujaim
- Sean Williams
- Sean Tindell
- Sean Nienow
- Sean Jerguson
- Sean Eberhart
- Scotty Campbell
- Scott Simon
- Scott Schneider
- Scott Rupp
- Scott Price
- Scott Plakon
- Scott Petri
- Scott Perry
- Scott Oelslager
- Scott Newman
- Scott Munsterman
- Scott Louser
- Scott Lautenbaugh
- Scott Largent
- Scott Jenkins
- Scott Hutchinson
- Scott Hammond
- Scott Frantz
- Scott Fitzgerald
- Scott Dieckhaus
- Scott DeLano
- Scott C. Bedke
- Scott Boyd
- Scott Beason
- Sarah Stevens
- Sarah Davis
- Sandy Crawford
- Sandra Major
- Sandra Greiner
- Sander Rue
- Samuel Smith
- Samuel 'Sam' Krone
- Sam Teasley
- Sam Slom
- Sam McCann
- Sam C Mims
- Salvatore R. Iaquinto
- Sally Doty
- Sal Esquivel
- S. Chris Jones
- Ryan Zinke

- Ryan Williams
- Ryan Wilcox
- Ryan Smith
- Ryan Silvey
- Ryan Mishler
- Ryan Maher
- Ryan Mackenzie
- Ryan Haynes
- Ryan Harmon
- Ryan Aument
- Ruth Teichman
- Ruth Samuelson
- Ruth R. Whitaker
- Ruth Briggs King
- Ruth Ann Petroff
- Rusty Glover
- Rusty Crowe
- Russell 'Russ' M. Fulcher
- Russell Olson
- Russell Black
- Russ Karpisek
- Russ Jones
- Russ Jones
- Royd Chambers
- Roy Schmidt
- Roxann L. Robinson
- Rowlie Hutton
- Ross, Richard
- Ross, George
- Ross Paustian
- Ross McGregor
- Rosie M. Berger
- Rosemary Brown
- RoseMarie Swanger
- Roscoe Streyle
- Rosa Rebimbas
- Ronnie W. Cromer
- Ronnie Johns
- Ronda Storms
- Ronda Rudd Menlove
- Ronald Sorvaag
- Ronald Schieber
- Ronald Sandack
- Ronald Richard
- Ronald Grooms
- Ronald G Johnson
- Ronald E. Hubert
- Ronald Collins
- Ronald A. Villanueva
- Ronald "Doc" Renuart
- Ron Young
- Ron Stephens
- Ron Miller
- Ron Marsico
- Ron Maag
- Ron Lollar
- Ron Justice
- Ron Jorgensen
- Ron Gould
- RON GEORGE
- Ron Carlisle
- Ron Bacon
- Ron Arthun
- Ron Amstutz
- Ron Alting
- Rogers Pope
- Roger Williams
- Roger West
- Roger Solum
- Roger Sherman
- Roger Reitz
- Roger Katz
- Roger Kahn
- Roger Hunt
- Roger Chamberlain
- Roger Brabandt
- Roger Barrus
- Rodney Whittemore
- Rodney Schad
- Rodney E. Anderson
- Rod Adair
- Roby Smith
- Robin Weisz
- Robert 'Wes' Wesley Hayes, Jr.
- Robert W. Lewis
- Robert Tata
- Robert Stivers
- Robert Sprague
- Robert Shadoin
- Robert Schaaf
- Robert Sampson
- Robert Olson
- Robert Nutting
- Robert McKim
- Robert Mayer
- Robert M Tomlinson
- Robert Kostelka
- Robert Kane
- Robert J. Genetski II
- Robert Hager
- Robert Godshall
- Robert G. Marshall
- Robert Frantsvog
- Robert Erbele
- Robert E. Dale
- Robert Dickey
- Robert 'Denny' Dennis Altes
- Robert D. Orrock, Sr.
- Robert D. Morris
- Robert D Robbins
- Robert Cowles
- Robert C Schenck
- Robert 'Bobby' W. Harrell, Jr.
- Robert 'Bob' Paul Nonini
- Robert 'Bob' Krist
- Robert 'Bob' G. Helm
- Robert 'Bob' E. Schaefer, Sr.
- Robert 'Bob' A. Bouchard
- Robert Behning
- Robert Bacon
- Robert B. Bell
- Robert Adley
- ROBERT A. COSTA
- Rob Orr
- Rob Kauffman
- Rob Johnson
- Rob Eissler
- Ritch Workman
- Rita Parks
- Rita Martinson
- Rita Campbell
- Riley E. Ingram
- Ried Holien
- Ricky Long
- Rick Womick
- Rick Stream
- Rick Snuffer
- Rick Saccone
- Rick Ripley
- Rick Outman
- Rick Olson
- Rick Murphy
- Rick Jones
- Rick Jasperse
- Rick Hardcastle
- Rick Gunn
- Rick Gray
- Rick Gray
- Rick Brinkley
- Rick Brattin
- Rick Bertrand
- Richard Stevenson
- Richard Stevens
- Richard Smith
- Richard Rosen
- Richard 'Rick' M. Quinn, Jr.
- Richard 'Rich' A. Wills
- Richard P. Bell
- Richard Montgomery
- Richard McArthur
- Richard Malaby
- Richard M. McClain

- Richard L. Morris
- Richard L. Cannady
- Richard L. Anderson
- Richard L Alloway
- RICHARD K. IMPALLARIA
- Richard H. Smith
- Richard H. Lawrence
- Richard Greenwood
- Richard Glorioso
- Richard Geist
- Richard Floyd
- Richard Dodge
- Richard 'Dick' J. Harwood
- Richard DeBolt
- Richard Corcoran
- Richard Burford
- Richard Bray
- Richard Bennett
- Richard Baughn
- Richard Arnold
- Richard Anderson
- Richard Adams
- Richard A. Westman
- Rich Zipperer
- Rich Wardner
- Rich J. Pahls
- Rich Golick
- Rich Crandall
- Rich Cebra
- Ric Killian
- Rhonda Rhoads
- Rex Damschroder
- Renee Schulte
- Rene Garcia
- Reed DeMordaunt
- Rebecca Lockhart
- Rebecca Kubacki
- Rebecca Edwards
- Rayne Brown
- Raymond 'Ray' E. Cleary III
- Raymond Garofalo
- Ray Weter
- Ray Wallace
- Ray Vandeveer
- Ray Rogers
- Ray Pilon
- Ray Merrick
- Ray Holmberg
- Ray A. Franz
- Raul Torres
- Randy Wood
- Randy Weber
- Randy Vulakovich
- Randy Truitt
- Randy Rushing
- Randy Richardville
- Randy P Boyd
- Randy Nix
- Randy McNally
- Randy Kirner
- Randy Head
- Randy Gardner
- Randy Frye
- Randy Feenstra
- Randy Davis
- Randy Burckhard
- Randy Boehning
- Randy Asbury
- Randolph 'Randy' D. Brock
- Randi Becker
- Randel Christmann
- Ralph Watts
- Ralph W. Norman
- Ralph Shortey
- Ralph Shellfield
- Ralph Sarty
- Ralph Ostmeyer
- Ralph Okerlund
- Ralph M. Foley
- Ralph Kilzer
- Ralph Hise
- RaeAnn Kelsch
- Rachel V Burgin
- R. Steven Landes
- R. 'Steve' Steven Bair
- R. Shawn Tornow
- R. Paul Lambert
- R. Michael Young
- R. Lee Ware, Jr.
- R Ray Peterson
- Prasad Srinivasan
- Poirier, Elizabeth
- Phyllis J. Pond
- Phyllis Henderson
- Phyllis Heineman
- Phillip 'Phil' W. Shoopman
- Phillip 'Phil' D. Owens
- Phillip Pavlov
- Phillip Johnson
- Phillip Gandy
- Phillip Dean Lowe
- Phillip D. Hinkle
- Phillip Boots
- Philip 'Phil' A. Nicholas
- Philip Moran
- Philip Gunn
- Philip Frye
- Philip C. Winters
- Phil Williams
- Phil Williams
- Phil R Shepard
- Phil Potvin
- Phil Lovas
- Phil Lovas
- Phil King
- Phil Jensen
- Phil Hart
- Phil Curtis
- Phil Berger
- Peterson, George
- Peter Stautberg
- Peter S. Brunstetter
- Peter Rioux
- Peter Pettalia
- Peter 'Pete' S. Illoway
- Peter Nehr
- Peter Miller
- Peter MacGregor
- Peter M. McCoy, Jr.
- Peter Knudson
- Peter Johnson
- Peter J. Lund
- Peter J. Fagan
- Peter F. Farrell
- Peter Edgecomb
- Peter E. Perley
- Peter Cownie
- Peter Beck
- Pete Pirsch
- Pete Livermore
- Pete Goicoechea
- Pete Brungardt
- Perry Lee
- Penny Houston
- Penny Bacchiochi
- Peggy Wilson
- Peggy Lehner
- Peggy Judd
- Peggy Judd
- Paulette Braddock
- Paula Dockery
- Paul Wieland
- Paul Waterhouse
- Paul Stam
- Paul Seaton
- Paul Schumacher
- Paul Sanford
- Paul Ray
- Paul R. Barnard
- Paul Muxlow
- Paul McKinley
- Paul Lee

- Paul Hornback
- Paul Hollis
- Paul Harris
- Paul Gazelka
- Paul Fitzwater
- Paul E. Shepherd
- Paul E. Opsommer
- Paul DeMarco
- Paul Davis
- Paul D. Workman
- Paul Curtman
- Paul Clymer
- Paul Bussman
- Paul Bennett
- Paul Beckman
- Paul Battles
- Patty Miller
- Patti Komline
- Patti J. Lewis
- Patti Anne Lodge
- Patrick Sheehan
- Patrick Rooney Jr
- Patrick Painter
- PATRICK N. HOGAN
- Patrick M. Brennan
- Patrick M Browne
- Patrick Lane
- PATRICK L. McDONOUGH
- Patrick Hatlestad
- Patrick Flood
- Patrick Connick
- Patrick Colbeck
- Patrick Anderson
- Patricia Stricherz
- Patricia Miller
- Patricia Harless
- Patricia H Vance
- Pat Ward
- Pat Somerville
- Pat Nelson
- Pat McElraft
- Pat Marsh
- Pat Hickey
- Pat Grassley
- Pat B Hurley
- Pat Apple
- Pamela Sawyer
- Pamela Althoff
- Pam Wolf
- Pam Roach
- Paige Kreegel
- Page Cortez
- P. 'Mike' Michael Forrester
- P. Eric Turner
- Owen Petersen
- Orrall, Keiko
- ON H. DWYER, JR.
- Oliver K. Olsen
- Oley Larsen
- Ogden Driskill
- O'Connell, Shaunna
- Norman W Sanderson
- Norman 'Norm' Wallman
- Norman H. McAllister
- Norman 'Doug' D. Brannon
- Norma Smith
- Norm Johnson
- Norine A. Kasperik
- Noreen Kokoruda
- Norby Chabert
- Nolan Mettetal
- Noel Torpey
- Nick Wagner
- Nick T. Manolakos
- Nick Moser
- Nick Marshall
- Nick Lorusso
- NICHOLAUS R. KIPKE
- Nicholas Micozzie
- Nicholas A Miccarelli III
- Nichi Farnham
- Nelson L. Hardwick
- Nelson Dollar
- Neil Riser
- NEIL C. PARROTT
- Neal Kedzie
- Neal Hunt
- Nathan Ballentine
- NANCY R. STOCKSDALE
- Nancy McLain
- Nancy McLain
- Nancy Landry
- Nancy Johnson
- Nancy E. Jenkins
- Nancy Detert
- Nancy Boettger
- Nancy Barto
- Nancy Adams Collins
- Nan Baker
- N Leo Daughtry
- Myron Neth
- Myra Crownover
- Monty J. Pearce
- Mitchell S Setzer
- Mitch Toryanski
- Mitch Gillespie
- Mitch Carmichael
- Missy Thomas Irvin
- Milton 'Pete' Peter Nielsen
- Milo Smith
- Mike Wilson
- Mike Walsworth
- Mike Vereb
- Mike Verchio
- Mike Vehle
- Mike Turzai
- Mike Tobash
- Mike Thomson
- Mike Speedy
- Mike Sparks
- Mike Schulz
- Mike Schatz
- Mike Reese
- Mike Peterson
- Mike Parson
- Mike Parry
- Mike Padden
- Mike Nathe
- Mike Moyle
- Mike Millican
- Mike McLane
- Mike McGhee
- Mike Mazzei
- Mike Madden
- Mike Leara
- Mike Lair
- Mike Kowall
- Mike Kelley
- Mike Kehoe
- Mike Karickhoff
- Mike Jones
- Mike Jacobs
- Mike Huval
- Mike Hubbard
- Mike Horner
- Mike Hill
- Mike Hewitt
- Mike Hawker
- Mike Haridopolos
- Mike Hamilton
- Mike Hager
- Mike Green
- Mike Greear
- Mike Gloor
- Mike Folmer
- Mike Flood
- Mike Fleck
- Mike Faulk
- Mike Fasano
- Mike Duffey
- Mike Dudgeon
- Mike Dovilla

- Mike Delph
- Mike Cierpiot
- Mike Cheokas
- Mike Chenault
- Mike Callton
- Mike C Stone
- Mike Brubaker
- Mike Bernkoetter
- Mike Bell
- Mike Ball
- Mike Armstrong
- Mike Alberts
- Miguel Diaz de la Portilla
- Micky Hammon
- Mickey Channell
- Michelle Ugenti
- Michelle Ugenti
- Michelle Fischbach
- Michelle Benson
- Michele Reagan
- Michele Brooks
- Michael Willette
- Michael Watson
- Michael Waddoups
- Michael Thomas 'Mike' Rose
- Michael Thibodeau
- Michael Shirkey
- Michael S Bennett
- Michael Ramone
- Michael Peifer
- Michael Nofs
- Michael Noel
- Michael Morley
- Michael Molgano
- Michael 'Mike' W. Gambrell
- Michael 'Mike' L. Fair
- Michael 'Mike' J. Hebert
- Michael 'Mike' Carrell
- Michael 'Mike' A. Pitts
- Michael McLachlan
- Michael McClellan
- Michael L Waugh
- Michael Jungbauer
- Michael John Lamoureux
- Michael J. Webert
- Michael J. Von Flatern
- Michael J. Marcotte
- MICHAEL J. HOUGH
- Michael Henne
- Michael Harrison
- Michael Ellis
- MICHAEL D. SMIGIEL, SR.
- Michael D Brandenburg
- Michael Celli
- Michael Bileca
- Michael Beaulieu
- Michael Baumgartner
- Michael B. Watson
- Michael B Weinstein
- MICHAEL A. McDERMOTT
- Mia Costello
- Merlynn Newbold
- Merlin Bartz
- Merle Flowers
- Merita Ann 'Rita' Allison
- Meredith Strang Burgess
- Melvin Newendyke
- Melvin Brown
- Melissa Woodbury
- Melissa Magstadt
- Melissa Leach
- Melinda S. Smyser
- Melanie Sojourner
- McLain 'Mac' R. Toole
- Maxine T. Bell
- Max C. Black
- Maureen S. Walsh
- Mauree Gingrich
- Matthias Greene
- Matthew Shepherd
- Matthew Klein
- Matthew J. Lori
- Matthew Hill
- Matthew H Caldwell
- Matthew Baker
- Matt Wingard
- Matt Windschitl
- Matt Wand
- Matt Ubelhor
- Matt Teeters
- Matt Shea
- Matt Ramsey
- Matt Murphy
- Matt Lynch
- Matt Lehman
- Matt Huuki
- Matt Huffman
- Matt Hudson
- Matt Hatchett
- Matt Gaetz
- Matt Gabler
- Matt Dollar
- Mary Sue McClurkin
- Mary 'Prissy' P. Hickerson
- Mary Pilcher-Cook
- Mary Lou Slinkard
- Mary Lazich
- Mary Jo White
- Mary Ann Hanusa
- Mary A. Throne
- Mary A. Morrissey
- Marva Beck
- Marv Hagedorn
- Marty Gearheart
- Martin Scott
- Martin Knollenberg
- Martin Causer
- Marti Coley
- Marsha Haefner
- Marlene Anielski
- Mark Willadsen
- Mark White
- Mark Wagoner
- Mark W Hollo
- Mark Venner
- Mark Tuggle
- Mark Taddiken
- Mark Sherwood
- Mark Shelton
- Mark Sanford
- Mark R. Christensen
- Mark Pody
- Mark Parkinson
- Mark Owens
- Mark Ouimet
- Mark Norris
- Mark Neuman
- Mark N. Willis
- MARK N. FISHER
- Mark Mustio
- Mark Messmer
- Mark Madsen
- Mark Lofgren
- Mark L. Cole
- Mark Kirkeby
- Mark K Keller
- Mark K Hilton
- Mark Johnson
- Mark Jansen
- Mark Hatfield
- Mark Hamilton
- Mark Gillen
- Mark G. Schoesler
- Mark G. Schoesler
- Mark Formby
- Mark Chelgren
- Mark Brandenburg
- Mark Boitano
- Mark Biviano
- Mark Baker
- Mark Allen
- Mark A. Semlek

- Mark A. Higley
- Mark A Dosch
- Marjorie 'Marge' A. Chadderdon
- Marion B. Frye
- Mario Scavello
- Marilyn Slaby
- Marilyn Giuliano
- Marilyn Avila
- Marguerite Quinn
- Margaret Sitte
- Margaret 'Peg' Flory
- Margaret Ellis Rogers
- Margaret E. O'Brien
- Margaret Dayton
- Margaret Conditt
- Margaret B. Ransone
- Margaret Ann Ruhl
- Marcy Toepel
- Marcia Hahn
- Marc Gibbs
- Manny Steele
- Manly Barton
- Mae Beavers
- Mack G. Shirley
- Mack "Bodi" White
- Mac McCutcheon
- Mac Huddleston
- Mac Butrram
- M. Kirkland Cox
- M. Keith Hodges
- Lyons, James
- Lynwood "Woody" Ireland
- Lynne Riley
- Lynn Wachtmann
- Lynn Smith
- Lynn M. Luker
- Lynn Greer
- Lynn D. Stewart
- Lynn D. Batchelor
- Lyndall Fraker
- Lynda Schlegel Culver
- Lyle Rowland
- Lyle Larson
- Lyle Hillyard
- Lydia N. Brasch
- Lydia Chassaniol
- Luther Olsen
- Luke A. Rankin, Sr.
- Luann Ridgeway
- Lt. Gov. Ron Ramsey
- Loy Mauch
- Lowry Snow
- Lowell Hazel
- Louis Terhar
- Louis Pate
- Louis Blessing
- Lorraine Quarberg
- Lori Klein
- Lori A. Benedict
- Lora Hubbel
- Lonnie Laffen
- Lon Burnman
- Lombardo, Marc
- Lois Snowe-Mello
- Lois Kolkhorst
- Lloyd K. Smucker
- Llewelyn Jones
- Lizbeth Benacquisto
- Livvy Floren
- Liston Douglas Barfield
- Lisa Posthumus Lyons
- Lisa Meier
- Lisa Baker
- Linden B. Bateman
- Lindell Shumake
- Linda Upmeyer
- Linda Sumner
- Linda P Johnson
- Linda Miller
- Linda K. Myers
- Linda K. Menard
- Linda Harper-Brown
- Linda Gray
- Linda Elam
- Linda Collins-Smith
- Lincoln Hough
- Lincoln D. Willis
- Lile Gibbons
- Liane Sorenson
- Lewis 'Gene' Eugene
- Levy, Steven
- Lester "Bubba" Carpenter
- Leslie Joan Nutting
- Leslie Donovan Sr.
- Lesley Vance
- Lesil L. McGuire
- Les 'Skip' Carnine
- Les Seiler
- Les Fossel
- LeRoy J. Louden
- LeROY E. MYERS, JR.
- Leonard Greene
- Leonard Fasano
- Leon E. Smith, Jr.
- Leo Harris Jr.
- Lenore Hardy Barrett
- Lenar Whitney
- Len Suzio
- Leland Christensen
- Lela Alston
- Leigh B. Larocque
- Lee Perry
- Lee Hein
- Lee Heider
- Lee Bright
- Lee Anderson
- Leah Vukmir
- Layton Freborg
- Lawrence Miller
- Lawrence 'Larry' K. Grooms
- Lawrence Klemin
- Lawrence Kit 'Kit' Spires
- Lawrence Cafero
- Lawerence E. Denney
- Lavon Lynn Heidemann
- LaVar Christensen
- Laura Hoydick
- Larry Tidemann
- Larry Taylor
- Larry S. Hicks
- Larry Rhoden
- Larry R. Brown
- Larry Phillips
- Larry Obhof
- Larry O`Neal
- Larry Metz
- Larry Luick
- Larry Haler
- Larry Gonzales
- Larry George
- Larry G Pittman
- Larry Dunphy
- Larry D. Kump
- Larry Crouse
- Larry Byrd
- Larry Bomke
- Larry Bellew
- Larry Ahern
- Larry A. Martin
- Lanham Lyne
- Lane Jean
- Lance Russell
- Lance Pruitt
- Lance Horbach
- Lance Harvell
- Lance Harris
- Lance Gooden
- Lance Carson
- Lake Ray
- L. Scott Lingamfelter
- L. Nick Rush
- L. Mark Dudenhefer

- Kymberly M. Pine
- Kyle McCarter
- Kyle Johansen
- Kurt Wright
- Kurt Wallace
- Kurt Schaefer
- Kurt Olson
- Kurt Masser
- Kurt Heise
- Kurt Damrow
- Kurt Bahr
- Kuros, Kevin
- Kristopher 'Kris' R.
- Kristina Roegner
- Kristin Conzet
- Kris Jordan
- Kraig Powell
- Kraig Paulsen
- Knapik, Michael
- Kit Jennings
- Kirk Talbot
- Kirk Schuring
- Kirk Pearson
- Kirk Dillard
- Kip Smith
- Kimberly Yee
- Kimberly Olsen
- Kimberley Rosen
- Kim Vanneman
- Kim Thatcher
- Kim Pearson
- Kim L Ward
- Kim Koppelman
- Kim David
- Kim D. Hendren
- Kim D. Hammer
- Kevin Witkos
- Kevin Van Tassell
- Kevin R. Ryan
- Kevin Pearson
- Kevin Parker
- Kevin Meyer
- Kevin McGee
- Kevin Mahan
- Kevin L. Bryant
- Kevin L Raye
- Kevin Koester
- Kevin Kelly
- Kevin J. Mullin
- Kevin Engler
- Kevin Elmer
- Kevin Daley
- Kevin Cotter
- Kevin Cooke
- Kevin Cameron
- Kevin Brooks
- Kevin Bacon
- Keven Stratton
- Kerry Roberts
- Kerry Rich
- Kerry Benninghoff
- Kerri Prescott
- Kermit C. Brown
- Kent Sorenson
- Kent Juhnke
- Kent Hampton
- Kenneth Winters
- Kenneth Sumsion
- Kenneth Sheets
- Kenneth L Roberson
- Kenneth Kurtz
- Kenneth 'Kenny' A. Bingham
- Kenneth Harvard
- Kenneth Fredette
- Kenneth B. Horn
- Kendell Kroeker
- Ken Yonker
- Ken Yager
- Ken Schilz
- Ken Paxton
- Ken Morgan
- Ken Johnson
- Ken Ivory
- Ken Haar
- Ken Goike
- Ken Andrus
- Ken A. Roberts
- KELLY M. SCHULZ
- Kelly Kite
- Kelly Keisling
- Kelly Hancock
- Kelly E Hastings
- Kelli Stargel
- Kelli Sobonya
- Kelley Linck
- Keith Marshall Gingery
- Keith Kempenich
- Keith Grover
- Keith Gillespie
- Keith Frederick
- Keith Faber
- Kay Mciff
- Katrina Asay
- Katie Stine
- Katie M. Dempsey
- Katie Eyre Brewer
- KATHY SZELIGA
- Kathy Rapp
- Kathy K. Richardson
- Kathy J. Byron
- Kathy Heuer
- Kathy Hawken
- Kathy Harrington
- Kathy Campbell
- KATHRYN L. AFZALI
- Kathleen 'Kathy' Sims
- Kathleen 'Kathy' A. Davison
- Kathleen Chase
- Kathleen C Passidomo
- Kathie Conway
- Katharine Watson
- Kate Sullivan
- Kate Harper
- Kate Brophy McGee
- Kate Brophy McGee
- Karen S. Hopper
- Karen M Rohr
- Karen Karls
- Karen K Krebsbach
- Karen Foster
- Karen Fann
- Karen Fann
- Karen Boback
- K.L. Brown
- Justin T. Harris
- Justin Simmons
- Justin Pierce
- Justin Pierce
- Justin P Burr
- Justin Olson
- Justin Olson
- JUSTIN D. READY
- Justin Cronin
- Julie Parrish
- Julie Harhart
- Julie Ellsworth
- Julie Denton
- Julie A. Rosen
- Julianne Ortman
- Julian Garrett
- Julia Lynn
- Julia Hurley
- Judy Manning
- Judy Lee
- Judy Emmons
- Judy Burges
- Judy Boyle
- Judson S. Gilbert II
- Judith 'Judy' Warnick
- Judd Matheny
- Jud McMillin
- Joyce Maker

- Joyce M. Broadsword
- Joyce Kingsbury
- Joyce Fitzpatrick
- Joshua Evans
- Joshua Byrnes
- Joshua A. Putnam
- Josh Johnston
- Josh Harkins
- Josh Clark
- Josh Brecheen
- Joseph Zakas
- Joseph Uecker
- Joseph R. Yost
- Joseph P. Zarelli
- Joseph Lopinto
- Joseph Leibham
- Joseph 'Joe' S. Daning
- Joseph 'Joe' M. Barbuto
- Joseph Haveman
- Joseph Hackett
- Joseph Graves
- Joseph E. Miro
- JOSEPH C. BOTELER III
- Joseph B Scarnati
- Jose R Olivia
- Jose Felix Diaz
- Jose Aliseda
- Joni Ernst
- Joni Cutler
- Jones, Bradley
- Jonathan T E Courtney
- Jonathan Perry
- Jonathan Nichols
- Jonathan Miller
- Jonathan McKane
- Jonathan Dismang
- Jonathan D. Barnett
- Jonathan C Jordan
- Jon Woods
- Jon Sonju
- Jon Scott Eubanks
- Jon Nelson
- Jon M. Hubbard
- Jon Lundberg
- Jon Hansen
- Jon G. Burns
- Jon Bumstead
- Johnny R. Key
- Johnny Nugent
- Johnny Anderson
- John Zerwas
- John Wood
- John Wightman
- John Westwood
- John Waterman
- John Wall
- John W. Patton
- John W. Goedde
- JOHN W. E. CLUSTER, JR.
- John Vratil
- John Vander Woude
- John Valentine
- John Tobia
- John Thrasher
- John Thomas "Trey" Lamar
- John Taylor
- John T. Smithee
- John shaban
- John Schroder
- John Schickel
- John Ryan
- John Rigby
- John Raney
- John Ragan
- John R Smith
- John R Gordner
- John Proos IV
- John Polk
- John Piscopo
- John Pippy
- John Picchiotti
- John Pederson
- John Payne
- John Pappageorge
- John P Yates
- John Overington
- John Otto
- John O Read
- John Nelson
- John N. Harms
- John N. Ellem
- John Moolenaar
- John Millner
- John Merrill
- John Meadows
- John McKinney
- John McComish
- John McCaherty
- John Mathis
- John Maher
- John M. O'Bannon, III
- John M Blust
- John Legg
- John Lawrence
- John Lamping
- John L Moore
- John Kuempel
- John Kissel
- John Kavanagh
- John Kavanagh
- John Jones
- John 'Jake' Milton Knotts, Jr.
- John J. Walsh
- John J. Hines
- John Howe
- John Hetherington
- John Hambrick
- John H. Tippets
- John H Eichelberger
- John Guinn
- John Garza
- John Frullo
- John Frey
- John Forgety
- John Ford
- John Fillmore
- John Fillmore
- John Faircloth
- John Evans
- John Elison
- John Eklund, Jr.
- John Eklund
- John E. Nelson
- John E. Davis
- John E. Courson
- John E. Ahern
- John E Huffman
- John Dougall
- John Diehl
- John D. O'Neal IV
- John Cauthorn
- John Carson
- John Carlson
- John C. Schiffer
- John C. Andreason
- John C Rafferty
- John C Morris
- John Burris
- John Brenden
- John 'Bert' A. Stevenson
- John Bear
- John B. Coghill, Jr.
- John Andrist
- John Alario
- John Adams
- John A. Cox
- John A. Cosgrove
- John A Torbett
- John A Berthelot
- Joey Hood
- Joey Hensley
- Joey Fillingane

- Joel Robideaux
- Joel Kretz
- Joel Johnson
- Joel Fry
- Joe Wilkinson
- Joe T. May
- Joe Straus
- Joe Schmick
- Joe Negron
- Joe N. Acinapura
- Joe Miller
- Joe Markley
- Joe Hune
- Joe Heilman
- Joe Harrison
- Joe Gimse
- Joe Faust
- Joe Emrick
- Joe Ellington
- Joe Driver
- Joe Carr
- Joe Bowen
- Joe Booth
- Joe Benning
- Joe Balyeat
- Joe A. Palmer
- Jody Amedee
- Jodie Anne Laudenberg
- Joan Nass
- JoAn E. Wood
- Joan B. Brady
- Jimmy Pruett
- Jimmy Patronis
- Jimmy Matlock
- Jimmy Holley
- Jimmy Higdon
- Jimmy Eldridge
- Jimmy Dixon
- Jimmie T Smith
- Jimmie Don Aycock
- Jim White
- Jim Weiers
- Jim Weiers
- Jim Weidner
- Jim Tracy
- Jim Tomes
- Jim Thompson
- Jim Summerville
- Jim Stamas
- Jim Smith
- Jim Smith
- Jim Shockley
- Jim Schmidt
- Jim Roers
- Jim Rice
- Jim Pitts
- Jim Peterson
- Jim Patterson
- Jim Norman
- Jim Nielson
- Jim Murphy
- Jim Merritt Jr.
- Jim McCune
- Jim McClendon
- Jim Marshall
- Jim Marriott
- Jim Lembke
- Jim Landtroop
- Jim Keffer
- Jim Kasper
- Jim Jackson
- Jim Hughes
- Jim Honeyford
- Jim Halligan
- Jim Guthrie
- Jim Gotto
- Jim Davis
- Jim Cox
- Jim Coley
- Jim Cobb
- Jim Christiana
- Jim Carns
- Jim Butler
- Jim Buchy
- Jim Boyd
- Jim Bolin
- Jim Bird
- Jim Beckett
- Jim Barton
- Jim Banks
- Jim Baird
- Jessica Sibley Upshaw
- Jery C. Dockham
- Jerry Weiers
- Jerry Weiers
- Jerry W Tillman
- Jerry Stevenson
- Jerry Stern
- Jerry R. Torr
- Jerry R Turner
- Jerry Nolte
- Jerry 'Nate' Nathan Bell
- Jerry Madden
- Jerry Lewis
- Jerry Knowles
- Jerry Klein
- Jerry Behn
- Jerome L. Delvin
- Jerome L. Delvin
- JeremyFaison
- Jeremy Young Hutchinson
- Jeremy Taylor
- Jeremy Peterson
- Jeremy Miller
- Jeremy H Oden
- Jeremy Gillam
- Jeremiah J. Nordquist
- Jenny Anderson Horne
- Jeffrey Timberlake
- Jeffrey S Guice
- Jeffrey Pyle
- Jeffrey McClain
- Jeffrey 'Jeff' D. Thompson
- Jeffrey Haverly
- Jeffrey Essmann
- Jeffrey E Piccola
- Jeffrey Brandes
- Jeffery Gifford
- Jeff Thompson
- Jeff Thompson
- Jeff Smith
- Jeff Smith
- Jeff Nesset
- Jeff Longbine
- Jeff Kruse
- Jeff King
- Jeff Kaufmann
- Jeff Grisamore
- Jeff Farrington
- Jeff Espich
- Jeff Dial
- Jeff Dial
- Jeff Delzer
- Jeff Collins
- Jeff C. Siddoway
- JEANNIE HADDAWAY-RICCIO
- Jeanie Riddle
- Jeanie Lauer
- Jeanette M Nunez
- Jean Schodorf
- Jean Preston
- Jean Leising
- Jean Hunhoff
- JD Alexander
- Jay Wasson
- Jay Scott Emler
- Jay Rodne
- Jay Roberts
- Jay Powell
- Jay Neal
- Jay Love
- Jay Houghton

- Jay Hottinger
- Jay Barnes
- JAY A. JACOBS
- Javan "J.D." Mesnard
- Javan "J.D." Mesnard
- Jason Welch
- Jason T Brodeur
- Jason Spencer
- Jason Spencer
- Jason Smith
- Jason Shaw
- Jason Schultz
- Jason Saine
- Jason Rapert
- Jason Priest
- Jason Perillo
- Jason Overstreet
- Jason Isaac
- Jason Crowell
- Jason Conger
- Jason Atkinson
- Jase Bolger
- Jarrod Martin
- Jarrod Crockett
- Jared Carpenter
- Jarad Klein
- Janice K. McGeachin
- Janice Giegler
- Janet H Adkins
- Janéa Holmquist
- Jane M Earll
- Jane Knapp
- Jane Cunningham
- Jan Tankersley
- Jan Jones
- Jan Angel
- Jamie Ison
- Jamie Boomgarden
- James White
- James W. (Will) Morefield
- James W "JW" Grant
- James Van Engelenhoven
- James Seymour
- James Schaefer
- James Roland Smith
- James Parker
- James P. (Jimmie) Massie, III
- James Morris
- James Marleau
- James M. LeMunyon
- James L. McNeil
- James L Boles Jr
- James 'Jim' Patrick
- James 'Jim' Hodges Harrison
- James 'Jim' H. Merrill
- James 'Jim' Eckhardt
- James 'Jim' C. Hammond
- James 'Jim' Anderson
- James 'Jay' H. Lucas
- James Hamper
- James Hahn
- James H Langdon Jr
- James Gillway
- James E. Edmunds, II
- James Dunnigan
- James C Frishe
- James Buck
- Jake Corman
- Jake Carter Files
- Jacqueline Sly
- Jackson H. Miller
- Jackie Winters
- Jack Williams
- Jack Whitver
- Jack W. Harper
- Jack W. Harper
- Jack Lutz
- Jack Latvala
- Jack Johnson
- Jack Goodman
- Jack Draxler
- Jack Drake
- Jack Donahue
- Jack Brandenburg
- J.T. Waggoner
- J.M. Lozano
- J.E. Putnam
- J. Randall Minchew
- J. Mark Johnston
- J. Gary Simrill
- J. Derham Cole, Jr.
- J Scott Raecker
- Israel D. O'Quinn
- Ira Hanson
- Hunter Greene
- Hunt, Randy
- Humason, Donald
- Hugh Kenneth Leatherman, Sr.
- Hugh D. Crawford
- Hugh Blackwell
- Hubert Houser
- Howitt, Steven
- Howard Walker
- Howard Stephenson
- Howard Sanderford
- Howard McFadden
- Howard Maxwell
- Howard 'Luke' A. Kenley
- Holly Hughes
- Hill, Bradford
- HERBERT H. McMILLAN
- Herb Frierson
- Henry Rayhones
- Henry 'Hank' H. R. Coe
- Henry Burns
- Heidi E. Scheuermann
- Hedlund, Robert
- Heather Sirocki
- Heather Carter
- Heather Carter
- Heath VanNatter
- Heath Mello
- HB Hank Zuber III
- Harvey T. Smith
- Harvey Smith Peeler, Jr.
- Harvey R. Kenton
- Harvey Hilderbran
- Harry Warren
- Harry Shiver
- Harry R. Purkey
- Harry Geisinger
- Harry Coates, Jr.
- Harry 'Chip' Bancroft Limehouse III
- Harry Brown
- Harry Brooks
- Harris Blake
- Harrington, Sheila
- Harold Sigler
- Harold J. Peterman
- Harold J Brubaker
- Hans Zeiger
- Hans Hunt
- Hank Lott
- Hal Wick
- H. WAYNE NORMAN, JR.
- H Marlene O'Toole
- Gwen E. Howard
- Guy Vander Linden
- Grey Mills
- Gretchen Hoffman
- Gregory S. Clark
- Gregory Miller
- Gregory 'Greg' L. Adams
- Gregory F. Lavelle
- Gregory D. Habeeb
- Gregory Cromer
- Gregg Blikre
- Greg Wren
- Greg Walker
- Greg Treat
- Greg Steuerwald
- Greg Snowden

- Greg Smith
- Greg Reed
- Greg Morris
- Greg MacMaster
- Greg Hinkle
- Greg Haney
- Greg Forristall
- Greg Evers
- Greg Childers
- Gray Tollison
- Gordon Dove
- Gordon Denlinger
- Gordon C. Helsel, Jr.
- Goeff Hansen
- Glenn Moniz
- Glenn Grothman
- Glenn Anderson
- Glen Massie
- Glen Klippenstein
- Glen Grell
- GLEN GLASS
- Glen Froseth
- Glen Casada
- Glen Bradley
- Giles Ward
- Gilbert R. Baker
- Gil Riviere
- Gifford, Susan
- Geroge Keiser
- Gerlad Long
- Gerlad Dial
- Gergory Hughes
- Gerald W. Hocker
- Gerald Uglem
- Gerald Stebelton
- Gerald S. Gay
- Gerald McCormick
- Gerald 'Gerry' E. Geis
- Gerald 'Gary' W. Reis
- Gerald E Greene
- Gerald Allen
- George R. Fontaine
- George R Moraitis Jr
- George Nodland
- George M. Hearn
- George Lavender
- George G Cleveland
- George E. Eskridge
- George Dunbar
- George 'Chip' E. Campsen III
- Geoff Michel
- Gene Yaw
- Gene Whisnant
- Gene Ward
- Gene Maddox
- Gene Digirolamo
- Gene Alday
- Gene Abdallah
- Gen Olson
- Geanie Morrison
- Gayle Manning
- Gayle L. Batt
- Gayle B Harrell
- Gay Kernan
- Gary Worthan
- Gary V Staples
- Gary Sukit
- Gary Stanislawski
- Gary Simpson
- Gary Scherer
- Gary Plummer
- Gary Paur
- Gary L. Stevens
- Gary Kreidt
- Gary Knight
- Gary Jackson
- Gary G. Howell
- Gary Fuhr
- Gary Elkins
- Gary E. Collins
- Gary Don Stubblefield
- Gary Deffenbaugh
- Gary Day
- Gary Dahms
- Gary Cross
- Gary C. Alexander
- Gary Aubuchon
- Gary A Lee
- Gary A Chism
- Garth Everett
- Garry R. Smith
- Garrett Richter
- Garrett Mason
- Garrett Love
- Galen Higdon
- Galen D. Hadley
- Gail Lavielle
- Gail Haines
- GAIL H. BATES
- Gail Griffin
- Gage Froerer
- G. Murrell Smith, Jr.
- G. M. (Manoli) Loupassi
- G. L. Pridgen
- Frost, Paul
- Fredrick W Costello
- Fred Wood
- Fred Romkema
- Fred Mills Jr
- Fred Keller
- Fred J. Dyson
- Fred Girod
- Fred F Steen II
- Fred Emerich
- Fred Cox
- Fred Camillo
- Franklin Foil
- Frank Simpson
- Frank S Niceley
- Frank Pratt
- Frank Pratt
- Frank N. Henderson
- Frank Morse
- Frank Lasee
- Frank LaRose
- Frank Iler
- Frank Howard
- Frank Hoffmann
- Frank Foster
- Frank Farry
- Frank D. Peasley
- Frank Artiles
- Frank Antenori
- Francis 'Topper' Matthew McFaun
- Francis 'Greg' Gregory Delleney, Jr.
- Francis Gibson
- Four Price
- Fletcher L Hartsell Jr
- Ferguson, Kimberly
- Fattman, Ryan
- F. 'Mike' Michael Sottile
- F. Bruce Holland
- Evelyn Lynn
- Evan Vickers
- Eugene Clarke
- Erwin Cain
- Erikka Storch
- Erik Simpson
- Erik Helland
- Erik Fresen
- Erick Moore
- Erich Ponti
- Eric Watson
- Eric Schmitt
- Eric R. Anderson
- Eric Nelson
- Eric Michael Bedingfield
- Eric L. Householder
- Eric J. Bikas
- Eric Hutchings
- Eric Feige
- Eric Eisnaugle

- Eric Burlison
- Eric A. Koch
- Emory Dunahoo
- Elwyn Thomas
- Ellyn Setnore Bogdanoff
- Ellis Black
- Elli Espling
- Ellen Brandom
- Elizabeth W Porter
- Elizabeth Kraus
- Elizabeth Jane English
- Eli Evankovich
- Eli D. Bebout
- Eldon Nygaard
- Elder A Vogel
- Elaine D. Harvey
- Eileen 'Lynn' G. Dickinson
- Eileen Kowall
- Efton M Sager
- Edwin B Erickson
- Edward Walker
- Edward van Gerpen
- Edward T. Scott
- Edward Southard
- Edward Lindsey
- Edward 'Eddie' R. Tallon
- Edward 'Ed' A. Buchanan
- Edward Clere
- Eduardo Gonzalez
- Edmond Soliday
- Edgar V Starnes
- Eddie Lambert
- Eddie Joe Williams
- Eddie Fields
- Eddie Farnsworth
- Eddie Farnsworth
- Ed Setzler
- Ed Rynders
- Ed Orcutt
- Douglas Thomas
- Douglas Sagers
- Doug Whitsett
- Doug Overbey
- Doug Miller
- Doug McLeod
- Doug McKillip
- Doug Magnus
- Doug LaMalfa
- Doug Holt
- Doug Holder
- Doug Gutwein
- Doug Funderburk
- Doug Ericksen
- Doug Eckerty
- Doug Damon
- Doug Collins
- Dorothy 'Sue' S. Landske
- Dorothy Pelanda
- Dorothy L Hukill
- Doris Goodale
- Doris Goodale
- Dorinda Connor
- Donnie Chesteen
- Donnie Bell
- Donna Sheldon
- Donna Oberlander
- DONNA M. STIFLER
- Donna Lichtenegger
- Donna Hutchinson
- Donald W. Merricks
- Donald Steinbeisser
- Donald Schaible
- Donald L Clark
- Donald E. Burkhart, Jr.
- Donald 'Don' Benton
- Donald C White
- DONALD B. ELLIOTT
- Donald A. Blakey
- Don Wells
- Don Vigesaa
- Don Shooter
- Don Ruzicka
- Don Philips
- Don Parsons
- Don Miller
- Don Lehe
- Don Kopp
- Don Ipson
- Don Gosen
- Don Gaetz
- Don East
- Don Carson Bowen
- Don Benton
- Don Barrington
- Dominic Pileggi
- Dolores Gresham
- Dixon Pitcher
- Diehl, Geoff
- Dickie Drake
- Dick Kelsey
- Dick Hess
- Dick Dever
- Dick Brewbaker
- Dick Anderson
- Dianne Tilton
- Diane Patrick
- Diane Franklin
- Derek Brown
- Denton C. Darrington
- Denny Hoskins
- Dennis Roach
- Dennis Richardson
- Dennis Pyle
- Dennis Powers
- Dennis M. Lake
- Dennis L Jones
- Dennis Kruse
- Dennis Keschi
- Dennis K Baxley
- Dennis Johnson
- Dennis J. Devereux
- Dennis DeBar
- Dennis Carroll Moss
- Dennis Bonnen
- Denis Grimsley
- D'Emilia, Angelo
- deMacedo, Viriato
- Delvis Dutton
- Delus Johnson
- Dell Raybould
- Del McOmie
- Del Marsh
- Dee Margo
- DebraLee Hovey
- Debra Young Maggart
- Debra 'Debbie' M. Hobbs
- Debra D Plowman
- Deborah Sanderson
- Deborah Hudson
- Deborah A. Long
- Debby Barrett
- Debbie Riddle
- Debbie Mayfield
- Debbie Lesko
- Debbie Lesko
- Deb Peters
- Deb Lynn Shaughnessy
- Deb Fischer
- Dean Wink
- Dean Sanpei
- Dean M. Mortimer
- Dean L. Cameron
- Dean Kirby
- Dean Cray
- Dean Cannon
- Dawn Pettengill
- Davy Carter
- David Yarde
- David Williams
- David W. Stevens
- David W. Stevens
- David Tribble, Jr.

- David Tjepkes
- David Simpson
- David Simmons
- David Sessions
- David Scribner
- David Scott
- David Sater
- David Rust
- David Rouzer
- David Robertson
- David Richardson
- David Ralston
- David R. Miller
- David R Lewis
- David Pearce
- David Novstrup
- David Nelson
- David Monson
- David Millard
- David Maloney
- David M. Meeks
- David Lust
- David Luetchefeld
- David Long
- David Lee Zwonitzer
- David Lawson
- David Labriola
- David L. Wilson
- David L. Thomas
- David L. Branscum
- David Knight
- David Johnson
- David Johnson
- David J. Sanders
- David I. Ramadan
- David Holt
- David Hogue
- David Hinkins
- David Hildenbrand
- David Hickernell
- David Heaton
- David Hawk
- David Hastings
- David Hann
- David Hall
- David Gowan
- David Gowan
- David Givens
- David G Argall
- David Frizzell
- David E. Yancey
- David Drovdal
- David Day
- David 'Davey' R. Hiott
- David Cotta
- David Casas
- David Butterfield
- David Burns
- David Burnell Smith
- David Burnell Smith
- David B. Albo
- David Alexander
- David Agema
- David A. Wolkins
- Dave Yaccarino
- Dave Weiler
- Dave Thompson
- Dave Syverson
- Dave Senjem
- Dave Schatz
- Dave Reed
- Dave Oehlke
- Dave Nething
- Dave Lewis
- Dave Hinson
- Dave F. Bloomfield
- Dave Deyoe
- Dave D. Bonner
- Dave Burke
- Dave Brown
- Daryl Metcalfe
- Daryl Cowles
- Darwin Booher
- Darrell Pollock
- Darrell G. Bolz
- Darrell G McCormick
- Darlene Taylor
- Darin LaHood
- Danny Bubp
- Danielle Conrad
- Daniel W. Marshall, III
- Daniel Thatcher
- Daniel McCay
- Daniel Martiny
- Daniel Huseman
- Daniel F McComas
- Daniel Davis
- Daniel 'Danny' B. Verdin III
- Daniel 'Dan' Paul Hamilton
- Daniel 'Dan' K. Zwonitzer
- Daniel B. Short
- Dana Dow
- Dana D Young
- Dan Williams
- Dan W Ingle
- Dan Truitt
- Dan Soucek
- Dan Seum
- Dan Saddler
- Dan Ruby
- Dan Rasmussen
- Dan P. Swecker
- Dan Newberry
- Dan Moul
- Dan Leonard
- Dan Lederman
- Dan Kristiansen
- Dan Johnson
- Dan Huberty
- Dan Hall
- Dan Flynn
- Dan Duffy
- Dan Dryden
- Dan Dockstader
- Dan Claitor
- Dan Carter
- Dan Brown
- Dan Branch
- Dan "Blade" Morrish
- Damon Thayer
- Dale W. Zorn
- Dale Schultz
- Dale Righter
- Dale R. Folwell
- Dale M Erdey
- Dale Ford
- Dale crafts
- D Craig Horn
- Cynthia Thielen
- Cynthia S. Denby
- Curtiss Kreun
- Curtis Sonney
- Curtis Olafson
- Curtis Oda
- Curtis King
- Curtis Johnson
- Curtis Halford
- Curtis 'Curt' D. McKenzie
- Curtis Bramble
- Curt Webb
- Curt Meier
- Curt Hofstad
- Curry Todd
- Cresent Hardy
- Craig Tieszen
- Craig Redmon
- Craig Newbold
- Craig Miner
- Craig Johnson
- Craig Headland
- Craig Frank
- Courtney Combs

- Corinne Ching
- Corinne Ching
- Corey Brown
- Conrad Appel
- Connie Scott
- Colin Bonini
- Cole McNary
- Colby Coash
- Cloria Brown
- Clinton Harden, Jr.
- Clifton Richardson
- Clifford G. "Biff" Lee
- Clifford 'Cliff' R. Bayer
- Cliff Rosenberger
- Cliff Hite
- Cliff Branan
- Cliff Bentz
- Cliff Aldridge
- Clel Baudler
- Clay Scofield
- Clay Schexnayder
- Clay Ingram
- Clay Ford
- Clark Jolley
- Clark Chapin
- Clarence J. Vranish
- Claire Robling
- Cindy Noe
- Cindy Kirchhofer
- Cindy Burkett
- Chuck Winder
- Chuck Williams
- Chuck Thomsen
- Chuck Soderberg
- Chuck Sims
- Chuck Purgason
- Chuck McGrady
- Chuck Martin
- Chuck Kleckley
- Chuck Hopson
- Chuck Gatschenberger
- Chuck Damschen
- Christy Perry
- Christopher T. Head
- Christopher P. Stolle
- Christopher Leopoid
- Christopher Lauzen
- Christopher K. Peace
- Christopher Herrod
- Christopher Davis
- Christopher Coutu
- Christopher 'Chris' J. Murphy
- Christopher Broadwater
- Christine Redogno
- Christine Johnson
- Christina Hagan
- Christie Carpino
- Christian Coomer
- Chrissy Sommer
- Chris Widener
- Chris Telfer
- Chris Steineger
- Chris Ross
- Chris Rector
- Chris Molendorp
- Chris McDaniel
- Chris Massey
- Chris Langemeier
- Chris Hagenow
- Chris Gerlach
- Chris Dorworth
- Chris Carney
- Chris Brown
- Chip Huggins
- Chip Baltimore
- Chet Pollert
- Chester Crandell
- Chester Crandell
- Cheryl Grossman
- Cheryl A. Pflug
- Chauncey 'Greg' Klugh Gregory
- Chas Vincent
- Charlie R. Huggins
- Charlie Janssen
- Charlie Howard
- Charlie Geren
- Charlie Denison
- Charlie Dean
- Charlie Davis
- Charlice Byrd
- Charles Turbiville
- Charles T. McIlhinney
- Charles Schwertner
- Charles R. Ross
- Charles Perry
- Charles 'Pat' P. Childers
- Charles Moss
- Charles Michael Sargent
- Charles McBurney
- Charles K. Scott
- CHARLES J. OTTO
- Charles Hoffman
- Charles E Van Zant
- Charles D. Poindexter
- Charles 'Charlie' S. Collins
- Charles Chaney
- Charles 'Butch' H. Shaw
- Charles Busby
- Charles "Doc" Anderson
- Charisse Millett
- Chad Nimmer
- Chad Fincher
- Cecile H. Bledsoe
- Cecil P. Ash
- Cecil P. Ash
- Cecil Dolecheck
- Cathy Munoz
- Cathy Dahlquist
- Cathy Connolly
- CATHLEEN M. VITALE, Esq.
- Catherine Cloutier
- Catherine 'Cathy' A. Giessel
- Casey Kozlowski
- Casey Guernsey
- Casey Eure
- Casey Anderson
- Cary Condotta
- Carroll Leavell
- Carroll Gibson
- Carolyn Whitney Branagan
- Carolyn McGinn
- Carolyn H Justice
- Carolyn Crawford
- Carole Pankau
- Carol Miller
- Carmine Mowbray
- Carlos V. Bilbao
- Carlos Trujillo
- Carlos Lopez-Cantera
- Carlin Yoder
- Carla Nelson
- Carl Walker Metzgar
- Carl Seel
- Carl Seel
- Carl Rogers
- Carl 'Bunky' R. Loucks
- Cameron Sexton
- Cameron Henry
- Cam Ward
- Calvin Hill
- Caleb Jones
- Cale Case
- C. Todd Gilbert
- C. Scott Bounds
- C. Matthew Fariss
- C Adam Harris
- Byron Cook
- Buzz Brockway
- Butch Parrish
- Burt Tulson
- Burt R. Solomons
- Burke J. Harr

- Buddy Harden
- Bubber Epps
- Bryce Marlatt
- Bryan Taylor
- Bryan Nelson
- Bryan K. Pedersen
- Bryan Hughes
- Bryan Cutler
- Bryan B. King
- Bryan Adams
- Bruce Wyche Bannister
- Bruce Williamson
- Bruce Westerman
- Bruce Tutvedt
- Bruce Starr
- Bruce Rampelberg
- Bruce R. Rendon
- Bruce L Hanna
- Bruce Goodwin
- Bruce Dammeier
- Bruce Cozart
- Bruce Chandler
- Bruce Caswell
- Bruce Burns
- Bruce Borders
- Bruce Bickford
- Bruan R Holloway
- Brooks Coleman
- Brock Greenfield
- Brice Wiggins
- Brian Savilla
- Brian Nieves
- Brian Munzlinger
- Brian Moore
- Brian Liss
- Brian Langley
- Brian Kelsey
- Brian K. Savage
- Brian Hill
- Brian Gosch
- Brian Ellis
- Brian Crain
- Brian C. Bosma
- Brian Boquist
- Brian Bingman
- Brian Aldridge
- Brett Harrell
- Brett Geymann
- Bret Allain
- Brent Waltz
- Brent Steele
- Brent Lasater
- Brent Jackson
- Brent J. Crane
- Brent Hill
- Brenda L. Pogge
- Brenda Kupchick
- Brenda J. Council
- Brenda Heller
- Brenda Barton
- Brenda Barton
- Brandt Hershman
- Brandon Smith
- Brandon Creighton
- Bradley Moulton
- Bradley Last
- Bradley Daw
- Bradford C. Jacobsen
- Brad Zaun
- Brad Wilson
- Brad Roae
- Brad Mayo
- Brad Lager
- Brad Galvez
- Brad Drake
- Brad Dee
- Brad Ashford
- Brad A Klippert
- Boldyga, Nicholas
- Bobby Shows
- Bobby B Howell
- Bob Skarphol
- Bob Rucho
- Bob Robson
- Bob Robson
- Bob Ramsey
- Bob Peterson
- Bob Nicholas
- Bob Nance
- Bob Morton
- Bob Mensche
- Bob Martinson
- Bob Marshall
- Bob Lynn
- Bob Lake
- Bob Jenson
- Bob Huff
- Bob Hensgens
- Bob Heaton
- Bob Hanner
- Bob Hackett
- Bob Gray
- Bob Dixon
- Bob Deelstra
- Bob Cherry
- Bob Brechtel
- Bob Ashley
- Bo Watson
- Blair Thoreson
- Blaine Galliher
- Billy Pat Wright
- Billy Maddox
- Billy Hudson
- Billy Horne
- Bill Zedler
- Bill Wright
- Bill White
- Bill Thomas
- Bill Taylor
- Bill Stouffer
- Bill Stoltze
- Bill Simanski
- Bill Seitz
- Bill Sanderson
- Bill Sample
- Bill Roberts
- Bill Reiboldt
- Bill Rabon
- Bill Pritchard
- Bill Poole
- Bill Pigott
- Bill Lant
- Bill Ketron
- Bill Kennemer
- Bill Holtzclaw
- Bill Hembree
- Bill Hayes
- Bill Hamilton
- Bill Hager
- Bill Garrard
- Bill G. Ingebrigtsen
- Bill Dunn
- Bill Dix
- Bill Devlin
- Bill Davis
- Bill Cook
- Bill Coley
- Bill Callegari
- Bill Burt
- Bill Brown
- Bill Bowman
- Bill Beagle
- Bill Anderson
- Beverly Woolley
- Beverly J. Sherwood
- Beverly Gard
- Betty Olson
- Betty De Boef
- Bette Grande
- Beth Turner
- Beth O'Connor
- Bert K. Stedman

- Bert Jones
- Bert Brackett
- Bernie O'Neill
- Bernard Ayotte
- Benjamin L. Cline
- Benjamin Kruse
- Ben Watson
- Ben Harbin
- Ben Glardon
- Ben Brooks
- Ben Albritton
- Becky Nordgren
- Becky Duncan Massey
- Becky Currie
- Beau McCoy
- Beaton, Matthew
- Bastien, Richard
- Bart M. Davis
- Bart Korman
- Barry Moore
- Barry Mask
- Barry D. Knight
- Barrows, F.
- Barrow Peacock
- Barrett Rich
- Barney Fisher
- Barbara Sims
- Barbara R Sears
- Barbara Nash
- Barbara J. Comstock
- Barbara C Marumoto
- Barbara Bailey
- B.J. Pak
- B. R. Skelton
- Austin M Allran
- Arthur Payne
- Arthur Orr
- Arthur O Neill
- Arthur Fryslie
- Art Wittich
- Art Swann
- Arlan Meekhof
- Aric Nesbitt
- April Weaver
- Anthony Sykes
- Anthony Ligi
- ANTHONY J. O'DONNELL
- Anthony Guglielmo
- Anthony G. Forlini
- Anthony DeVitis
- Anthony D Amelio
- Annette Sweeney
- Annette M. Dubas
- Anne Zerr
- Anne J. Thayer
- Anne Gonzales
- Anne B. Donahue
- Anne B. Crockett-Stark
- Anna Fairclough
- Anna Border
- Ann V. Clemmer
- Ann Rivers
- Ann Purcell
- Anitere Flores
- Angie Chen Button
- Angela Hill
- Andy Tobin
- Andy Tobin
- Andy Thompson
- Andy Olson
- Andy Mayberry
- Andy Holt
- Andy Hill
- Andy Gipson
- Andy Gardiner
- Andy Billig
- Andy Biggs
- Andrew Roraback
- Andrew Maragos
- Andrew Koenig
- Andrew J. Welch
- Andrew C. Brock
- Andrew Brenner
- Andrew 'Andy' S. Patrick
- Andrew 'Andy' Patrick Donaghy
- ANDREW A. SERAFINI
- Andrea Lea
- Andrea LaFontaine
- Andre Cushing
- Ana Rivas Logan
- Amy Volk
- Amy T. Koch
- Amy L. Edmonds
- Amy Carter
- Amos Amerson
- Amanda Price
- Amanda Pasdon
- Amanda M. McGill
- Amanda A. Reeve
- Amanda A. Reeve
- Alon Wieland
- Allen W. Kerr
- Allen Treadaway
- Allen Peake
- Allen Paul
- Allen M. Jaggi
- Allen Fletcher
- Allen Farley
- Allen Christensen
- Allan Ritter
- Alice Kerr
- Alex Willette
- Alex Monsour
- Alex Atwood
- Alberta Darling
- Albert 'Chuck' Pearce
- Alan Seabaugh
- Alan Powell
- Alan Olson
- Alan Olsen
- Alan Hays
- Alan Harper
- Alan Dick
- Alan Delk Clemmons
- Alan C. Boothe
- Alan Baker
- Alan Austerman
- Al Pscholka
- Al Novstrup
- Al Melvin
- Al Landis
- Al DeKruif
- Al Carlson
- Al Adinolfi
- AJ Griffin
- AG Crowe
- ADELAIDE C. (ADDIE) ECKARDT
- Adams, Paul
- Adam Driggs
- Adam B. Howard
- Acree, Cindy
- Abbie Cornett
- Aaron Pena
- Aaron Osmond
- Aaron Ling Johanson
- Aaron Libby
- A. WADE KACH
- A. Shane Massey
- Ruth Rowan
- Ron Walters
- Robert A. Watson
- Ray Canterbury
- Randi Becker
- Patricia L. Morgan
- Nicholas D. Kettle
- Michael W. Chippendale
- Linda R. Evans Parlette
- Laurence W. Ehrhardt
- Joseph A. Trillo
- John A. Savage
- Joe Fain
- J.T. Wilcox

- Glenford J. Shibley
- Francis T. Maher, Jr.
- Doreen Marie Costa
- Dennis L. Algiere
- Dawson Tucker Hodgson
- David V. Taylor
- David E. Bates
- Daniel Patrick Reilly
- Daniel P. Gordon Jr.
- Christopher Scott Ottiano
- Brian C. Newberry
- Bill Hinkle
- Bill Anderson
- Bethany L. Moura
- Allen V. Evans
-
- Alex McFarland
- President, Southern Evangelical Seminary (Charlotte, NC)
-
- Most Rev. George Dallas McKinney
- Bishop, & Founder and Pastor, St. Stephen's Cathedral, Church of God in Christ (San Diego, CA)
-
- Most Reverend Dale J. Melczek
- Bishop, Roman Catholic Diocese of Gary, IN
-
- Rt. Rev. John E. Miller, III
- Missionary Bishop, Anglican Mission in the Americas
-
- Rt. Rev. Martyn Minns
- Missionary Bishop, Convocation of Anglicans in North America (Herndon, VA)
-
- Dr. C. Ben Mitchell
- Graves Professor of Moral Philosophy, Union University (Jackson, TN)
-
- Dr. R. Albert Mohler, Jr.
- President, Southern Baptist Theological Seminary (Louisville, KY)
-
- Most Rev. Salvatore R. Matano
- Bishop, Roman Catholic of Burlington, VT
-
- Dr. Russell D. Moore
- Senior VP for Academic Administration & Dean of the School of Theology, Southern Baptist Theological Seminary (Louisville, KY)
-
- Bishop Robert C. Morlino
- Bishop, Roman Catholic Diocese of Madison, WI
-
- Richard J. Mouw
- President, Fuller Theological Seminary (Pasadena, CA)
-
- Thomas D. Mullins
- Christ Fellowship Church, Palm Beach, FL
-
- J. Todd Mullins
- Christ Fellowship Church, Palm Beach, FL
-
- Rt. Rev. Charles H. Murphy, III
- Missionary Bishop of Rwanda and Chairman of the Anglican Mission in the Americas
-
- Most Rev. John J. Myers
- Archbishop, Roman Catholic Archdiocese of Newark, NJ
-
- Most Rev. Joseph F. Naumann
- Archbishop, Roman Catholic Diocese of Kansas City, KS
-
- David Neff
- Editor-in-Chief, Christianity Today (Carol Stream, IL)
-
- Tom Nelson
- Senior Pastor, Christ Community Evangelical Free Church (Leawood, KS)
-
- Dr. Jerry Newcombe
- Host/Senior Producer, Coral Ridge Ministries (Fort Lauderdale, FL)
-
- Niel Nielson
- President, Covenant College (Lookout Mt., GA)
-
- Most Rev. John Nienstedt
- Archbishop, Roman Catholic Archdiocese of Saint Paul and Minneapolis, MN
-
- Nikolas T. Nikas, Esq.
- President and General Counsel, Bioethics Defense Fund
-
- Michael Novak
- Author, Philosopher, & Theologian
-
- Most Rev. Edwin F. O'Brien
- Archbishop, Roman Catholic Archdiocese of Baltimore, MD
-
- Dr. Tom Oden
- Theologian, United Methodist Minister and Professor, Drew University (Madison, NJ)
-
- Most Rev. Jerry Ogles
- Anglican Orthodox Communion Worldwide (Enterprise, AL)
-
- Marvin Olasky
- Editor-in-Chief,World Magazine and provost, The Kings College (New York City, NY)
-
- Rev. Neftali "Charles" Olmeda
- Pennsylvania Chapter Director, National Hispanic Christian Leadership Conference (Allentown, PA)
-
- Most Rev. Thomas J. Olmsted
- Bishop, Roman Catholic Diocese of Phoenix, AZ
-
- Rev. William Owens
- Chairman, Coalition of African-American Pastors (Memphis, TN)
-
- Dr. J.I. Packer
- Board of Governors, Professor of Theology, Regent College (Canada)
-
- Metr. Jonah Paffhausen
- Primate, Orthodox Church in America (Syosset, NY)
-
- Most Rev. Richard E. Pates
- Bishop, Roman Catholic Diocese of Des Moines, IA
-
- Tony Perkins
- President, Family Research Council (Washington, D.C.)
-
- Metr. Archbishop Stephan Petrovich
- Ukrainian Autocephalous Orthodox Church of North & South America
-
- Eric M. Pillmore
- CEO, Pillmore Consulting LLC (Doylestown, PA)
-
- Dr. Everett Piper
- President, Oklahoma Wesleyan University (Bartlesville, OK)
-
- Todd Pitner
- President, Rev Increase
-
- Dr. Cornelius Plantinga
- President, Calvin Theological Seminary (Grand Rapids, MI)
-
- Dr. David Platt
- Pastor, Church at Brook Hills (Birmingham AL)
-
- Rev. Jim Pocock
- Pastor, Trinitarian Congregational Church (Wayland, MA)
-
- Fred Potter
- Executive Director & CEO, Christian Legal Society (Springfield, VA)
-
- Archbishop Andre J.W. Queen, SCR
- Catholic Apostolic National Church
-
- Dennis Rainey

- President, CEO, & Co-Founder, FamilyLife (Little Rock, AR)
-
- Fr. Patrick Reardon
- Pastor,All Saints Antiochian Orthodox Church (Chicago, IL)
-
- Bob Reccord
- Executive Director, Council on National Policy

- Dr. Harry L. Reeder
- Sr. Pastor, Briarwood Presbyterian Church (Birmingham, AL)
-
- Most Rev. Kevin C. Rhoades
- Bishop, Roman Catholic Diocese of Fort Wayne-South Bend, IN
-
- Most Rev. David Ricken
- Bishop, Roman Catholic Diocese of Green Bay, WI
-
- His Eminence Justin Cardinal Rigali
- Archbishop, Roman Catholic Archdiocese of Philadelphia, PA
-
- Rev. Eugene F. Rivers
- Senior Policy Adviser to the Presiding Bishop, Chuch of God in Christ
-
- James and Betty Robison
- Founder and President, LIFE Outreach International (Fort Worth, TX)
-
- Most Rev. Thomas J. Rodi
- Archbishop, Roman Catholic Archdiocese of Mobile, AL
-
- Rev. Samuel Rodriguez
- President, National Hispanic Christian Leadership Conference

- Stewart Epperson,
- Chairman, Council on National Policy

-
- Most Rev. Val E. Rose
- Presiding Bishop,Conservative Anglican Church of North America

- Right Reverend Robert Ruiz
- Bishop, Houston Diocese of the Conservative Anglican Church of North America
-
- David Schuringa
- President, Crossroads Bible Institute (Grand Rapids, MI)

- Rick Santorum
- Former U.S. Senator (PA)
-
- Tricia Scribner
- Author (Harrisburg, NC)
-
- Dr. Dave Seaford
- Senior Pastor, Community Fellowship Church (Matthews, NC)
-
- Alan Sears
- President, CEO, & General Counsel, Alliance Defense Fund (Scottsdale, AZ)
-
- Randy Setzer
- Senior Pastor, Macedonia Baptist Church (Lincolnton, NC)
-
- Kelly Shackelford, Esq.
- Chief Counsel, Liberty Legal Institute (Plano, TX)
-
- Most Rev. Michael J. Sheehan
- Archbishop, Roman Catholic Archdiocese of Santa Fe, NM
-
- Rev. Louis P. Sheldon
- Founder and Chairman, Traditional Values Coalition (Anaheim, CA)
-
- Most Rev. Michael J. Sheridan
- Bishop, Roman Catholic Diocese of Colorado Springs, CO
-
- Dr. Ron Sider
- Director, Evangelicals for Social Action (Wynnewood, PA)
-

- Fr. Robert Sirico
- Founder, Acton Institute (Grand Rapids, MI)
-
- Dr. Robert Sloan
- President, Houston Baptist University (Houston, TX)
-
- Rev. Paul T. Stallsworth
- Taskforce of United Methodists on Abortion and Sexuality/Lifewatch (Cottleville, MO)
-
- Charles Stetson
- Chairman of the Board, Bible Literacy Project (New York, NY)
-
- Dr. David Stevens
- CEO, Christian Medical & Dental Association (Bristol, TN)
-
- John Stonestreet
- Executive Director, Summit Ministries (Manitou Springs, CO)
-
- Dr. Joseph Stowell
- President, Cornerstone University (Grand Rapids, MI)
-
- Rev. Peter M.J. Stravinskas
- Editor, The Catholic Response (Pine Beach, NJ)
-
- Dr. Sarah Sumner
- Professor of Theology and Ministry, Azusa Pacific University (Azusa, CA)
-
- Dr. Glenn Sunshine
- Research Fellow of the Action Institute (Grand Rapids, MI)
-
- Chuck Swindoll
- Founder and Chairman of the Board, Insight for Living, Senior Pastor—Stonebriar Community Church (Frisco, TX), Chancellor—Dallas Theological Seminary
-
- Joni Eareckson Tada
- Founder and CEO, Joni and Friends International Disability Center (Agoura Hills, CA)
-
- Luiz Tellez
- President, The Witherspoon Institute (Princeton, NJ)
-
- Dr. Timothy C. Tennent
- Professor, Gordon-Conwell Theological Seminary (South Hamilton, MA)
-
- James R. Thobaben
- Professor of Bioethics and Social Ethics, Asbury Theological Seminary (Wilmore, KY)
-
- Dr. Greg Thornbury
- Dean of the School of Christian Studies, Union University, Fellow at the Wilberforce Forum (Washington, D.C.)
-
- Michael Timmis
- Chairman, Prison Fellowship and Prison Fellowship International (Naples, FL)
-
- Michael Timmis, Jr
- Chairman of the Board, Ave Maria University (Ave Maria, FL)
-
- Mark Tooley
- President,Institute for Religion and Democracy (Washington, D.C.)
-
- H. James Towey
- President, St. Vincent College (Latrobe, PA)
-
- Most Rev. Donald W. Trautman
- Bishop, Roman Catholic Diocese of Erie, PA
-
- Juan Valdes
- Middle and High School Chaplain, Florida Christian School (Miami, FL)
-
- Most Rev. Allen Vigneron
- Archbishop, Roman Catholic Diocese of Detroit, MI
-
- Most Rev. John G. Vlazny

- Archbishop, Roman Catholic Archdiocese of Portland, OR
-
- Todd Wagner
- Pastor, WaterMark Community Church (Dallas, TX)
-
- Dr. Graham Walker
- President, Patrick Henry College (Purcellville, VA)
-
- Rev. William J. Waltersheid
- Secretary for Clergy and Consecrated Life, Roman Catholic Diocese of Harrisburg, PA
-
- Most Rev. Michael W. Warfel
- Bishop, Roman Catholic Diocese of Great Falls-Billings, MT
-
- Fr. Alexander F. C. Webster, PhD
- Archpriest, Orthodox Church in America and Professorial Lecturer, The George Washington University (Ashburn, VA)
-
- George Weigel
- Distinguished Senior Fellow, Ethics and Public Policy Center (Washington, D.C.)
-
- David Welch
- Houston Area Pastor Council Executive Director, US Pastors Council (Houston, TX)
-
- Most Rev. Thomas Wenski
- Bishop, Roman Catholic Diocese of Orlando, FL
-
- Dr. James Emery White
- Founding and Senior Pastor, Mecklenberg Community Church (Charlotte, NC)
-
- Luder Whitlock
- Excelsis (Orlando, FL)
-
- Dr. Hayes Wicker
- Senior Pastor, First Baptist Church (Naples, FL)
-
- Don Wildmon
- American Family Association
-
- Mark Williamson
- Founder and President, Foundation Restoration Ministries/Federal Intercessors (Katy, TX)
-
- Parker T. Williamson
- Editor Emeritus and Senior Correspondent, Presbyterian Lay Committee
-
- Dr. Craig Williford
- President, Trinity International University (Deerfield, IL)
-
- Dr. John Woodbridge
- Research professor of Church History & the History of Christian Thought, Trinity Evangelical Divinity School (Deerfield, IL)
-
- Don M. Woodside
- Performance Matters Associates (Matthews, NC)
-
- Dr. Frank Wright
- President, National Religious Broadcasters (Manassas, VA)
-
- Most Rev. Donald W. Wuerl
- Archbishop, Roman Catholic Archdiocese of Washington, D.C.
-
- Paul Young
- COO & Executive VP, Christian Research Institute (Charlotte, NC)
-
- Dr. Michael Youssef
- President, Leading the Way (Atlanta, GA)
-
- Ravi Zacharias
- Founder and Chairman of the Board, Ravi Zacharias International Ministries (Norcross, GA)
-
- Most Rev. David A. Zubik
- Bishop, Roman Catholic Diocese of Pittsburgh, PA
-
- Archbishop Stephen Enea
-
- Primate, Italo- Greek Orthodox Church
- Gerald R. Adams
- Pastor, Life Tabernacle, Hopkinsville, KY
-
- Mark Ammerman
- In The Light Ministries (Lancaster, PA)
-
- Rev. Dale A.P. Anderson
- Founder of Joshua's Gate Ministries and a Trucking Evangelist
-
- Edwin Anderson
- Senior Pastor, Impact Family Church, High Springs, FL
-
- Greg Anderson
- Pastor, Impact Family Church
-
- Pastor Jonathan Archer
- First Baptist Church, Brawley CA
-
- Aaron Auer
- ROAR Ministries (Reviving Oregons Amazing Roots)
-
- Peter William John Baptiste, SFO
- Christian Unity in Diversity Central (Donum Veritatis - The Gift of Truth Ministries)
-
- Fr. John Barbella
- Metuchen, NJ
-
- Matt Barber
- Director of Cultural Affairs, Liberty Counsel and Associate Dean of Liberty University School of Law
-
- Robert M. Barge
- Founder of Wherever Ministries and "the Jesus test"
-
- Patrick C. Beeman
- Catholic Medical Students Association
-
- Laurence D. Behr
- Association for Arch of Triumph
-
- Rev. Brent Bergman
- Grace Community Church (PCA), Palm Harbor, FL
-
- Rev. Bill Bergstrom
- Webb Chapel United Methodist Church
-
- Dr John Henry Beukema
- King Street Church
-
- Pastor Marcia Bilyue
- Manimal Ministeries
-
- Bishop Daniel Blanton
- Victorious Living Chapel (Columbus, OH)
-
- Dr. John Bolt
- Professor of Systematic Theology, Calvin Theological Seminary, Grand Rapids, MI
-
- Rev. Frank Boone
- Wesley Chapel United Methodist Church
-
- Bob Borger
- Associate Pastor, Annapolis Evangelical Presbyterian Church, Annapolis, MD (PCA)
-
- John F. Brehany, Ph.D.
- Catholic Medical Association
-
- Ronn Brooks
- Pastor, Florissant Valley Baptist Church, Florissant, MO
-
- Dean R. Broyles
- President and Chief Counsel, The Western Center for Law & Policy (Escondido, CA)
-
- Reverend Stephen O'Neal Brunson, II

- Lifeway Apostolic Ministries
-
- Rev. Christopher E. Burcham
- Senior Pastor, Union Hill Baptist Church (Clemmons, NC)
-
- Rev. Howard K. Burgoyne
- Superintendent, The East Coast Conference of The Evangelical Covenant Church
-
- Rev. Donavon Burton
- Woodstock Baptist Church
-
- Howard Cameron
- Pastor, Trinity Church, Beaumont, TX
-
- Philip Carlson, MD
- Pastor, Bethany Church of Sierra Madre
-
- Dr. Thomas K. Carr
- Chair, Philosophy and Religious Studies Department, Mount Union University (OH)
-
- Rev. David Cheng
- President, Professional Ministry International
-
- Rt. Rev. Mitred Protopresbyter Andriy Chirovsky
- Pastor, St. Michael Ukrainian Catholic Church and Provessor, Sheptytsky Institute of Eastern Christian Studies (Tempe, AZ)
-
- Rev. Dennis Chitwood
- Genesis Ministry
-
- Rev. LeRoy Christoffels
- Christian Reformed Church
-
- Rev. Timothy Clayton
-
- St. Paul's Anglican
-
- AnnMarie & Larry Clutter
- White Stone Ministry International
-
- Dana Cody
- Life Legal Defense Foundation
-
- Rev. William B. Coker, Jr.
- Kent 1st Church of the Nazarene and Director for Children's Ministries for the Washington-Pacific District of the Church of the Nazarene
-
- Andy Comiskey
- Desert Stream Ministries
-
- Reverend Mr. Rick Condon
- Roman Catholic Diocese of Des Moines, IA
-
- Dr. Timothy F. Conklin
- South Bay Bible Fellowship, East Moriches, NY
-
- Darrell Conley
- Minister, Folkston Georgia Church of Christ
-
- Rev. Edward B. Connolly
- Pastor, St. Joseph Parish and St. Vincent dePaul Parish (Girardville, PA)
-
- Rev. Dennis J. Cooney
- St Raphael Catholic Church, Lehigh Acres, FL
-
- The M. Rev. Raymond W. Copp
- Chancellor, Saint Ambrose College and Prelate, Order of St. Ambrose
-
- Rev. Eric Costa
- Ascension Presbyterian Church (PCA), Beaverton, OR
-
- Dr. King A. Counts
- Carlisle Reformed Presbyterian Church
-
- Brad Dacus
- Pacific Justice Institute (Sacramento, CA)
-
- Donny H. Davis
- Mills Community Baptist Church (Rienzi, MS)
-
- Rev. Ben and Melinda Deckert
- Word of Truth International
-
- Edmund C. de la Cour, Jr.
- First Baptist Church of Pocasset, MA
-
- Rev. Rick Dunn
- Global Frontiers Project
-
- Dr. Gary Dyer
- First Baptist Church, Midland TX
-
- Garrin W. Dickinson
- Holy Nativity Church
-
- Paul C. Dinolfo
- President, Sword of the Spirit - North America
-
- Rt. Rev. Barron Lee Dixon, D.D.
- Trinity Anglican Now
-
- Rev. Harry Edenhofer
- People's Bible Church
-
- Rev. Adam DJ Egan
- Pastor, Blessed Virgin Mary Polish National Catholic Church (Albany, NY)
-
- Barbara J. Elliott
- President, Center for Renewal
-
- Rev. Christopher S. Esget
- Immanuel Evangelical-Lutheran Church (Alexandria, VA)
-
- Brian Farmer
- Catholic Ultreyea Leader, St. Mary's of the Annuciation Roman Catholic Church (Danvers, MA)
-
- Pastor Neil Farrar
-
- Church on the Rock, Topsham, ME
-
- Pastor Rob Fisk
- Heart of the Hills Christian Church, Rochester, MI
-
- Norm Fox
- The Times and the Scriptures
-
- Reverend Canon Terry Gensemer
- Charismatic Episcopal Church for Life (CEC For Life)
-
- Pastor Richard Gerten
- Family Bible Church
-
- Brian Gibson
- Pro-Life Action Ministries
-
- Pastor Bob Gilbert
- Dalkeith Baptist Church
-
- Rev. Frank J. Glenn, Jr
- Founder & Senior Pastor, Glenn Christian Foundaiton Church (Warren, OH)
-
- Dr. Fernando A. González
- Iglesia Alianza Cristiana y Misionera, Magnolia Gardens (Bayamón, Puerto Rico)
-
- Tom Grantham
- Pastor, Purpose Baptist Church (Opelika, AL)
-
- Fr Joseph Grimaldi
- St. Mark Roman Catholic Church, Sheepshead Bay (Brooklyn, NY)
-
- Greg Grooms
- Hill House

- Ed Herald
- Victory Christian Center

- Matthew Harner
- Swanton Alliance Church (Swanton, OH)

- Bob Harrington
- Pastor, Harpeth Community Church

- Cory Hartman
- First Baptist Church of Hollidaysburg, PA

- Mark Hartman
- Senior Pastor, Sugar Creek Baptist Church, Sugar Land, TX

- Zester Hatfield
- Founder & President, Reformation Ministries International Corp.

- Dr. Jody Hice
- Candidate for U.S. Congress, Georgia Seventh District, Bethlehem, GA

- Mark S Hickinbotham
- St. Stephen's Anglican Church, Oak Harbor, WA

- Stephen J. Higgins
- President, Williamson Christian College, Franklin, TN

- Monica Janssen

- Faith Formation Assistant and Parish Book Keeper, Ss. Peter and Paul Parish (Hortonville, WI)

- The Rev. Dr. John K. Hill
- Center for Care and Counseling, Inc.

- Art Hobba
- Founder, Core 300 Men's Ministry (Agoura Hills, CA)

- The Rev'd David S. Houk
- St. John's Episcopal Church and School

- Stephanie O. Hubach
- Mission to North America (MNA)Special Needs Ministries Director

- Dr. Michael B. Hughes
- First Baptist Church (Sunnyside, WA)

- Keith S. Jackson
- Marshall Church of the Nazarene

- Dennis Janson
- His Will, His Way Ministries

- Rev. Joshua D. Johnson
- Hope Wesleyan Church of Fowler, IN

- Rev. David Jolman
- 1st Hudsonville Christian Reformed Church

- Rev. Richard L Jones
- The Uprising

- Rev. Yngve Kalin
- The Church Coalition for the Bible and Confession in the Church of Sweden

- Rev. Christopher Keefer
- First Baptist Church of Poolville, TX

- Rev. James W. Keller
- District Superintendent, Missionary Church, Michigan District

- Alex M. Knight
- Christ United Methodist Church

- Ron Knox
- First Baptist Church, Royalton, IL

- Les Kuiper
- Pastor, First Christian Reformed Church

- Andrea Lafferty
- Traditional Values Coalition

- Rev. Don Lare
- Community United Methodist Church (Elyria, OH)

- Neal Laybourne
- Senior Pastor,Barre Evangelical Free Church (Barre, VT)

- Rev. Maria D. Lancaster
- Embryo Adoption Services of Cedar Park

- Rev. Samuel Laswell
- Interim Minister, New Hope Church, Southfield, MI

- Rev. Dr. David Scott Lee
- Paston, Newbury Bible Church (SBC), Newbury, VT

- Gail Levin
- Founder/Executive Director Generational Crossroads

- Dr. Scott Lively
- Abiding Truth Ministries

- Bob Lord
- TV Host, EWTN Global Network

- Penny Lord
- TV Host, EWTN Global Network

- Rev. Matthew Lorfield
- Messiah Lutheran Church, La Crescent, MN

- Rev. Robert E. Louden
- North Baptist Church, Ottawa, KS

- The Rev'd Darin R. Lovelace
- St John's Anglican Church (Park City, UT)

- Rev. Mr. Dennis Lovell
- St. Anne's Parish (Logan, IA)

- James MacDonald
- Senior Pastor, Harvest Bible Chapel, Rolling Meadows, IL

- Rev. Larry Mangone
- Radiant Christian Assembly of God

- Tom A. Marcum
- CrossPointe (Mooreland, OK)

- Charles & Valerie Portwood
- Pastors, House on The Rock Church FCF, Inc.

- Kent Prater
- LifePoint Church

- Bishop Scott Rathbone
- Church of God, Hickory, NC

- Dr. Ricky Ray
- Senior Pastor, Highlawn Baptist Church (Huntington, WV)

- Rev. Wayne P. Riddlebaugh
- American Heritage Ministry, Inc

- Burt Rosen
- Knox Area Rescue Ministries

- Michael F. Ross
- Senior Pastor, Christ Covenant Church (PCA), Matthews, NC

- Jerry A. Rowley
- Emerald Coast Messianic Ministries, Inc (E.C.M.M.)

- Jeff Russell
- President, The Kardia Foundation

- Dr. Philip G. Ryken
- Senior Minister, Tenth Presbyterian Church, Philadelphia, PA
-
- Gerry Schanckenberg
- Senior Missionary Priest of Epiphany Anglican Fellowship (Longmont,CO)
-
- Dr. Thomas Schirrmacher
- International Institute for Religious Freedom
-
- Robert Shank
- Founder and CEO of The Master's Program - A ministry of Priority Living, Inc.
-
- Rev. Bobby A. Sharp
- Brookview Baptist Church
-
- Charles Sharpe
- Pastor, Heartland Academy Community Church
-
- Fr Daniel E. Siepker
- Pastor, SS Peter & Paul Catholic Church (Atlantic, IA)
-
- George Siler
- Social Science Department Head, The First Academy, Orlando FL
-
- Fr. Martin Slaughter
- St. Gerard Majella Roman Catholic Church (Los Angeles, CA)
-
- Rev. Leonard A. Smith
- St. Vincent de Paul Catholic Church
-
- Right Rev. Fr. Michael T. Smith D.D., OHI, SSJE
- Founder,Ante-Nicene Restoration Catholic Church; Chancellor, St. Paul the Apostle Ante-Nicene School of Theology; and Pastor of New Corinth Fellowship (Niagara Falls, NY)
-
- Warner Smith
- First Baptist Church of Emerson
-
- Dr. Matthew R. St. John
- Bethel Church (Fargo, ND)
-
- Rev. Paul T. Stallsworth
- President, Taskforce of United Methodists on Abortion and Sexuality (aka Lifewatch)
-
- Rev. Mr. Thomas W. Starbuck
- St. Anthony Roman Catholic Church (Des Moines, IA)
-
- Rev. Edward J. Struzik
- (Retired)
- Maria Regina Residence for Retired Priests, Somerset, NJ
-
- Rev. Tony Taylor
- Hilltop Lakes Chapel (Hilltop Lakes, TX)
-
- Nicole Theis
- Delaware Family Policy Council
-
- Dr. William K. Thierfelder
- President, Belmont Abbey College (Belmont, NC)
-
- Larry Thompson
- Pastor, Living Waters Mission (Marlin, TX)
-
- Dr. Gregory Thompson
- America ASLEEP kNOw MORE
-
- Dr. Mark Toone
- Chapel Hill Presbyterian Church
-
- Rev Fr John Trigilio, Jr, PhD, ThD
- Confraternity of Catholic Clergy
-
- Robert Benn Vincent
- Pastor, Grace Presbyterian Church (Alexandria, LA)
-
- Rev. Aaron Vriesman
- North Blendon Christian Reformed Church
-
- Rev'd. Dr. Wm. Beau Wagner
- Rector, St. Matthew's Episcopal Church (Lisbon Falls,ME)
-
- Rev. Paul Waldmiller
- Global Family Outreach Ministry
-
- The Most Rev. Philip E. P. Weeks
- Charismatic Episcopal Church and Barnabas Ministries, Inc
-
- Rev. Christian White
- Paris Church of God, Paris, IL
-
- Daniel P. Whitley
- Clintondale Friends Christian Church
-
- Dr. Jeremy D. Wilkins
- University of St Thomas School of Theology at St Mary's Seminary
-
- Rev. Allen Winn
- Butler Baptist Association
-
- Rev. Timothy J. Wolf
- New Horizon Christian Fellowship
-
- Jon A. Wright
- Metro Church of Kansas City
-
- Jon Wymer
- York Evangelical Free Church
-
- John M. Wynne
- Director of Restoring Truth Ministries
-
- Fr. Zachary of the Mother of God, SOLT
- Roman Catholic Priest Director of Formation
-
- Deacon Dick P. Ziller
- Panora, IA
-
-

www.ingramcontent.com/pod-product-compliance
Lightning Source LLC
Chambersburg PA
CBHW081157270326
41930CB00014B/3195
9780985872366